McGinnis, Terri

Well cat book: the classic comprehe
sive handbook of cat care

Also by Terri McGinnis

The Well Dog Book:
The Classic Comprehensive Handbook of Dog Care
Dr. Terri McGinnis's Dog & Cat Good Food Book

THE WELL CAT BOOK

RANDOM HOUSE NEW YORK

THE

WELL CAT

BOOK

THE CLASSIC COMPREHENSIVE HANDBOOK OF CAT CARE

Terri McGinnis, D.V.M.

ILLUSTRATED BY PAT STEWART

The information in this book, if followed carefully, will enable you to deal with a
wide range of cat care problems. However, this book is not designed to substitute
for care by a veterinarian, and if you have any questions about whether the
advice or procedures in this book are appropriate for your cat, consult a
veterinarian.

This work was originally published in different form in 1975 by Random House,
Inc., New York.

Library of Congress Card Catalog Number: 92-56834
ISBN: 0-394-58769-3

Manufactured in the United States of America
24689753
Revised Edition

Book design by Lilly Langotsky

Dedication for the Second Edition

FOR TED AND JAKE

PREFACE TO THE SECOND EDITION

In the many years since *The Well Cat Book* was originally published, veterinary medicine has changed in extraordinary ways. Not only have new illnesses such as feline infectious peritonitis (see page 197) and feline immunodeficiency virus infection (see page 195) appeared, but medical procedures once restricted to the diagnosis and treatment of human maladies are now commonplace in veterinary practice. Blood tests, urinalysis, radiographs (X-ray pictures), electrocardiograms, computers, and the most modern anesthetics are used daily in animal hospitals around the world. Sophisticated medical equipment once reserved for use in humans such as endoscopes, ultrasound machines, CAT scanners, and magnetic resonance imagers aid in the diagnosis and treatment of conditions as diverse as bronchitis, heart ailments, and brain tumors. Veterinarians specializing in diseases of the eye or skin, internal medicine, surgery, neurology, emergency care, or dentistry can be found in most major cities. Nevertheless, the core of veterinary medicine remains the same. This new edition of *The Well Cat Book* reflects these changes in veterinary medicine while still addressing the common problems and concerns of every pet owner.

Although the ability to diagnose and treat disease in cats is becoming ever more sophisticated, the cat has basically been unchanged for more than 5,000 years. Although many individual breeds of cats have been developed, all cats resemble one another more than they differ. This book is, therefore, useful for all types. By learning the basic information contained in this volume and by learning how to use this book as a quick reference, you will be able to be more self-reliant and confident that you are giving your cat the best daily care. The times you will need a veterinarian's help will be reduced, and those instances when a visit to a veterinary hospital is required will become less distressing and mysterious. Everyone should have the pleasure of living with a well cat!

ACKNOWLEDGMENTS

Books are rarely published without the efforts of many individuals. *The Well Cat Book* is no exception. Don Gerrard, my original editor and copublisher, was most important in the publication of the first *The Well Cat Book*. It was his cat who became injured late one night and caused Don to search for a book that could be used to decide when and if help from a veterinarian was needed. When no useful book could be found, he gave me the opportunity to write one that could fill such a need. Thank you, Don, for your insight, encouragement, and honesty.

Tom Reed, a good friend, veterinarian, and illustrator of the original *The Well Cat Book* and original *The Well Dog Book,* also deserves special thanks for all his efforts. His drawings, freely given, provided the basis for the current illustrations found in both books. Diane and George Ahlgren, Nancy Ehrlich, Michael Floyd, the late Jay Fuller, and Madeline Reed also helped by reviewing the manuscript for the first edition.

The second edition of *The Well Cat Book* followed discussions with Dan Johnson, who wisely arranged for Olga Tarnowski to shepherd the book to completion. Thank you, Dan, for your interest and advice. I hope the book you launched is satisfying and useful to you.

Transformation of *The Well Cat Book* from the first to the second edition would have been impossible without my editor, Olga Tarnowski. Her unflagging good cheer, attention to detail, and continuing interest despite her claims of being mainly a "dog person" attest to her professionalism. Every author should have such a fine editor.

The book's illustrator, Pat Stewart; the book's designer, Lilly Langotsky; the production editor, Nancy Inglis; and copy editor, Martha Schwartz, were also vital to its completion. Thank you all.

Finally special thanks go to my professors; my clients and their pets; the staff, veterinarians, and owner of the Albany Veterinary Clinic; some very special cats; and my friends and family. The education the professors at the University of California School of Veterinary Medicine gave me has never let me down and has taught me that a veterinarian's learning never ends. Dr. Niels Pederson, an expert on feline viral diseases and professor of medicine at U.C. Davis Veterinary School has generously given his time for consultation and moral support. My loyal clients and their pets help keep me up-to-date, remind me what pet owners need, and sustain my practice. The clinic staff and veterinarians give me and my patients daily support and good cheer in sometimes difficult circumstances. My thanks is insufficient recognition of their skills and dedication. Tigger, Dr. Gomez, Split, Huey, Boggs, Perry, Big Al, Buckwheat, and Andy have all taught me different lessons and have been living reminders of every cat's individuality. For my friends and family, who know some of my talents and all of my shortcomings, I reserve the most important thanks of all. Thanks especially to Bruce who is always there for me and to Harry who helps me wake up and smell the coffee. What a great bunch of nice people you are!

CONTENTS

INTRODUCING THE WELL CAT

Cats have a long and obscure history. Over thirty-five million years ago the cat's first ancestors appeared. It is thought that they originated from a weasellike meat eater that was a member of an animal family called Miacidae (also thought to be the ancestor of, among others, the dog, raccoon, bear, skunk, and hyena). From these first cat ancestors arose two branches of recognizably catlike creatures. One included the saber-toothed cats that eventually became extinct; the other included the ancestors of all the Felidae (cat family) alive today. Exactly when cats became humans' companions is not known. It is well documented, however, that cats closely resembling those alive today were an important part of the Egyptian culture, where as early as 2500 B.C. they were revered and considered sacred. From Egypt it appears that domestic cats spread to the Far East and Europe and, much later (around the seventeenth century), were imported to North America from Europe. Although the cat was condemned as a symbol of evil during the Middle Ages in Europe and at the time of the witch hunts in North America, for most of history the cat has maintained the position of an important companion to people and a natural means of rodent control.

In fact, cats have gained steadily in popularity and numbers since the eighteenth century. Today in developed countries they seriously compete with dogs for the public's affection. Over fifty-two million cats reside in the United States alone!

Although cats have been humans' companions for so long, it is only within the last thirty-five years or so that veterinarians and cat owners have become interested in and able to provide very specialized health care for them. Many pet owners today want to take an active part in preserving and maintaining their cat's good health. This book is written for them.

The Well Cat Book differs from other books on cat care because it tells you how to understand the signs of illness or injury your cat may develop and how to evaluate those signs in order to begin proper treatment. It resembles its companion book, *The Well Dog Book*. Both are intended to help you understand what your veterinarian is talking about when he or she discusses your pet's health, to enable you to treat some illnesses at home, to prevent others, and truly to help your veterinarian get your pet well when an illness is too severe to be treated without professional skills. Think of this book as a kind of paramedic's manual for cats that will help you treat many problems on your own. It should help you save money wasted in unnecessary veterinary visits without endangering your pet's health.

For the most part only common health problems affecting cats are covered here. I've tried to include the basic things I as a cat owner most wanted to know before I became a veterinarian, and I've tried to answer the questions cat owners most often ask me about cat health care. I've tried not to oversimplify things, but in many cases technical information I thought the average cat owner would not be likely to use is not included. If you are interested in details of certain subjects, refer to some of the books mentioned in the text or ask your veterinarian for titles of other books that might help you. Use the information in this book to learn how to use your veterinarian as a resource. Remember, however, that the book is not intended as a substitute for visits to the veterinarian, but rather as a supplement to them. Show this book to your veterinarian as a sign that you are interested in taking an active part in maintaining your cat's health.

You don't need to buy any specialized equipment to use this book. Your eyes, hands, ears, and nose, and an understanding relationship with your cat are your most important tools. Don't be afraid to use them. There are more similarities between cats and people than many pet owners realize. As you read, you will probably find out that you know a lot more about "cat medicine" than you think you do.

The best way to use this book is to read it through once from beginning to end. In this way you will learn what is normal for your cat and how to care for a healthy cat, then you will learn the signs that can indicate illness and what you should do about them. With this first reading you will find out which sections of the book you would like to read again and which sections you will only need to refer to if a specific problem arises. When you want to use this book to learn about a specific problem your cat may have, look for the problem in the General Index (page 313) and in the Index of Signs (page 305). To learn how to use these indices, see page 125.

Anatomy is the place to begin. With this chapter as a guide you will gain a ready familiarity with your cat's body and learn how to give a physical exam. You may wish to refer back to this section when diagnosing an illness as well.

Preventive Medicine is a general health care chapter covering important aspects of your cat's daily life. It and the following sections have been designed for easy, frequent reference by the use of sub-heads.

Diagnostic Medicine is the heart of the book. Be sure to read enough of this chapter to understand how it is organized and how to use the Index of Signs. Then, when your cat shows any sign of illness or injury, use this section as a guide to proper action.

Home Medical Care tells you the basics of home treatment. It includes general nursing procedures and advice on drugs. Since in most cases of illness or injury your cat will have some treatment at home, you may want to become familiar with the information here before beginning to diagnose signs.

Breeding and Reproduction contains facts about the cat's reproductive cycle. Use it to learn how to prevent or plan pregnancy; how to care for a female before, during, and after birth; and how to care for newborn or orphan kittens.

You, Your Cat, and Your Veterinarian will help you if you don't yet have a veterinarian or are dissatisfied with your present one. Use it to learn what characteristics good veterinarians share and what you can do to motivate most veterinarians to provide good service.

The body always tries to heal itself. This important fact will help your treatment when your cat is sick. In many cases your cat will not need veterinary aid. Remember, though, that by electing to treat your cat at home, you are taking responsibility for the results. Learn to recognize when the body is losing the battle to heal itself. If you can't be *sure* you are really helping your cat, discuss the problem with a doctor of veterinary medicine. Another caution: Medicine is not always black or white. Often there are several equally good ways to approach a health problem. I've recommended the approach that works for me; your veterinarian may disagree and get equal success with other methods. Trust your veterinarian and your common sense.

1

ANATOMY:

∽

Getting to Know Your Cat's Body

**MUSCLE AND BONE
(MUSCULOSKELETAL SYSTEM)**

SKIN (INTEGUMENTARY SYSTEM)

EYES

EARS

**DIGESTIVE SYSTEM
(GASTROINTESTINAL SYSTEM)**

**REPRODUCTIVE AND
URINARY ORGANS
(GENITOURINARY SYSTEM)**

RESPIRATORY SYSTEM

**HEART AND BLOOD
(CIRCULATORY SYSTEM)**

LYMPHATIC AND IMMUNE SYSTEMS

NERVOUS AND ENDOCRINE SYSTEMS

PHYSICAL EXAMINATION

Physical examination consists of applying knowledge of anatomy to a routine and thorough inspection of all or part of your cat's body. Each person (including every veterinarian) develops his or her own method for giving a physical examination. The best routine to develop is one that prevents you from forgetting to examine any part and one with which you feel most comfortable.

Example: Examine your cat by systems as set out in this chapter (muscle and bone, digestive system, etc.) Then return to examine miscellaneous items such as eyes, ears, and lymph nodes. Then take the cat's temperature.

Example: Take the cat's temperature (see page 242). Proceed with examination starting with the head and working toward the tail. In addition to examining special structures in the area—e.g., ears, eyes, mouth, and nose for the head, claws and pads for the limbs—don't forget to examine the skin in each area and to look for the lymph nodes associated with each area. Follow up by watching your cat in motion.

Special tools needed for physical examination: A rectal thermometer is the only special tool necessary for performing a routine physical examination of your cat at home. Your other tools are your five senses, particularly the senses of touch, sight, and smell.

Special terms used in physical examination: Except for anatomical names of body parts that are mentioned and illustrated in this chapter, there are few special terms that you need to learn to help you with a physical examination. Refer to this page if any of the following words are confusing in the text.

Palpate—to examine with your hands. This is one of your most important methods of physical examination and is why you are asked to *palpate* or *feel* parts of your cat's body so frequently throughout this book.

Terms which indicate direction in reference to the body are illustrated on the facing page.

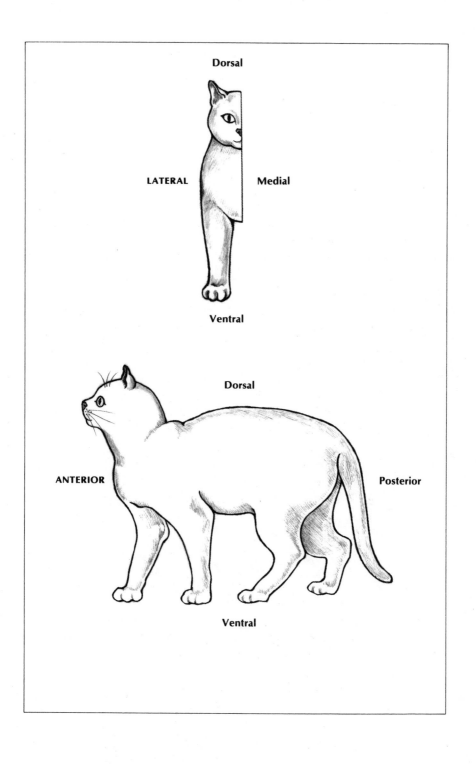

Dorsal

LATERAL Medial

Ventral

Dorsal

ANTERIOR Posterior

Ventral

You can do a better job of giving your cat health care at home with some basic knowledge of *anatomy* and *physiology. Anatomy* is the study of your cat's body structure and the relationship among its parts. For example, knowing the location of your cat's eyes and ears and their normal appearance is knowing anatomy. *Physiology* is the study of how the parts of your cat's body function. Understanding how your cat's eyes and ears function to enable your cat to see and hear are examples of understanding physiology. Although you will be able to examine and understand anatomy easily, physiology is much more difficult. Brief descriptions of how your cat's various body parts work are given here, but it takes intensive study, such as that your veterinarian has given the subject, to really understand physiology well.

You will be most concerned with the external anatomy of your cat, but some internal anatomy is included as well, since an introduction to it will help you understand your veterinarian more easily as you discuss health problems your cat may have. The easiest and fastest way for you to become familiar with what you need to know is to get together with your cat and the following pages of this book. Handle your cat as you read the anatomical descriptions and look at the drawings. If you have a kitten, examine him or her several times during growth. You will see many changes over several months, and the physical contact will bring you emotionally closer to one another.

Looking carefully at your cat's anatomy and encouraging your cat to sit quietly while he or she is examined are extremely important in preparing both yourself and your cat for times when you will have to give health care at home. Also, the maneuvers you go through in examining your cat at home are the same ones your veterinarian uses when giving your cat a physical examination. A cat who has become accustomed to such handling at home is usually more relaxed and cooperative at the veterinary office.

Place your cat on a smooth-surfaced table in good light for examination. The smooth surface prevents good traction and, therefore, a "quick getaway," and the novelty (at least for some cats) of being on a table will entice many cats to stay put rather than attempt an escape. Use a gentle touch and a minimum of restraint. Most cats respond poorly to heavy restraint: A hand placed gently over or in front of the shoulders or under the chest is usually sufficient. If your cat squirms and tries to get away, interrupt the exam, lift the cat quickly off his or her feet while voicing the command "No!" firmly, then replace the cat on the table. Don't give up. Although cats don't seem to be as naturally inclined to respond to obedience training as dogs, they can and do learn to respond to your wishes if you make them known clearly and you are consistent. Be sure to praise your cat whenever he or she cooperates, and repeat the correction procedure wherever he or she tries to escape. The best procedure for a very uncooperative cat is to start out with very short exam periods, repeated frequently. As the cat becomes accustomed to the procedure and reassured that no injury is going to occur, cooperation improves and the examination time can be increased. There are several methods of firm restraint to use with cats (see page 251), but these should be reserved for use in the veterinarian's office or when you have to administer "disagreeable" treatment to your cat. Rely on consistent repetition and gentle handling to establish a good working relationship with your cat.

MUSCLE AND BONE
(MUSCULOSKELETAL SYSTEM)

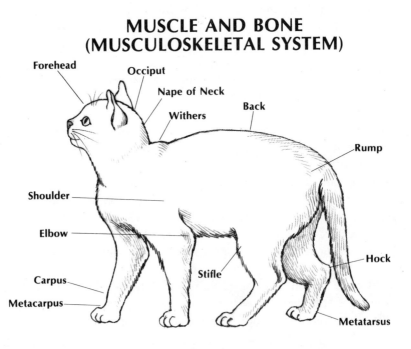

Muscle tissue is composed of contractile units that provide the power for voluntary movement, breathing, blood circulation, digestion, glandular secretion, and excretion of body wastes, as well as many other more minor functions. There are three types of muscle tissue in your cat's body. *Smooth* or *unstriated* muscle is involved in a host of primarily involuntary body functions such as the *peristaltic* (wavelike) movements of the digestive tract. *Cardiac* (heart) muscle, which is capable of independent rhythmic contraction, is found only in the heart, the pump for the circulatory system. *Skeletal* or *striated* muscle makes up the rest of the muscles in the body, including the diaphragm and certain trunk muscles responsible for breathing. An illustration of the muscles in your cat's body is not included in this book because knowing their positions and names is not important in giving routine health care at home.

Bone is a continually changing and actively metabolizing tissue in the living animal. It is composed primarily of the minerals calcium and phosphorus in an organic connective tissue framework that is mainly protein. The outstanding physical functions of bone are to form the skeleton, which supports and protects the soft tissues (e.g., organs, muscles, fat) of the body, and to provide levers against which the various skeletal muscles move. The bones have other functions as well. Mineral storage is provided in the hard bone itself, and fat storage and the formation of blood cells and antibodies (see page 86) occur in the marrow present inside the bones.

Each cat has about 244 bones in the skeletal structure, not in-

SKELETON

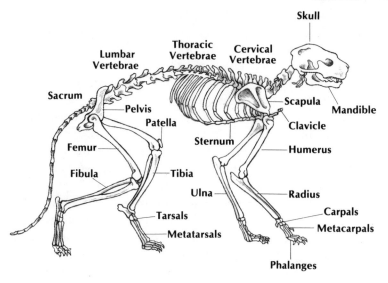

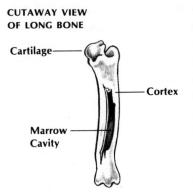

Cartilage

Cortex

Marrow
Cavity

cluding tiny bones called *sesamoids* normally associated with certain tendons. Names of bones that might be important to you in understanding your veterinarian's diagnosis are marked on the skeletal drawing. See whether you can locate each of them on your cat with your hands.

Start with the *skull* (head). Notice its compact, round shape and short, powerful jaws. Thick and thin layers of muscle and connective tissue overlie the bones of the skull, but these tissues are not very prominent, and you may have difficulty distinguishing between the soft tissues and bone. You may be able to feel the relatively thick, paired *temporal* muscles over the top of the head between the ears and the *masseter* muscles that lie in the area of your cat's cheeks. These two pairs of muscles function together with smaller muscles to close the mouth. The rest of the skull feels very bony. Trace the bony area between the temporal muscles back to its end behind the ears. This small, hard bump at the end is called the *occipital protuberance* and is a normal part of every cat's skull. Another bony area easy to identify is the *mandible,* the lower jaw. You move this bone when opening and closing your cat's mouth (see page 22).

The skull is attached to the rest of the skeleton by the *cervical vertebrae.* Try to feel these neck bones by moving your fingers firmly over the sides and top of the neck. You will find it very difficult to feel any bony structures because of the well-developed muscles that cover the neck. The cervical vertebrae, along with the lower vertebrae, form your cat's *spinal column* (backbone).

The *thoracic vertebrae* start in the area between the edges of the shoulder blades. You can feel the curved upper edge of each *scapula* (shoulder blade) near the middle of the back at the *withers.* Each scapula and the muscles that cover it can be seen to move freely when your cat walks and runs. Use your index finger to feel the spines of the thoracic vertebrae between the shoulder blades. Unless your cat is pretty fat you will be able to trace these bones with your finger down the center of your cat's back. They become the spines of the *lumbar vertebrae* in the area behind the last rib and disappear near the hip where several vertebrae are joined to form the *sacrum.*

You can feel only the spines of the vertebral bones but not the rest of the bones themselves because a heavy group of muscles lies on each side of the spinal column down the back. These *epaxial* muscles are most prominent in the *lumbar* region where you can feel them easily by running your fingers along each side of the spinal column. Unless your cat is tailless, you will probably be able to feel each *coccygeal* (tail) vertebra under its covering muscles.

Now examine each leg starting at the foot. The average cat has five *digits* (toes) on each of the front feet and four each on the back feet. Cats affected with *polydactyly,* an inherited trait, may have from one to four extra digits on the front feet; but extra toes on the rear feet are quite rare. Feel each toe carefully. You will find that each consists of three bones (*phalanges*). These correspond to the bones in your fingers and toes. The first toe bone (first phalanx) and nail are covered by a fold of skin in the relaxed foot. These retractile nails allow your cat to walk quietly. To examine these, grasp the leg in the palm of your hand, place your index finger on the pad of the toe you want to examine and your thumb over the top of the same toe at the joint between the first and second phalanx, then squeeze your fingers together. When you do this you will find that the toenail and first phalanx come into view and will remain extended until you release your fingers. Move your fingers slowly up each toe to the middle of the foot. In this area each toe is attached to a long bone that corresponds to the bones that form the palm of your hand and the sole of your foot. These bones are called *metacarpals* in the front feet and *metatarsals* in the rear.

EXTENDING THE CLAW

The *forepaw* (front foot) attaches to the *foreleg* (front leg) at the *carpus* (wrist). Gently flex

Claw Mechanism

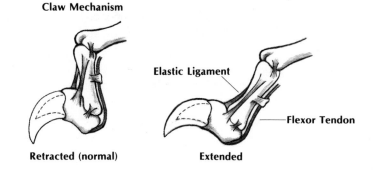

Retracted (normal)   Extended

Elastic Ligament

Flexor Tendon

and extend this joint. If you *palpate* (examine with your hands) carefully, you may be able to feel the small, individual bones that form this joint. Above the carpus are the long bones of the *foreleg*, the *radius* and *ulna*. These bones are well covered by muscles on the *lateral* (outside) surfaces except in the region of the elbow, but if you feel deeply you will be able to feel bone through the muscle layers. On the *medial* (inside) surface you can easily feel a bone (the radius) near the wrist. Place the fingers of one hand over the elbow. Grasp the foreleg below the elbow with your other hand, and flex and extend the joint. A normal joint moves smoothly with no grating or grinding vibrations felt by your fingers. The *humerus* is the bone that forms the foreleg above the elbow. It is well covered with muscles that correspond to those of your upper arm. The humerus is most easy to feel at the point of the shoulder, but if you feel deeply in other areas you can also find it underlying the muscles.

Another bone you may feel under the skin on the cat's upper chest near the point of the shoulder is the *clavicle*. This tiny bone is the vestigial equivalent of the human clavicle (collarbone) that no longer serves an important anatomic purpose for cats.

In the *hindlimb* (rear leg) the foot attaches to the leg at the *hock*. This joint corresponds to your ankle. Flex and extend the joint to learn its normal movement. The fibrous band that attaches prominently on the posterior surface of the hock is the Achilles tendon. It is part of a mechanism that causes the hock to flex or extend whenever the *stifle* (knee joint) is flexed or extended and vice versa.

REAR LEG

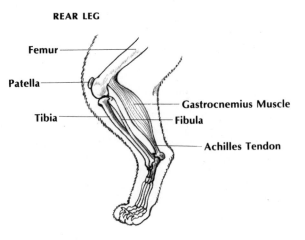

Femur
Patella
Tibia
Gastrocnemius Muscle
Fibula
Achilles Tendon

The *tibia* and *fibula* are the bones that lie between the knee and the hock. Muscles cover the *lateral* (outside) surface of these bones, but you can feel them through the muscles and can easily feel the tibia on the inside surface of the leg in this area. The tibia helps to form the stifle joint along with the *femur* and *patella* (kneecap). Place the fingers of one hand over the patella and flex and extend the knee joint. You should be able to feel the patella move freely and smoothly as you manipulate the joint. Now move up the leg to the thigh. The *femur* is the long bone of the thigh. It is well covered by heavy muscles, so you will be unable to feel it easily except near the knee. Feel the muscles of the thigh and try to feel the femur under them. The femur *articulates* (forms a joint) with the pelvis at the hip. To test this joint, grasp the thigh with the fingers and palm of one hand and place your thumb over the area of the hip joint, then flex and extend the joint. This leaves one hand free to control your cat. You can perform this part of the examination either with your cat standing on three legs or lying on one side. Complete your examination of the musculoskeletal system by running your fingers over the sides of your cat's chest. You should be able to feel each rib easily under a freely movable coat of skin, fat, and muscle. If you can't easily feel the ribs, your cat is too fat. Pick a rib and follow it with your fingers down the side of the *thorax* (chest) to its end. If you have chosen one of the first nine ribs you will find that it attaches to a bone forming the *ventral* (bottom) surface of the chest. This is the *sternum.* The last four ribs do not attach directly to the sternum.

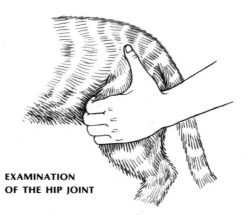

EXAMINATION OF THE HIP JOINT

In male cats a small bone called the *os penis* is present inside the penis. An equivalent structure is not present in the clitoris of the female cat.

After you have examined the major parts of your cat's musculoskeletal system (or before, if you like), stand back and look at your cat as a whole. Are the legs straight? Are the wrist joints erect? Are there any unusual lumps or bumps? Most normal cats are very similar in *conformation* (bony and muscular structure) to the drawings in this book.

Now watch your cat move. All motion should be free and effortless. Do you see any signs of lameness? If you have any particular questions about your cat's conformation or movement be sure to discuss them with your veterinarian.

SKIN (INTEGUMENTARY SYSTEM)

The *integumentary system* consists of the skin and its specialized modifications: the hair, the foot pads, the claws, and the anal sacs. Your cat's skin protects his or her body against environmental changes, trauma, and germs. In the skin vitamin D is synthesized; below the skin (in the *subcutaneous* tissues) fat is stored. Skin is both an organ of sensation and an organ (via certain skin glands) for waste excretion. Unlike humans' skin, however, the cat's body skin plays only a minor role in heat regulation. Skin disease does occur in cats, and the condition of your cat's skin and hair can sometimes tell you a great deal about his or her general state of health.

If your cat is healthy, the skin should be smooth, pliable, and free of large amounts of scales (dandruff), scabs, odorous secretions, and parasites (see page 106). Normal skin coloration ranges from pale pink through shades of brown to black. Spotted skin is completely normal and may be seen in cats without spotted coats. The skin (and hair) color comes from a dark-colored pigment called *melanin,* which is produced and stored in special cells in the bottom layer of the *epidermis* (outer skin layer).

Examine your cat's skin carefully. To do this, part the fur of long-haired cats in several places and look carefully at the skin itself. In short-haired cats run the thumb of one hand against the grain of the hair to expose the skin. Be sure to examine the skin in several places over the body, on the legs, under the neck, and on the head. When you are examining the head, note how there is a distinct thinning of hair in front of the ears. This is called *preauricular alopecia;* although the degree varies between cats, its presence is normal. It marks the site of the temporal glands, microscopic skin glands thought to be important in scent marking. Similar glands are present in the skin at the corners of the mouth, on the chin, and on the tail.

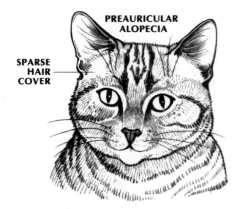

PREAURICULAR
ALOPECIA

SPARSE
HAIR
COVER

Any buglike creatures you see attached to your cat's skin or hair or that quickly move away as you part the hair are *external parasites* and should not be there. They are likely to be fleas (see page 106), but may be lice (see page 117), mites (see page 117), or ticks (see page 116). Small salt- and pepperlike, white and black granules may be flea eggs and flea feces.

A specialized area of skin of particular interest to owners of mature tomcats is the *supracaudal organ* (tail gland). This is an area of numerous and large oil-producing glands located on the upper surface of the tail. Although it is present in all cats, it is not particularly evident unless there is excessive accumulation of the gland's oily secretion. If this has occurred in your cat, you will find an area of greasy, brownish secretion as you part the hair on the top of the tail. This may be accompanied by stringy, oily hairs. This unsightly condition is commonly referred to as *stud tail* (feline tail gland hyperplasia) and is sometimes relieved by castration (see page 273) and fastidious grooming (see page 50).

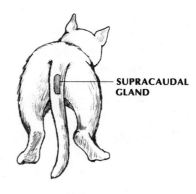

SUPRACAUDAL GLAND

Roll your cat on his or her side or back to see where the skin forms the nipples of the *mammary glands* (breasts). The mammary glands themselves are skin glands that have become modified for the pro-

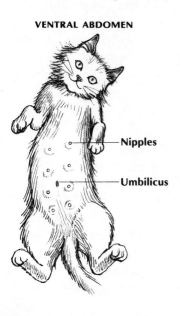

VENTRAL ABDOMEN

Nipples

Umbilicus

duction of milk. Male as well as female cats normally have four nipples on each side, although some cats have as many as five pairs. The prominence of the nipples and mammary glands in the *queen* (female cat) varies with age and stage of the *estrous cycle* (see page 267). Examine your cat's mammary glands by feeling the areas between the nipples and a wide area around them. In a normal male or *anestrous* female (see page 267) you should not be able to feel any lumps or bumps. If you find *any,* discuss their importance with your veterinarian.

If you have a young cat with short abdominal hair, you may notice a faint scarlike area on the skin at the midline near the area where the chest meets the *abdomen* (belly) while you are examining the breasts. This is your cat's *umbilicus* (belly button). If you see a lump in this area, it may be an *umbilical hernia.* (See page 294 and decide whether or not you need a veterinarian's help.)

Now return to the head to examine your cat's nose. The skin is modified over the nose so that its superficial layers are thick and tough. This skin has no glands, but is usually moist from nasal secretions and feels cool as a result of evaporation. A cool, moist nose or a warm, dry one, however, is not an accurate gauge of your cat's body temperature; use a thermometer (see page 242). Cats' noses vary widely in coloration. Colors anywhere from salmon or pale pink through brown to black are normal, as are spotted noses. A brightly colored nose that becomes pale or white can be a sign of illness (see page 186), so be sure to become familiar with the normal appearance of your cat's nose.

The skin is also modified to be thick and tough over the foot pads. The deepest layer of the foot pads is very fatty and acts as a cushion to absorb shock. The middle layer (*dermis*) contains *eccrine glands,* the only skin glands in the cat equivalent to humans' heat-regulating sweat glands. If you feel your cat's foot pads when he or she becomes excited (e.g., on a trip to the veterinarian's office) you will find that the pads become damp with eccrine gland secretion. These glands are also responsible for the steamy footprints you may see when your cat crosses the sidewalk on a warm day.

The foot pads are named according to which bones they overlie—*digital, metacarpal* (*metatarsal* in the rear feet), and *carpal* (none in the rear). Examine your cat's foot pads and learn their names. Knowing the names may help you describe the location of a problem to your veterinarian.

Two unusual modifications of the skin are the *anal sacs.* They are located internally under the external sphincter muscles of the anus at about the four o'clock and eight o'clock positions. If you lift your cat's tail directly upward you

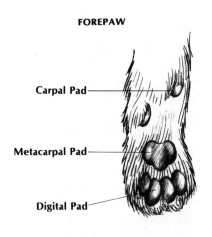

FOREPAW

Carpal Pad

Metacarpal Pad

Digital Pad

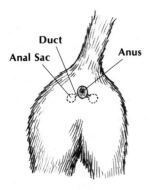

can see the small opening where each duct empties on each side near the opening of the anus. If the glands are full, a drop or two of brownish fluid will often drip from the openings as you lift the tail. This odorous anal sac secretion may serve to mark your cat's stool with his or her particular identification tag. They are also often emptied explosively in stressful situations. You may be able to feel the full anal sacs by placing your thumb externally on one side of the anus and your index finger on the other side, then gently moving your fingers up and down. Full glands feel like firm, dried pea-sized objects beneath the skin. Occasionally a cat's anal sacs don't empty properly on their own; then you or your veterinarian must empty them (see page 173).

Claws (toenails) are specialized in cats for digging, traction, hunting, and protection. To examine your cat's claws, extend them as explained on page 9. The outer layer of the claw is horny and may be pigmented or unpigmented. The inner layer is the *dermis* (quick), which is highly *vascular* (contains many blood vessels) and is continuous with the connective tissue covering the third phalanx. Even in a

dark-nailed cat you can usually see the dermis as a pink area inside the claw when it is held in front of a light. Cats normally keep their claws sharp by constant conditioning by which the old, dulled, and worn outer layers of the claws are pulled off. This normal scratching behavior sometimes becomes undesirable in cats confined indoors. Providing a cat with his or her own scratching post or nail trimming or declawing (see page 57) are ways to help solve the problem.

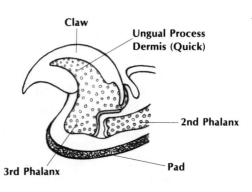

CROSS SECTION OF CLAW

Cats have three basic types of hair: guard hair, fine hair, and tactile hair. *Tactile hairs* (whiskers) grow out of very large sensory hair follicles on the muzzle and chin, at the sides of the face, over the eyes, and from large hair follicles located on the back of the foreleg just above the carpal pad. Their sensory function is a significant aid to your cat's vision and hearing and is thought to be of particular importance in helping cats orient themselves in poor light. *Guard hairs* are the longer, coarser hairs that comprise the immediately visible outer part of your cat's coat. *Fine hairs* are the soft hairs that make up the undercoat present beneath and between the guard hairs. Fine hairs consist of two types of soft hairs, *awn* and *down* or *wool.* Unless your cat is *Cornish Rex,* a special breed with a coat composed only of fine, curly hairs, whether the coat is long or short there are both guard hairs and fine hairs present. Try to distinguish between them in your cat's coat.

Although you may notice a particular increase in the numbers of hairs your cat sheds in the spring, all cats' coats are replacing themselves continuously. At any one time some hairs are falling out, some are in a resting phase, and others are growing in. Don't consider shedding excessive unless you begin to see bare skin areas developing in normally haired sites. A healthy cat's coat is neatly groomed and clean (although tomcats often look very dirty and unkempt when healthy). The coat should appear glossy and unbroken. Dark-colored coats usually seem to have more natural sheen, so take this into consideration before judging your cat's coat. After clipping or shaving, the average cat's coat takes three to four months to grow back fully, but it can take much longer, especially in long-haired cats.

EYES

Your cat's eyes are similar in structure and function to your own. Light entering the eye passes through the cornea, anterior chamber, pupil, lens, and vitreous body before striking the retina. Specialized cells in the retina (the rods and cones) convert light striking them into nerve signals that pass to the brain via the optic nerve. In cats these impulses result in an image thought to be perceived in various shades of gray and perhaps some blue, green, and red, and various degrees of brightness. Although color-vision is present to some degree, it is so limited as to be insignificant in the daily life of the cat. Located behind the retina is an area of tissue called the *tapetum lucidum.* Its function is to reflect light that has already passed through the rods and cones back to them (increasing visual acuity in dim light). It is the structure that is responsible for the appearance of cats' eyes "glowing in the dark." As you examine your cat's eyes you will see that each is surrounded by two modified skin folds, the eyelids. The

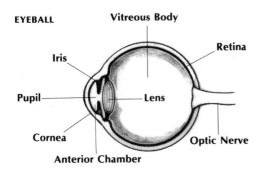

EYEBALL

Vitreous Body

Iris

Retina

Pupil — — Lens

Cornea

Optic Nerve

Anterior Chamber

edges of the lids should be smooth, even, and not rolled in (*entropion*) or out (*ectropion*). Cats do not normally have eyelashes. Look for lashes on your cat's eyelids and if any are present, be sure that they do not turn in abnormally to rub against the eye. Between the

Normal Eyelids   **Entropion**   **Ectropion**

eyelids at the *medial canthus* (corner of the eye near the nose) you can see the third eyelid (*nictitating membrane*). It may be pale pink or partially pigmented. Its normal position over the eye varies from cat to cat and has some relationship to the presence of disease (see

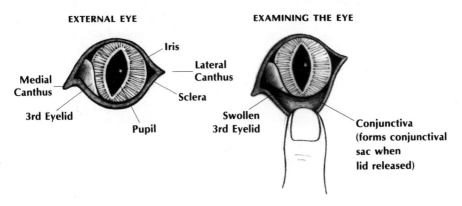

EXTERNAL EYE   **EXAMINING THE EYE**

Iris

Lateral
Canthus

Medial
Canthus

Sclera

3rd Eyelid

Pupil

Swollen
3rd Eyelid

Conjunctiva
(forms conjunctival
sac when
lid released)

page 148). Roll back the upper or lower eyelid by placing your thumb near its edge and gently pulling upward or downward. This allows you to view the inner lining of the lids, a pale pink mucuous membrane called the *conjunctiva*.

The visible part of the eyeball consists of the cornea, bulbar conjunctiva, anterior chamber, iris, and pupil. The *bulbar conjunctiva* is a continuation of the lining of the eyelids that covers the surface of the eyeball except for the area of the cornea. If it contains pigment the area may look spotted or dark. In unpigmented areas the bulbar conjunctiva is transparent, allowing the eye's white fibrous coat (*sclera*) and the fine blood vessels that traverse it to be seen through it. The *cornea* should be completely transparent. Through it you see

Dilated Pupil

Constricted Pupil

the anterior chamber, iris, and pupil. The color of the iris varies widely among cats. Greens and yellows predominate, but many other iris colors are possible, among them orange, blue, and lavender. Sometimes cats have a different iris color for each eye. White cats with this condition ("odd eyes") or with two blue irises are often deaf or hearing impaired (Waardenburg syndrome). The iris controls the size and shape of the pupil. Along with the eyelids, the pupil controls the amount of light allowed to enter the eye. Pupils should constrict simultaneously in bright light and dilate in dim light. When only one eye is exposed to light or darkness, the pupil of the remaining eye should constrict or dilate when the exposed one does. If your cat's eyes are normal when you test their response to light you will find that the pupils are round when dilated, slitlike (vertically) when constricted.

EARS

The external part of the ear, which you can see when casually looking at your cat, is called the *pinna*. The pinna receives air vibrations and transmits them via the ear canal to the eardrum. The outside of the pinna is covered with haired skin like that covering the rest of your cat's body. The inside is also partially haired, although the hair there is more sparse than that on the outside. Any visible unpigmented skin lining the inside of the pinna and ear canal should be pale pink in color. Bright pink or red is abnormal. All visible parts of the ear should be fairly clean. Normal accumulations consist of very small amounts of clear to slightly yellowish brown waxy material. Large amounts of this material, black waxy material, or sticky foul-smelling secretions are abnormal. If your cat's ears look normal to you, or your veterinarian tells you that your cat's ears are normal, smell them. This odor is the smell of a healthy ear. Deviations from this smell may indicate ear trouble even if you can't see any external indication of it.

Notice on the drawing that the ear canal is vertical for a distance, then becomes horizontal before it reaches the eardrum. This makes it impossible for you or your veterinarian to see very deeply into the ear canal without a special instrument called an *otoscope*. An advantage of this type of ear canal structure is that it allows you to clean quite deeply into the ear canal without fear of damaging the eardrum as long as you clean vertically (see page 53).

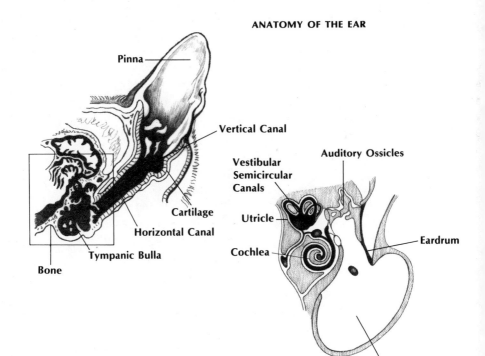

ANATOMY OF THE EAR

Pinna

Vertical Canal

Auditory Ossicles

Vestibular Semicircular Canals

Cartilage

Utricle

Horizontal Canal

Cochlea

Eardrum

Tympanic Bulla

Bone

Tympanic Bulla

The structure and function of your cat's middle and inner ear are very similar to your own. Vibrations reaching the eardrum are transmitted through the middle ear by small bones, the *auditory ossicles,* to the vestibular window. From the vestibular window the vibrations enter the inner ear where the *cochlea* converts these mechanical stimuli to nerve impulses that travel to the brain via the auditory nerve. In addition to the cochlea, the *semicircular canals* and *utricle* occupy the inner ear. These organs are important in maintaining the cat's sense of balance.

Hearing is present in cats when the ear canal opens at twelve to fourteen days. In general cats can distinguish among sounds better than either people or dogs. They can also hear higher pitched sounds (up to 65 kHz) than humans, whose hearing range extends to about 23 kHz.

INTERNAL ANATOMY

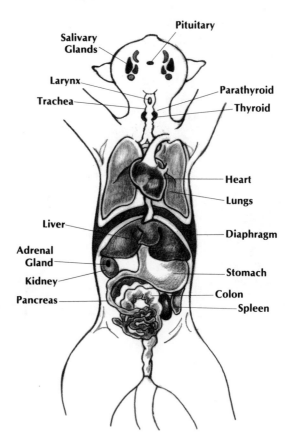

Pituitary

Salivary
Glands

Larynx

Trachea

Parathyroid

Thyroid

Heart

Lungs

Liver

Diaphragm

Adrenal
Gland

Kidney

Stomach

Pancreas

Colon

Spleen

DIGESTIVE SYSTEM
(GASTROINTESTINAL SYSTEM)

The digestive system consists of the digestive tube (mouth, pharynx, esophagus, stomach, small and large intestines, and anus) and the associated salivary glands, liver, gallbladder, and pancreas. Few of the foodstuffs necessary for growth, life, and work enter the body in a form that can be absorbed directly by the intestines and put straight to use by the body. Therefore it is the digestive system's function to convert foodstuffs to absorbable nutrients, using both mechanical and chemical means.

Anatomically you will be primarily concerned with the beginning and the end of the digestive tract—the mouth and the anus. The locations of the other structures are indicated on the drawing of internal anatomy. With practice you may become quite familiar with the shape and feel of some of the internal organs because most cats are small enough and have relaxed enough abdomens to make palpation easy. Feel *gently* and carefully; too firm or rough an examination can cause injury to your cat. With your cat standing, feel for the liver and stomach by running your fingers down the edges of the ribs bordering the abdomen. You may feel the firm, sharp edge of a normal liver most easily along the rib edge on the right side. Round liver edges or a liver that extends for some distance beyond the rib may be abnormal. When full, your cat's stomach will be felt as a

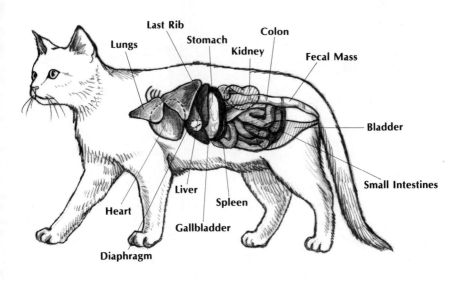

doughy or lumpy mass against the left side of the abdomen near the rib. You will also encounter the spleen (see page 34) on the left side. Feel your cat's intestines by grasping the abdomen between the thumb and fingers of one hand. Reach up along each side of the abdomen, bring your thumb and fingers toward one another, then move them downward toward the umbilicus. The intestines will slip through your fingers like wet noodles. If you reach high up in the posterior (towards the tail) part of the abdomen you may be able to feel your cat's colon full of stool. It will feel firm and somewhat sausage-shaped. If you become familiar with the shape and feel of a normal stool in your cat's colon, it may help you in the diagnosis of diarrhea (see page 169) or constipation (see page 170). As you perform your examination of the digestive system, you are likely to encounter the kidneys and bladder. For information about these organs turn to page 30.

MOUTH

Most cats are reluctant to have their mouths examined, especially the first time. Don't give up if your cat objects and tries to squirm away as you start your examination. Make your intentions clear and proceed with an air of confidence. If you are hesitant in your motions most cats will be quick to take advantage of the situation. Begin the examination by lifting each upper lip individually with the cat's jaws closed. Use one hand to steady your cat's head, if necessary, while examining with the other. This allows you to examine the *buccal* (outer) surfaces of the teeth and gums.

HEALTHY GUMS

SEVERE GUM DISEASE

Healthy gums feel firm and have edges so closely applied to the teeth that they look as if they are actually attached to the teeth. Gums fill the upper part of the spaces between the teeth, forming a "V" (an inverted "V" with the lower teeth) you can see between each front tooth and its neighbors. In unpigmented areas healthy gums are pink. Very pale pink or white gums, yellowish gums, red gums, or a red line along the tooth edge of pink gums is abnormal. Many normal cats have black-spotted gums, some with so much pigment that it is difficult to find a pink area to examine.

Cats' teeth are designed for grasping, tearing, and shredding. They are typical of an animal designed by nature to eat a carnivorous diet. In a normal mouth, the upper front teeth (incisors) just overlap the lower ones. An excessive overlap (overbite) is abnormal, as is a mouth structure in which the lower front teeth extend beyond the upper ones (underbite). A mild overbite or underbite doesn't seem to cause functional problems. However, cats bred for short faces such as Persians may have extreme underbites which are functionally unsound and are related to health problems. Be sure to check your cat's bite and the surface of each tooth. Abnormal tooth placement in young cats can affect jaw development and the later placement of adult teeth, so any problems you find should be immediately brought to your veterinarian's attention. The surfaces of the teeth are white in young cats and get yellower as the cat ages. A fingernail scraped along tooth surfaces should pick up little debris. Try it. Mushy white stuff that may scrape off is called *plaque,* a combination of saliva, bacteria, their by-products, and food debris. This can be removed easily by "brushing" your cat's teeth (see page 58). Hard white, yellow, or brown material is *tartar* or *calculus* (mineralized plaque) and must usually be removed by your veterinarian.

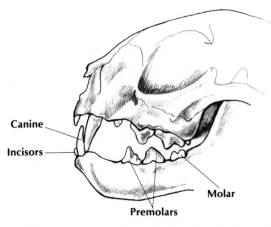

Teeth are categorized into four types: incisors (I), canines or cuspids (C), premolars (P), and molars (M). Veterinarians use a formula to indicate the number and placement of each kind of tooth in the mouth. The letter indicates the kind of tooth; the numbers placed next to the letter indicate how many of that particular kind of tooth are present in the upper and lower jaw of one half of the mouth. The average kitten has twenty-six *deciduous* teeth (baby teeth) arranged in the following manner. Starting at the middle of the front teeth (incisors)

$$\frac{\text{Upper teeth of half mouth}}{\text{Lower teeth of half mouth}} \;=\; (i\tfrac{3}{3}\;\; c\tfrac{1}{1}\;\; p\tfrac{3}{2}) \times 2 = 26$$

A kitten has no molars. Therefore the emergence of these baby teeth and their replacement by permanent ones is a convenient way to estimate the age of a young cat (see table, page 25).

The average adult cat has thirty permanent teeth:

$$\frac{\text{Upper teeth of half mouth}}{\text{Lower teeth of half mouth}} \;=\; (I\tfrac{3}{3}\;\; C\tfrac{1}{1}\;\; P\tfrac{3}{2}\;\; M\tfrac{1}{1}) \times 2 = 30$$

It is not unusual to find cats with fewer teeth than this "standard" number. Many cats never develop the full number of incisor teeth, others lose their teeth relatively early in life. Others are missing premolars or molars. If the other teeth and the gums are healthy, a few missing teeth don't seem to cause any problems. Once a cat's permanent teeth have erupted it is more difficult to use them as a guide to age.

Now examine the inner (*lingual*) surfaces of the teeth, the tongue, and the posterior part of the mouth. *To open your cat's mouth,* place one hand around the upper part of his or her head and push inward on the upper lips with your fingers and thumb as if you were trying to push them between the teeth. As your cat starts to open the mouth, use the index finger of your other hand to pull open the lower jaw by pushing downward on the lower incisor teeth. Look inside. You will see the rough surface of the tongue below, the hard palate above, and the inner teeth surfaces.

An unusual sense organ, the *vomeronasal organ,* opens into the mouth at a small bump on the hard palate just behind the upper

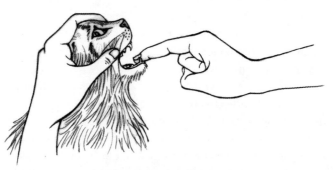

OPENING THE MOUTH

teeth. The rest of the organ is located in the soft tissues above the palate. When cats investigate objects with their mouths held slightly open (the *Flehman* or gape response) they are directing scents to this organ for evaluation.

If you move quickly you can use your finger to push the tongue to one side or the other to look under it. Using the index finger of the same hand you used to open the lower jaw, press down on the tongue. As you press down, try to move the tongue slightly forward. If you do this properly, you will mimic your doctor's use of a tongue depressor, allowing you to see the soft palate as a continuation of the hard palate, and the palatine tonsils. Cats' tonsils reside in a pocket (the *tonsilar fossa* or *sinus*), so they aren't easily seen unless they are enlarged. Be very careful when examining a cat's mouth. If there is any significant resistance withdraw your hands immediately to avoid injury.

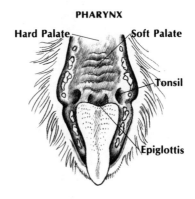

PHARYNX

Hard Palate — Soft Palate

Tonsil

Epiglottis

TEETH AS A GUIDE TO YOUR CAT'S AGE

AGE   **TEETH PRESENT**

AGE	TEETH PRESENT
Birth	None
2–3 weeks	Deciduous teeth coming in
4–5 weeks	All deciduous teeth in except second upper premolar
8 weeks	Second upper premolar in
3½–4½ months	Permanent incisors coming in
5 months	Permanent canines start erupting
6 months	Canines fully erupted, premolar 3 and molars present

Rarely, deciduous teeth may be retained as the permanent ones erupt. These may have to be removed by a veterinarian if they interfere with normal adult tooth placement.

After one year of age some staining and tartar accumulations are usually present on the teeth. There is no reliable way to use teeth as a guide to age, however, after a cat is mature.

LYMPH NODES

Tonsils are a type of specialized *lymphoid* tissue (containing many special cells called lymphocytes, see page 34 and 86) similar to your lymph nodes and to lymph nodes located in other parts of your cat's body. You can feel some lymph nodes on your cat's head in the area located below your cat's ear and behind the cheek where the head attaches to the neck. They are very small, firm, smooth-surfaced lumps associated with a larger similar lump. The larger lump is one of the cat's several salivary glands, and the only one you will be able to feel. After you feel the normal salivary gland and its associated lymph nodes and become familiar with them, try to feel the other lymph nodes indicated on the drawing. (You may need your veterinarian's help with this; unless the nodes are enlarged they can be difficult to find the first time you try to feel them.) When you find one, learn its normal size and shape. Lymph node changes (most commonly enlargement) should alert you to have your cat examined by a veterinarian since they are often a sign of serious illness or infection.

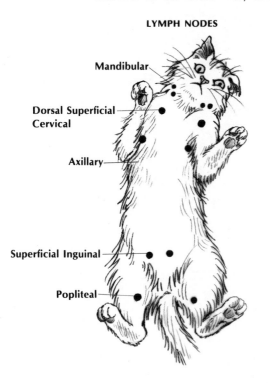

LYMPH NODES

Mandibular

Dorsal Superficial Cervical

Axillary

Superficial Inguinal

Popliteal

ANUS

The anus is the specialized terminal portion of the digestive tract through which indigestible material and waste products pass as stool. Most adult cats have one or two bowel movements daily. The number of bowel movements and the volume of stool passed, however, are dependent to a great degree on the amount of indigestible material in the diet. Cats eating dry food will tend to pass more feces than cats eating a highly digestible muscle meat, egg, and milk product diet, due to the higher fiber content of dry cat food. Normal stools are well formed and generally brown colored, although some diet ingredients may make them darker (liver) or lighter (bones). Extremely large volumes of stool, unformed, abnormally odorous stools, or unusually colored stools may indicate digestive tract disease. Be sure to try to observe your cat's stools several times a week.

Anal sacs have been discussed with the skin; see page 14. If you have not yet examined them, do it now while learning the normal appearance of your cat's anus. You may also want to learn to take your cat's temperature at this time since it should be a routine part of any physical examination and is usually taken rectally (see page 242).

REPRODUCTIVE AND URINARY ORGANS (GENITOURINARY SYSTEM)

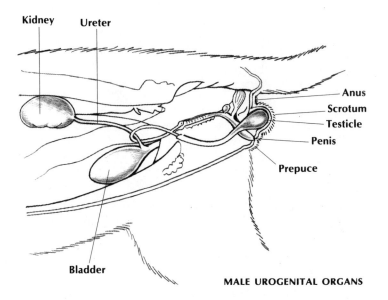

MALE UROGENITAL ORGANS

Major portions of the male cat's reproductive system are located externally within reach of your examination. Many cats resist a thorough examination of their genitals, however, so don't feel dismayed if you can't examine all parts as described. The *testes* (organs that produce sperm) are located in the *scrotum* (skin pouch) of the male kitten at birth or very shortly thereafter and should be relatively easy to feel by six weeks of age. Normally there are two testicles present, each of which feels firm, smooth, and relatively oval beneath its loose covering of skin. If your cat has one or no testicles in his scrotum (unilateral or bilateral *cryptorchidism*) the condition may need veterinary attention (see page 275). If you palpate carefully, you can feel a small lump protruding off the posterior end of each testicle. This is the tail of the *epididymis,* which stores sperm. To examine your cat's penis you must first retract the skin fold which covers it (the *prepuce* or *sheath*). To do this, grasp the prepuce gently but firmly between the index finger and thumb of one hand. Then push the skin fold anteriorly toward your cat's head. As you do this you will see the pink tip of the penis start to protrude posteriorly;

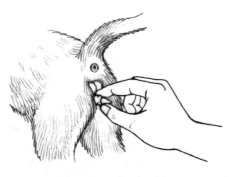

EXTRUDING THE PENIS

a cat's penis points in the same direction as the tail. If you have gotten a successful grip the first time, the rest of the penis will protrude once the skin fold is pushed fully forward, and it will remain protruded as long as you hold the retracted skin in place. If you have difficulty retracting the sheath the first time, try getting a better grasp. Try several positions before giving up.

The surface of the penis is covered by a pink mucous membrane. Prominent curved, horny *papillae* protrude from its surface in the area of the *glans* (expanded end of the penis) in mature, uncastrated males (tomcats). It is thought that these rough projections may be involved in stimulating the female cat to ovulate following mating; they may also provide additional sexual stimulation to the male and act as a holdfast. If your cat is very young or castrated, you will find that the surface of the glans penis is smooth. The spines begin to develop at about six months of age and have usually disappeared by six months following castration. The *urethra* (tube through which urine and reproductive secretions pass) can be seen to open at the end of the penis. It is extremely narrow in all male cats. If you see your cat urinate, notice what a thin stream of urine this produces. Any secretions present on the surface of the penis should be clear, not cloudy or colored.

Sperm are produced in the seminiferous tubules of the testicles. From the testes the sperm travel to the epididymis for storage and maturation. During ejaculation sperm travel through the *vas deferens* into the urethra where they are mixed with secretions from the prostate gland and bulbourethral glands, which are located internally and are not accessible for routine examination.

The vulva and clitoris are the only female cat's genitals that can be seen externally. The internal portions of the female reproductive tract—*uterus, cervix, ovaries,* and *fallopian tubes*—can be found on the illustrations here. The urethra empties into the vagina anterior

FEMALE REPRODUCTIVE SYSTEM

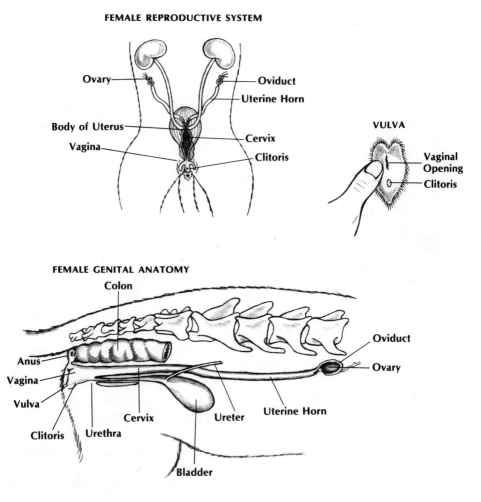

VULVA

FEMALE GENITAL ANATOMY

to a point you can see without special instruments. You may be able to see the tiny, dark pink clitoris in its fossa by gently spreading the vulvar lips with your fingers. This also allows you to see some of the lining of the vulva and vagina. These mucous membranes should be pink in color; any secretions present are normally clear.

You can find additional information on reproduction in the chapter *Breeding and Reproduction,* starting on page 265.

The urinary system of both male and female cats consists of two kidneys, two ureters, the bladder, and the urethra. Look for these organs on the illustrations. *Nephrons* (units of specialized cells) in the kidneys filter the blood to remove toxic metabolic wastes and are also important in maintaining the body's proper electrolyte and water balance. Urine formed in the kidneys passes through the ureters to the bladder where it is stored until it is eliminated through the urethra during urination. Normal cat urine is yellow and clear and has a distinctive odor. This odor is extremely intense in tomcats and is used to mark territory during the act of spraying (see page 273). The intensity of the yellow color of urine increases as the amount of water excreted decreases and vice versa. If your cat is not fat you will probably be able to feel the bladder and kidneys. With your cat standing, provide restraint with one hand under the chest while using the other one to feel for the bladder in the posterior abdomen between the rear legs. A bladder containing urine will feel somewhat like a water-filled balloon varying anywhere from about the size of a Concord grape to the size of a large lemon. Feel *gently* for the kidneys by grasping the abdomen with both hands, left on the left side, right hand on the right side. Reach high into the mid-lumbar area, then bring your fingers toward one another. Each kidney should feel firm, smooth, and relatively oval in shape. Most normal adult cat's kidneys are about the size of a small apricot, but there is much individual variation with body size and with the amount of body fat, since a layer of fat normally covers the kidneys. You may find the right kidney somewhat more anterior than the left one, but both move rather freely and will not be found in exactly the same position in each examination.

RESPIRATORY SYSTEM

The cat's respiratory system consists of two lungs, the air passages leading to them (nasal cavity, mouth, pharynx, larynx, trachea, bronchi), the diaphragm, and the muscles of the thorax. The system's main function, as in humans, is to supply oxygen to the body and to remove excess carbon dioxide produced by metabolism. In conjunction with the tongue and the mucous membranes of the mouth, the respiratory system has a secondary but extremely important function of heat regulation, since the cat has no highly developed mechanism for sweating. Unlike dogs, however, cats rely on panting for cooling only under extreme heat stress. The nostrils and nasal passages are also important to the cat's highly developed sense of smell.

The only parts of your cat's respiratory system you can see are the mouth and nostrils. Special instruments are needed to look into the nasal cavity; and this is difficult, even with special instruments, because the passages are so small. Look at your cat's nostrils. Any secretions from them should be clear and watery; sticky, cloudy, bloody, yellowish or greenish nasal discharge is abnormal.

You can feel your cat's larynx (Adam's apple) by grasping the neck on the undersurface where it meets the head. The larynx feels like a small, hard, fairly inflexible mass of tissue. It helps control the flow of air through the trachea and lungs and is the location of the vocal cords responsible for your cat's meow. The purr also originates in the larynx. When certain muscles within it contract narrowing its opening (the *glottis*), the air turbulence created during breathing results in the purring sound.

Notice the character of your cat's respirations at rest and after exercise. A normal cat at rest breathes about twenty to thirty times per minute. The movements of the chest are smooth and unstrained. After exercise, of course, the rate is much faster, and on very hot days or during periods of extreme excitement the rate increases above normal and panting may occur. Changes in the rate and character of a cat's respiration may indicate disease. Be sure to become familiar with your cat's normal breathing at rest, on cool and warm days, and during and after exercise so you can tell when changes have occurred.

HEART AND BLOOD (CIRCULATORY SYSTEM)

Your cat's circulatory system is similar to your own. It consists of a four-chambered heart that serves as a blood pump, arteries that carry blood away from the heart to the capillaries where molecular exchange occurs, and veins that return blood to the heart. There are no direct methods you can use to examine this system. A stethoscope (available at medical supply houses) will aid you in listening to your cat's heart, but one is not necessary to deal with everyday health problems you may encounter. The normal heart beats about 130 times per minute in the resting cat. Slightly agitated or nervous

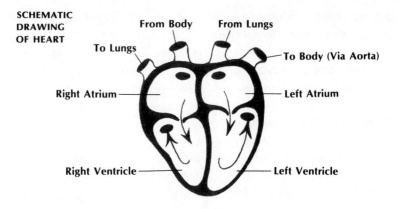

SCHEMATIC DRAWING OF HEART

From Body

From Lungs

To Lungs

To Body (Via Aorta)

Right Atrium

Left Atrium

Right Ventricle

Left Ventricle

but normal cats often have heart rates between 165 to 200 beats per minute. You can feel the heartbeat by placing your fingers or the palm of your hand against your cat's chest just behind the point of the elbow. Placing your hand completely around the lower part of the chest with your fingers on one side and your thumb on the other is another simple and easy way to feel your cat's heart beat. If you

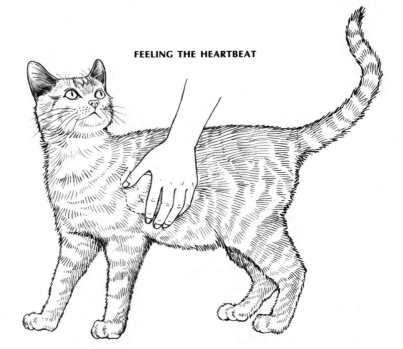

FEELING THE HEARTBEAT

cannot feel the heartbeat, you can usually hear it by placing your ear (or a stethoscope) against the chest. Each heartbeat consists of a strong, low-pitched thud, followed by a less intense, higher pitched thud, followed by a pause—lub-dup . . . lub-dup . . . lub-dup. In most healthy cats this rhythm is very regular, unlike dogs who usually have a variable heartbeat rhythm.

To take your cat's pulse, place your fingers at the middle of the inside surface of the rear leg near the point where the leg meets the body. This is the area where the femoral artery passes near the skin, allowing you to feel the pulse. The heart rate and pulse rate should be the same; true discrepancies be-

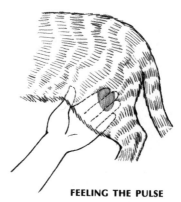

FEELING THE PULSE

tween them indicate serious circulatory problems. It is easiest to count the heart rate or pulse for fifteen seconds, then multiply by four to calculate the rate per minute.

A measure of capillary circulation is *capillary refilling time.* To measure this, press one finger firmly against your cat's gums. When you lift it away you will see a pale area that should refill with blood almost instantaneously. This measure of circulatory effectiveness can be helpful in evaluating possible shock (see page 202).

Blood is the fluid transported by the circulatory system. Blood consists of plasma, platelets, red blood cells, and white blood cells. The composition of the liquid portion of the blood, *plasma,* is very complex. It carries nutrients throughout the body, removes wastes, including carbon dioxide, and provides a means of transport for the hormones produced by the endocrine glands, as well as transporting the particulate blood constituents, the platelets and the red and white blood cells. *Platelets* are produced primarily in the bone marrow of the adult cat. These small bodies help prevent hemorrhage when a blood vessel is injured by aggregating together to form a physical barrier to blood flow and by stimulating clot formation. *Red blood cells* carry oxygen to the tissues and to a much lesser degree transport carbon dioxide away. They give blood its red color. They also determine the cat's *blood group* (type). Cats have three blood types A, B, and AB. Cats in group B have the greatest risk of reaction to unmatched blood transfusions since blood type A is most common. Ideally the blood type of both the donor and recipient should be known prior to blood transfusion. A veterinarian can have your cat's blood typed in anticipation of an emergency requiring blood transfusion or donation. There are several kinds of *white blood cells,* and each type has a particular function. As a group the white blood cells are most important in preventing and fighting infection. The red blood cells and white blood cells often change in number and in type when a cat becomes sick. The measurement of these cells by means of a *complete blood count* (CBC) performed by your veterinarian is frequently necessary for correct diagnosis and treatment of cat health problems.

The *spleen* is an abdominal organ that, although not necessary for life, has many functions related to the blood. You may have felt this organ during your examination of the digestive system (see page 21). In the adult cat the spleen produces some white cells, and, in times of need, it can produce red cells as well. It is a blood reservoir that can supply large numbers of red cells rapidly when the body needs oxygen. The spleen also removes old and abnormal red blood cells from circulation and stores some red cell components, such as iron.

LYMPHATIC AND IMMUNE SYSTEMS

The lymphatic system consists of lymph nodes and a network of thin-walled, permeable lymph channels and collecting ducts distributed throughout the body and associated with localized lymph nodes (see page 26). The lymph nodes filter the tissue fluids (which constantly bathe all body cells), removing foreign particulate matter and returning the fluids and blood cells they may contain to the general circulation via lymphatic channels that eventually empty into the great veins associated with the heart. Through its immune functions the lymphatic system also provides a way for the body to detect, identify, and destroy foreign material that invades it.

Simply put, the immune system processes foreign materials such as viruses, bacteria, other microbes, and environmental proteins through specialized white blood cells. *Neutrophils,* produced in the bone marrow and normally suspended in blood, can migrate quickly to the site of an infection to destroy and engulf some foreign materials and microbes. *Macrophages* can engulf invaders not destroyed by neutrophils and can signal other cells in the immune system to respond. Two types of *lymphocytes, T cells* and *B cells,* play central roles in the immune process. These cells are distributed throughout the body but are found aggregated in the lymph nodes, bone marrow, and spleen.

T cells arise in the fetal bone marrow and must be processed in the thymus gland to become functional. They play a major role in the body's ability to recognize itself and are, therefore, important in eliminating cancer cells and infectious agents. They also play a major role in graft rejection and in certain allergic responses. T cells *elabo-*

rate complex protein substances that act on other cells in the immune process in a wide range of biological activities.

B cells mature in the bone marrow, which serves as a continuing source of this kind of lymphocyte throughout life. B cells are activated to produce proteins called *antibodies* that are very specific for the *antigens* (proteins identified as foreign) that provoke them. B cells can produce their antibodies only with the aid of specific T cells (called *helper* T cells) acting together with specific stimulated macrophages that present the antigen to both the T and B lymphocytes. As time passes, the immunostimulated B lymphocytes differentiate into *plasma cells,* which are short-lived but capable of producing large quantities of antibodies, and long-lived *memory* B cells. These memory cells retain the ability to respond rapidly with antibody production specific for the same invader should reexposure occur.

Although you cannot detect most parts of the immune system during your physical exam, its normal daily functioning is vital to your cat's health. For information on how the immune system affects preventive vaccination of your pet, see page 87.

NERVOUS AND ENDOCRINE SYSTEMS

Integrating the functions of the various parts of the body is the main function of the nervous system and of the endocrine system. You cannot normally see or feel any of the components of these systems when you examine your cat. Nonetheless, if one system or the other is functioning abnormally it is usually not long before some striking change will occur in your animal. In general, the *nervous system* (brain, spinal cord, and peripheral nerves) is responsible for rapid body adjustments to environmental and internal stimuli. The *endocrine system,* for the most part, is responsible for more gradual responses that are mediated by chemical substances secreted by endocrine glands into the bloodstream *(hormones).* Complete neurological and endocrine examinations are not a routine part of your or your veterinarian's physical exams. For your information a brief outline of the functions of the various endocrine glands is listed on pages 36–37. Look at the drawings of the internal anatomy to see where these various glands are located. For very detailed information about these glands and other parts of your cat's anatomy and physiology you may want to consult the following books:

Cunningham, James G., *Textbook of Veterinary Physiology,* W.B. Saunders Company, Philadelphia, Penn., 1991.

Gilbert, Stephen G., *Pictorial Anatomy of the Cat,* University of Washington Press, Seattle, Wash., 1968.

McClure, Robert C., Mark J. Dallman, and Phillip G. Garrett, *Cat Anatomy,* Lea and Bebiger, Philadelphia, Penn., 1973.

Swenson, Melvin J., ed., *Dukes' Physiology of Domestic Animals,* Cornell University Press, Ithaca, N. Y., 10th ed., 1984.

ENDOCRINE GLAND	FUNCTION
Adrenal glands	*Cortex:* influences fat, carbohydrate, protein, and electrolyte metabolism. Affects water excretion and blood pressure; stimulates stomach acid secretion; inhibits inflammation and the immune system. *Medulla:* secretes *adrenaline* and *noradrenaline,* which raise blood sugar and help adaptation to stress.
Enteroendocrine cells of digestive tract	Secrete various hormones that regulate digestive tract motility and secretion of digestive enzymes. Some control over insulin secretion and the regulation of satiety.
Heart	*Atrial natriuretic peptide:* affects salt and water balance.
Islet of cells of the pancreas	Secrete *insulin, amylin,* and *glucagon,* which affect blood sugar level and fat and protein metabolism. Insulin also stimulates the appetite at the brain hypothalamus level.

ENDOCRINE GLAND	FUNCTION
Kidney	*Renin:* Affects blood pressure and sodium balance. *Erythropoietin:* Enhances red cell production.
Ovaries	Influence development of feminine characteristics; influence sexual behavior, estrus, and pregnancy.
Parathyroid glands	Influence calcium and phosphorus metabolism.
Pineal body	Affects sexual development and sexual cycles by sensing photoperiods.
Pituitary–hypothalamus	Regulates the activity of the ovaries, testes, thyroid, and adrenal cortex. Secretes *growth hormone,* which stimulates growth of body tissues. Controls milk secretion and milk letdown. Affects body water balance and thermoregulation. May modulate both short- and long-term memory.
Testes	Influence development of masculine characteristics; influence sex drive.
Thyroid	Controls metabolic rate and affects calcium and phosphorus metabolism.

Don't be surprised if your first examination of your cat takes an hour or two. If you have a kitten or an adult cat who has not been handled frequently before, it may take a full day to complete the exam because you may have to divide it into several parts separated by rest periods to compensate for your cat's reluctance to hold still for examination. Repeat your physical examination at least once a week while you are learning what is normal for your cat. By doing this you will train your cat to cooperate, and you will soon find that you no longer need to refer to this book so often. The time it takes for you to perform the examination will shorten considerably as you practice. You should eventually be able to finish it in about fifteen minutes. Most veterinarians become so skilled at physical examination that, until you become aware of what they are doing, you may not even realize that a physical examination is being performed. Your veterinarian may easily perform a routine physical in five or ten minutes. Special examinations, of course, take much longer.

Once you are familiar with your cat's anatomy, how frequently you repeat certain parts of a physical examination varies. You can get a good idea of your cat's general health by just being aware of his or her appetite and activity level. Be sure to examine the ears, eyes, teeth, and skin at least every two weeks. And examine the mammary glands of females, in particular, monthly. If your cat spends a considerable portion of time outside, you will probably have to make more of a conscious effort to do the examinations. Be sure to set aside several times a week to study your cat's condition; most illnesses are best treated if discovered early.

2

PREVENTIVE MEDICINE:

How to Care for a Healthy Cat

TRAINING

GROOMING

NUTRITION

**TRAVELING WITH OR SHIPPING
A CAT**

BOARDING YOUR CAT

**PREVENTIVE VACCINATION
PROCEDURES**

INTERNAL AND EXTERNAL PARASITES

**THE VALUE OF PREVENTIVE
MEDICINE**

PREVENTIVE MEDICINE CALENDAR

Daily: Feed a balanced diet. See page 60.

Groom cat as demanded by coat type and cat's habits. See page 50.

Observe cat's general external appearance, attitude, activity, and appetite. Any change may indicate a need for complete physical examination.

Clean litter pan, observe cat's stool, and, if possible, also observe the urine. For outdoor cats, look for evidence of abnormal stool on coat or behavior that may indicate urinary obstruction. See page 178.

Clean teeth if necessary. See page 58.

Weekly: Examine for external parasites and treat as necessary. See page 92 through 121.

Examine ears. See page 53.

Clean teeth if necessary. See page 58.

Administer hairball preventative. See page 168.

Every two weeks: Check claw length and appearance and trim, if necessary. See page 56.

Examine teeth if weekly cleaning is not necessary. See page 57.

Monthly: Examine mammary glands. See page 13.

Bathe, if necessary. See page 50.

Every six months: Perform a complete physical examination if one has not been indicated earlier.

Take a fecal sample to a veterinarian, particularly if there is an internal parasite problem in your area. See page 93.

Yearly: Take your cat to a veterinarian for a physical examination and booster vaccinations as necessary. See page 85.

$\mathbf{P}$reventive medicine is the best kind of medicine. Your veterinarian practices it when he or she vaccinates your cat for certain communicable diseases (see page 85). You can practice it by giving your cat good regular care at home, as discussed in this section. If you practice preventive medicine regularly, the occasions when your cat will need the care of a veterinarian can often be limited to yearly physical examinations and booster vaccinations. In the long run, preventive medicine will save you money and result in fewer stresses on your cat's body.

One of the best preventive medicine practices for cats is to keep them inside. This applies particularly to city cats and to cats who live in neighborhoods heavily populated with other cats, dogs, and people. Strict enclosure is not necessary; a system whereby your cat spends the most time indoors and is supervised outdoors is just about as satisfactory in health terms. However, do not allow your cat to roam without restriction or force your cat outdoors if you would like to avoid frequent trips to the veterinarian. Also be sure to provide your cat with a safe collar, an identification tag, and a collar bell if he or she is allowed outdoors. As long as their owners give them enough opportunities for physical and mental stimulation, indoor cats and cats that stick close to home when outdoors miss out on nothing necessary for a happy, healthy life; and they experience infectious disease, automobile accidents, poisoning, gunshot wounds, and cat fights much less frequently than their roaming peers. Roaming cats are responsible for serious predation of small wildlife and songbirds, so the least an owner who allows his or her cat outdoors without supervision can do is provide an effective collar bell. Make the decision whether your cat is to have access to the outdoors early, then stick to it. Cats kept indoors when young usually show little desire to roam, even when allowed outside later in life.

INDOOR VERSUS OUTDOOR CATS

TRAINING

The training necessary to make a cat easy to live with is minimal when compared with what the average dog requires in order to become a pleasant companion. Training for many cats includes only housebreaking (housetraining) and teaching them to come in response to their names, but many other things can, and sometimes must, be taught. Cats need to learn that curtains, houseplants, tabletops, and kitchen counters are off limits. They need to learn that biting and scratching are unacceptable ways to play with people. Some cats shake hands, retrieve balls, sit on command, and do other tricks that are amusing but not necessary for good companionship. Since only a small part of this book is devoted to understanding your cat's behavior and modifying it when necessary, you may find the following books interesting and useful:

Bohnenkamp, Gwen, *Manners for the Modern Cat,* Perfect Paws, P.O. Box 885214, San Francisco, Calif. 94188.

Dunbar, Ian, and Gwen Bohnenkamp, Series of behavior booklets that include *Litterbox Training, Household Destruction, Social Problems, Hyperactivity and Nocturnal Activity, Biting and Scratching,* and *Cat Training,* James and Kenneth Publishers, 2140 Shattuck Avenue, #2406, Berkeley, Calif. 94704. Also available are a series of audiocassettes on feline behavior and a cat behavior booklist.

Fox, Michael W., *Understanding Your Cat,* St. Martin's Press, N. Y., 1992.

In order to have a good relationship with your cat and to have success in any training you choose to do, you must be able to understand your cat's body language. Failure to do so not only prevents you from really appreciating the nuances of your cat's disposition but also can result in serious scratches and bites to you. Cats' body language can be most easily understood if you remember that relatively subtle alterations in pupil size, body hair, ear, mouth, whisker, tail, and body position can combine with vocalization in numerous ways to indicate your cat's mood. The following information describes only the most basic and obvious ways a cat uses his or her body to communicate.

NEUTRAL POSTURE   The neutral posture is assumed by a relaxed cat calmly observing his or her environment. The cat's mouth may be held open or closed.

The tail is usually held in a relaxed, lowered position, and both ears are pointed forward.

When alert, a cat's whole body becomes more rigid, the ears are held erect, and the tail becomes slightly raised. Often the tail twitches and the cat holds his or her mouth closed as the whiskers are brought forward. Alert cats may purr when they are relaxed with the person (or object) that draws their attention. **ALERT POSTURE**

As an alert cat moves forward to greet you, the tail will move to the straight-up position. Although the back may be slightly arched, a friendly cat saying hello always keeps the fur lying smooth. He or she may purr and/or rub the side of his or her head against you. **GREETING**

Unlike the alert cat who pushes forward to give a friendly greeting, the frightened (threatened) but self-confident cat may rush forward and attack. This cat's facial expression becomes menacing as the pupils constrict and direct eye contact is maintained. Both the ears and whiskers may be directed forward when there is a clear intention to attack. The tail may stand straight up, but most often it extends out from the body and its tip flicks back and forth, expressing disturbance with the situation. Hissing, growling, and spitting complete the threatening picture. Should you need to handle a cat exhibiting this body language, be prepared to risk a bite or severe clawing. Unless the aggressive cat can be left undisturbed for at least thirty minutes, this mood is difficult to change. **OFFENSIVE THREAT**

Cats who feel threatened but are less self-confident may adopt similar body language but turn their bodies to the side to appear larger than they would in a head-on approach. They also draw their whiskers back and flatten their ears against the backs of their heads. The pupils dilate and the mouth is opened wide to display the fangs. The cat will often scream and hiss. (This is a typical Halloween cat posture.) Sometimes a cat displaying the defensive threat type of body language can be gradually calmed down with soft talking and cautious attempts at petting, but there are many gradations and variations in this body language pattern, especially if the cat is in a situation that elicits conflicted emotions. Misguided attempts to handle or calm the cat can result in injury. To complicate matters further, male cats may display similar body language in play. **DEFENSIVE THREAT**

Fearful cats often assume a crouched position while maintaining the ruffled fur, flattened ears, and vocalizations of a more aggressive cat. **FEAR/ SUBMISSION**

Extremely fearful cats who are willing to defend themselves may roll onto their backs with their claws unsheathed and their legs ready to kick and scratch. When fear turns to complete submission, however, the cat will become quiet, smooth his or her fur, and avoid eye contact with you. It is usually safe to handle a fearful cat once he or she has become submissive as long as you are careful not to scare the cat again.

CAT BODY LANGUAGE

Neutral

Alert

Greeting

Defensive Threat

Offensive Threat

Fear/Submission

TEACHING A CAT HIS OR HER NAME

Use your cat's name frequently during training. Be sure to use it at pleasurable times such as during feeding, play, and when giving affection. Although you must use it as well to get your cat's attention before correction, your cat will learn his or her name much more quickly when it has pleasant associations. If you associate it consistently with good things such as special food treats, your cat will soon come running when you call his or her name. One caution: Never punish your cat after he or she comes in response to his or her name. Your cat may think you are giving punishment for coming and learn to avoid you when called by name.

BEHAVIOR CORRECTION

Although many cats do not seem to respond to punishment as correction for misdeeds, most do. Each time you get a new cat you will have to determine what method is best for that individual. In general, avoid physical punishment; instead get your cat to respond to gentle words and petting as positive rewards for acceptable behavior. Use a sharp "No!" when you find your cat doing something undesirable and see if this is sufficient to stop the behavior and prevent its recurrence. Be sure, however, to avoid punishing a cat after the fact for something he or she has done, since delayed correction is not only ineffective but confusing to your pet.

If harsh words are not sufficient correction, a loud hand clap is startling and sometimes quite effective. In some instances you may have to resort to picking your cat up by the scruff of the neck and giving a shake. A spank on the rump should be a last resort. Cats are intelligent creatures, and this type of physical punishment sometimes results in a cat who will "behave" when you are around, but immediately do the forbidden when you leave the room or the house. Also some cats may become aggressive toward people who administer physical punishment. A squirt from a water gun or spray bottle will often work better than punishment more directly associated with you. Keep a filled implement at hand. When your cat chews on your plants, gets into the fireplace, climbs on the curtains, jumps onto the stove or into the toilet, or does something else equally as dangerous or irritating in exploration, give a squirt to his or her face. The unwanted behavior will usually stop after a few corrections, and the squirt gun method often produces long-lasting results. Booby traps are another means of correction useful for preventing misbehavior in your absence. Ask your veterinarian and/or consult the book list for information on the use of mousetraps, deodorants, alcohol or perfume, aluminum foil, empty soda cans, motion sensors, and mothballs as aids to behavior correction.

TOYS

Be sure to provide your cat with sufficient diversions at home. A bored cat is a cat who gets into trouble. Continued correction will never result in a "perfectly behaved" cat if you fail to provide permissible entertainment. Many commercial cat toys are good, but be sure to inspect them well before assuming they are safe. All cats' toys should be big enough so that they cannot be swallowed (even with difficulty) and sturdy enough so that they cannot be torn apart and eaten. Avoid string and thread and also balls of yarn, as many cats unroll them and chew on the strands. Cats often swallow these materials, which can cause serious gastrointestinal problems including intestinal obstruction followed by perforation. A patch of fresh catnip, catnip-stuffed toys, paper bags, empty thread spools, stuffed socks, and bones that can be chewed on but not swallowed are good inexpensive toys that many cats enjoy. A cloth- or carpet-covered cat "tree" is more expensive, but is often immediately adopted as favorite perch and scratching area instead of your furniture. (For more information about scratching posts, see page 54.)

AGE TO GET A KITTEN

If you have a choice, probably the best time to bring home a new kitten is when he or she is between eight and ten weeks of age. Although a critical period for socialization has not been firmly established for the cat as it has for the dog, there is ample evidence that kittens who do not receive normal contact with other cats when young (before six weeks of age) tend to develop abnormal behavioral patterns such as extreme shyness or aggressiveness and may never relate well to other cats. By waiting to bring your cat home until he or she is eight to ten weeks of age you allow time for proper social interaction with the littermates and the mother, while still acquiring a kitten young enough to be able to adapt well to you and to the new environment in your home.

HANDLING IS IMPORTANT

Although this period of socialization to other cats is important, of equal importance is proper socialization to people. Since it has been shown that cats between the ages of three and seven weeks handled daily by people are generally much less aloof and more willing to accept restraint than those who have not been handled, be sure to choose a kitten that has had lots of interaction with and attention from people. Continue to handle your new kitten for at least an hour a day when you bring him or her home. Playing with your kitten with toys is not enough. Stroking, handling the feet, head, ears, and mouth and teaching your cat to accept (and even enjoy) gentle restraint is very important. Cats with naturally more confident personalities will blossom with this sort of handling even if their early socialization could have been better, and those with more timid or aggressive temperaments can usually be significantly rehabilitated with time and patience.

GIVE YOUR CAT A PLACE OF HIS OR HER OWN

Unless you want to share your bed with your cat, give your kitten a place of his or her own from the first night with you. Get a cat bed or use a cardboard box and line it with a clean, washable towel or blanket. Place this bed in your cat's special area. If your kitten does not yet know how to use a litter pan, it is probably best to choose an area that is large enough to contain your kitten's bed, his or her food and water dishes, and a litter pan. Try to provide some significant distance between the litter pan and the feeding area. Cats prefer to eliminate away from feeding areas and will usually use the pan more consistently and effectively if it is not placed near the food. Enclose the kitten in his or her special place at night and whenever you are not around to provide supervision to avoid elimination accidents and accidental injuries. A large dog-sized shipping crate is ideal to use as a temporary enclosure, but a small room will work as well and is better when your kitten grows larger and becomes more active. A room provides plenty of space for indestructible toys, safe climbing objects, and a scratching post, all of which are necessary for proper release and channeling of a normal kitten's activities. Be firm and consistent with any arrangement you choose in order to avoid encouraging any mischief-making habits and to reserve your bed for yourself. It's easy to take a charming, tiny kitten to bed for a few nights; it's just about impossible to keep an adult cat off a cozy bed once he or she has claimed it.

HOUSETRAINING

Because cats are instinctively fastidious about where they eliminate, housetraining (housebreaking) the average cat is usually very easy.

Often a kitten will already be using a litter pan when you first bring him or her into your home. If not, you will probably be able to train your cat to use one very quickly.

Get a smooth-surfaced pan (plastic or enamel-surfaced ones are best) that can be easily cleaned and disinfected or use disposable litter boxes. Newspapers or chemically untreated sawdust or wood shavings are sanitary materials to use for litter, but commercial clay, silica, or cellulose litters are best. They are clean, absorbent, tend to reduce odors, and most cats seem to like them (especially litters with a sandlike texture). Line the pan with the litter material, then put it in a place easily accessible to your cat but not directly adjacent to food or water bowls. If you have a kitten be sure he or she doesn't have to go too far to find the litter pan at first and be sure the sides of the pan aren't too high to climb over easily, or you may have trouble with housebreaking. If your cat doesn't use the litter pan correctly from the start as most cats do, you can help teach the proper behavior by placing the kitten into the pan after eating, when he or she awakens, and after play. Give praise when you see the desired result and administer correction if elimination begins in the wrong place by saying "No!" sharply and firmly and placing the cat back in the litter pan to finish.

If you choose to allow your cat free access to the outdoors, you can use the litter pan to teach your cat to eliminate outdoors. Once your cat has become accustomed to going in and out, move the litter pan gradually from its original site toward the cat's usual exit. If at any time during this procedure your cat does not use the pan, move it back to the last place where it was used for a day or two before continuing. In a few days your cat should be using the pan right next to the exit. Then move the pan to a place just outside the exit and then to the selected outdoors spot for elimination. After your cat has been using the pan outside for a few days, remove it entirely. Most cats will continue to choose to eliminate outside. Cat feces in the garden can be a human health hazard, however (see page 93). If your cat uses your garden as a toilet, wear gloves while gardening or at least wash your hands and fingernails thoroughly afterward. Children, whose habits tend to be less sanitary than adults', should not play in areas where your cat may bury stools.

Remove stools from the litter pan daily. This is best accomplished with a spoonlike litter strainer that can be purchased at a pet store or supermarket. If you use disposable litter pan liners or completely disposable litter pans, discard them at least every fourth day. Otherwise, wash the litter pan thoroughly at least every fourth day. (Do this outdoors or in a sink not used for washing dishes or bathing.) Use hot water, detergent, and chlorine bleach, then rinse the pan well and allow it to dry before replacing the litter. *Do not* use disinfectants containing phenol (carbolic acid), cresols, resorcinol, or hexylresorcinol; they can be toxic to cats. Also avoid products containing ammonia; these may smell like urine to your cat and discourage him or her from using a pan because it doesn't smell clean. If this cleaning schedule is not sufficient to keep odors at an acceptable level, baking soda is a safe product to try. Place a layer of it equal to about one third the weight of the litter in the bottom of the litter pan each time you change it.

Sometimes a litter pan acceptable to you won't be one acceptable to your cat. Most cats do not like wet or dirty litter pans and will begin to eliminate in abnormal places when dissatisfied with their normal toilet area. So be sure to remove litter from the pan and replace soiled with fresh material whenever it becomes wet, even if this occurs more frequently than your normal cleaning schedule. The ideal schedule is to empty and clean the litter box daily. It is also important to have *at least* one litter pan per cat if you have two or more. In fact, it is a good idea to have two litter pans even if you have just one cat, since it has been shown that feral (wild) cats rarely urinate and defecate in the same place.

LITTER BOX PROBLEMS MAY CAUSE HOUSE SOILING

Elimination in abnormal places may also occur when the litter pan is clean and dry. Sometimes this is because you have changed litter material after using one kind for a long period of time, or sometimes the cat has developed a preference for a material such as carpet instead of cat litter. If you must change brands of litter do it gradually by mixing the new kind with the old since abrupt changes will induce as many as 50% of cats to begin to urinate (and/or defecate) outside their litter pan. A change from normal use of the litter pan to house soiling may also be caused by psychological stress. Be sure the litter pan is located away from heavy traffic areas and that your cat has not developed a behavior problem caused by separation anxiety, conflicts with other pets, or harassment by children. Since cats do not like to eliminate where they eat or sleep, confinement to a small room or a cage often encourages the use of the litter pan instead of another site and can help calm a cat that is disturbed by others in the household. Illness can also cause problems with housetraining. For more information see pages 179, 234, and 273.

GROOMING

Whether you will need to follow a particular grooming schedule with your cat will depend greatly upon the length and density of his or her coat, whether he or she spends the majority of time indoors or outdoors, and whether he or she self-grooms well. In general, cats who spend time outdoors will need baths and brushing more frequently in order to make them pleasant companions than cats spending all their time indoors. Indoor cats may need their nails trimmed frequently. Read this section and decide for yourself which grooming schedule you need to apply to your cat.

BATHING

Although cats groom themselves, not all do it sufficiently often or sufficiently well to remain free of fleas, to keep themselves clean enough to be pleasant companions, and to have a healthy and good-looking hair coat and skin. Tomcats who spend a great deal of time outside seem to be the worst offenders, but any cat may need a bath on occasion when he or she becomes dirty, for flea control, or for other health reasons. Accustom your cat to bathing early in life so it won't be difficult to do later when the necessity arises.

WHEN TO START BATHS It is best to give a young cat a bath about once a month, starting around three months of age, just so he or she becomes adjusted to the bathing procedure. You can, however, bathe a kitten as young as seven or eight weeks of age if you do it quickly and prevent chilling. Bathing itself does not cause illness, but the stress of being chilled can predispose any cat, particularly a young one, to disease. Once your cat has become familiar with bathing and is cooperative, use the appearance, feel, and odor of the skin and fur as guides to bathing frequency.

HOW OFTEN TO BATHE Once a month is usually sufficient for an average cat with healthy skin. However, once a week may be necessary to achieve good flea control (see page 110). Bathing once a week also significantly decreases the allergens in cat's fur that are usually responsible for human allergies to cats.

SHAMPOO TO USE Unless your cat has a specific skin problem requiring medicated shampoos recommended by a veterinarian, use a good quality cat shampoo or a gentle human shampoo (e.g., baby shampoo) for bathing. Cats generally have a skin pH of 7, so shampoos with a neutral pH are best. Avoid bar soap and dishwashing detergents since they seem to be particularly drying and very irritating to some cat's skin and hair. A cream rinse (products for humans or for pets) can be used following shampooing to make the comb-out of long-haired cats easier.

Before the bath it is a good idea—but not absolutely necessary—to protect your cat's ear canals and eyes from the soap and water. This can be done by placing large wads of cotton firmly inside the ears and by applying a nonmedicated ophthalmic ointment to the eyes. (To learn how to apply eye ointment, see page 249.) Long-haired cats should be combed out before bathing to make grooming afterward easier.

Place your cat in a sink or bathtub and use warm water. If your cat is an adult and a little uncooperative, gain control and avoid scratches to yourself by grasping the cat with one hand around the base of the head just behind the ears or by the scruff of the neck (see page 252.) Then use your free hand for soaping and rinsing. If your cat is extremely insecure, a narrow nylon harness put on the cat and attached to a leash that is tied to a fixture (never a hot water faucet) will keep the cat in the tub. Never leave a cat tied in this manner alone. Better than this, though, is a window screen placed in the tub. Most cats will cling to this with their claws, remaining in the tub, leaving both your hands free for the job at hand. Praise your cat if he or she cooperates, and try to correct with a "No" if not. Another technique that can be useful is to wash the cat with his or her body placed in a nylon net bag that has a drawstring closure that can be drawn up snugly to the cat's neck. As a last resort, your veterinarian can provide tranquilizers to use when it is necessary to bathe an extremely unmanageable cat.

Start the bath by wetting your cat thoroughly starting at the base of the skull and working toward the tail, then apply the shampoo and suds it up. Two shampoo applications may be necessary if your cat is very dirty. Follow the sudsing with a thorough rinsing, since any soap left on the skin can be irritating and any stunned parasites (see page 110) left on the skin may wake up later and continue their activities. Once the fur is free of shampoo apply a cream rinse, if necessary, then rinse again thoroughly. This may be followed by a flea dip (see page 110). Towel drying is usually sufficient, but, if you accustom your cat to the sound, you can use a hair drier to speed the drying process.

GROOMING BETWEEN BATHS

The kind of grooming your cat's coat needs between baths depends on its length and character. Short-haired cats usually need little grooming, but you may want to give them a bi-weekly brushing to distribute the oils of the coat and to remove loose hair, lessening the amount you find around the house and the amount they ingest while self-grooming. A grooming mitt or slicker brush works well for this. Long-haired cats usually need frequent (preferably daily) brushing to prevent matted coats and to lessen the possibility of hairball formation (see page 168).

HAIR MATS Mats of hair often develop behind the ears and under the legs, so don't forget to brush or comb these areas thoroughly. When you find small mats, they can often be teased apart with a comb. If they become large, cut them away with scissors or clippers.

TAR, PAINT, OIL Tar, paint, and oil can be difficult substances to remove from the coat. *Do not* use gasoline, turpentine, kerosene, paint remover, or other similar substances in an attempt to remove them. Cut out small accumulations of tar or paint. Large amounts of tar can be removed without cutting by soaking the affected hair in vegetable or mineral oil or ointments containing the surface-active agent polyoxethylene sorbitan (polysorbate) for twenty-four hours (e.g., bandage tar-covered feet soaked in oil), then washing with soap and water. Small patches of oil on the coat can be removed by sprinkling them with cornstarch, allowing the starch to soak up the oil, then brushing it out. Large amounts can be treated with mineral oil as you would for tar. As a last resort (e.g., if your cat is covered with oil) use a gentle dishwashing detergent as a shampoo.

SKUNK ODOR If your cat gets sprayed by a skunk, use shampoo and water for a bath, then follow with a milk or tomato juice soak. Pour the milk or juice on straight; let it sit for about ten minutes, then rinse it out. If you don't have access to milk or tomato juice, you can follow the bath with a rinse of lemon or lime juice mixed with equal parts of water or 1 teaspoonful of household ammonia in 1 quart of water. If you rinse with lemon or lime juice or ammonia, be sure to keep it out of your cat's eyes, nose, and mouth while waiting to perform the final clear water rinse. Commercial products for the removal of skunk odor are also available at pet stores.

GROOMING TOOLS

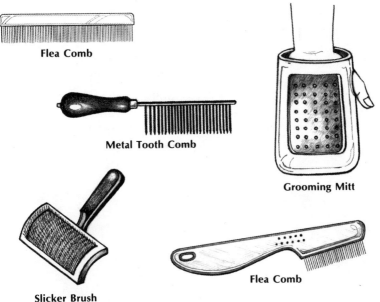

Flea Comb

Metal Tooth Comb

Grooming Mitt

Slicker Brush

Flea Comb

In areas such as California where *foxtails* (wild barley) or other **FOXTAILS** troublesome plant awns grow, longer haired cats with access to the outdoors need to have their coats examined for them daily in the late spring, summer, and fall. Although cats' grooming habits usually prevent problems with plant awns, those not discovered and removed easily penetrate the skin, causing irritation and infection.

Cats affected with stud tail (see page 13) may benefit cosmetically **STUD TAIL** if you apply cornstarch to the affected area every other day during the brushing process. Washing the affected area two or three times a week with a shampoo that contains benzoyl peroxide is also beneficial. Stubborn cases can often be kept under control by a daily cleansing with rubbing alcohol. Apply it by gently scrubbing the affected skin with an alcohol-soaked cotton ball.

EARS

Most cats who groom themselves adequately keep their ears extremely clean and need no help from you. Small accumulations of wax are normal. If your cat doesn't remove them you can do it easily following a bath by using a damp towel or soft cloth. Wrap the cloth over your index finger, then clean out the excess wax and dirt as far down the ear canal as your finger will reach. Any folds or crevices you cannot reach into with your finger can be cleaned using a cotton-tipped swab dry or moistened as needed with water, rubbing alcohol, or mineral oil. You cannot damage your cat's eardrums by cleaning in this manner unless you are extremely forceful, since the canals are very narrow and deep and do not allow ready penetration by a cotton-tipped swab.

If your cat has an inflammation or infection of the ear (otitis) special ear cleaning may be necessary (see page 250).

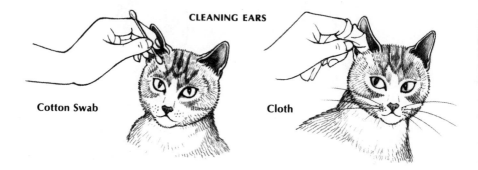

CLEANING EARS

Cotton Swab

Cloth

CLAWS

SCRATCHING—
A NORMAL
BEHAVIOR

As part of their inherited behavioral tendency to groom themselves, cats condition their claws (toenails). They do this by scratching on objects that catch the outer, worn claw covering and remove it, exposing the sharp, new claw beneath. As well as sharpening the claws, the claw marks help cats visually mark their territories, and the scent glands on the feet may also mark the scratched area. This is a completely normal feline behavior. It can, however, be a problem for owners of cats confined indoors. Cats who are not provided with a scratching post or board will use rugs, furniture, and draperies for their scratching, damaging or ruining these furnishings completely. (Cats also remove their worn outer claw coverings with their teeth, but this is seen less frequently and doesn't cause problems for owners as does scratching behavior.)

PROVIDE A
SCRATCHING
POST AT A
YOUNG AGE

Provide your cat with a scratching post or board while he or she is very young in order to avoid problems later. You can use a commercial scratching post—horizontal or vertical posts usually covered with carpet—or you can make a scratching post yourself. A board about eight inches wide and twelve to eighteen inches long, bare or fabric covered, can be attached to the wall. It should be at a height

such that your cat can rest comfortably on the rear feet while
scratching and stretching, so it
may have to be raised as your
cat grows. A good scratching post
can be made of a bare or fabric-
covered board built freestanding
horizontally or vertically. Many
cats seem to prefer a log with the
bark still on it or sisal doormats
that can be hung vertically or left
on the floor. Whichever scratching object you choose, be sure it is
stable to prevent it from coming
loose or falling over onto the cat
during a vigorous scratching ses-
sion.

SCRATCHING POST

Place the scratching object near
your cat's sleeping or resting area when first beginning training,
because cats usually stretch and scratch just after awakening. Then
praise and pet your cat whenever he or she uses it. Whenever your
cat scratches at furniture or other undesirable objects, give a correction and take the cat to the scratching post. However, be sure to
emphasize positive reinforcement by giving your cat food, play, and
affection whenever he or she is scratching at the post. Too much
punishment will only result in a cat who will learn never to scratch
anything (including the post) in front of you. Encourage play with
toys that can be dangled from the post. This will give you an opportunity to give praise for jumping and clawing at the post. With consist-
ency and repetition your cat should soon be using the scratching
article and leaving other objects alone.

If you have an adult cat whom you have failed to condition to a
scratching post while young, your problem may be more difficult.
The basic principles of correction and praise are the same, but it may
take much longer for you to achieve the desired results. You may also
have to temporarily move favored but inappropriate scratching objects, such as couches, and replace them with a scratching post
and/or booby trap the areas and objects which are off-limits. Try to
provide a scratching post covered with a material at least as desirable
as the things your cat has been scratching on before, or you may not
get far at all. Animal behaviorists feel that loosely woven rough
fabrics with longitudinally oriented threads are preferred by cats, but
you may have to experiment a little before finding just the right one.

During the training period you may have to trim your cat's claws in order to avoid furniture damage.

HOW TO TRIM CLAWS Trimmers for human nails are satisfactory for trimming cats' claws, or you may use nail trimmers designed especially for pets, such as the White's type. Resco trimmers, usually used for dogs' toenails, also work fine for cats. To trim your cat's nails, extend the claw as described on page 9. If you do this in good light and your cat's claws are not darkly pigmented, you will be able to see the pink *dermis* (the quick). Cut the nail just beyond the point where you see the dermis end. If you cut into the dermis, it is painful to the animal, and some bleeding will usually occur. The bleeding stops, but the pain will make your cat reluctant to have a nail trim the next time. Pigmented nails are harder to trim, since the color obscures the quick. However, with good, intense light you can often see the quick even if the nail is dark colored. If you can't see the dermis, the easiest rule to follow is to cut the nail just beyond the point where it starts to curve downward. If you accidentally trim the nail into the quick and the bleeding doesn't stop quickly, you can apply a styptic powder or pencil, Monsel's solution (ferric subsulfate, available from pharmacists), cornstarch, or a black tea bag that has been moistened then squeezed out, or you can bandage the foot firmly for about an hour (see page 256).

RESCO NAIL TRIMMER

WHITE'S NAIL TRIMMER

If you have accustomed your cat to being handled at a young age, nail trimming should be a one person job. If your cat seems particularly disagreeable, try to accustom him or her to the procedure gradually, trimming a few nails at a time and correcting bad behavior before resorting to a second person for aid. Cats who are overrestrained for nail trimming will become aggressive before having a chance to learn to cooperate. An alternative to nail trimming is the application of commercially available tiny wooden or shell beads or clear plastic nail covers to the cat's claws with adhesive. These nail protectors need to be replaced every few weeks.

CROSS SECTION OF CLAW

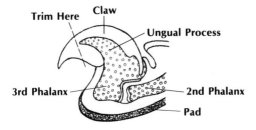

Trim Here   Claw

Ungual Process

3rd Phalanx

2nd Phalanx

Pad

Declawing *(onchyectomy)* is a surgical procedure that can be re-sorted to when nail trimming and attempts to train a cat to use a scratching post have failed. It may also be necessary for cats who are not careful to keep their claws sheathed during play. It should not, however, be a routine procedure for pet cats. It is too painful a procedure to be performed unnecessarily, and cats who have been declawed are at a disadvantage in some situations. They are unable to protect themselves well against dogs or other cats and often cannot climb as well as normal cats to escape danger. Therefore, declawed cats should not be allowed outdoors unsupervised. When you and your veterinarian agree that declawing is necessary, the surgery is performed under general anesthesia in the veterinary hospital. The front claws are removed completely so regrowth is impossible, and the feet are usually bandaged for a day or two. The rear claws can be removed if desired, but this is unnecessary, since they do not usually cause a problem in scratching behavior or accidental injury to the cat's owner during play and are necessary for a cat to scratch him or herself. Once the bandages are removed, your cat will be able to return home and within two weeks should be free from pain.

An alternative surgery is one in which the tendons that extend the claws are cut. This procedure has not found general favor, as regular nail trimming to avoid growth of the toenails into the paw pads is required afterward.

TEETH

Almost all cats need special attention given to their teeth to preserve them and to minimize mouth odors. Most cats, like most people, develop deposits called dental *tartar* or *calculus* on their teeth. When present it is most obvious on the premolars and molars as a hard yellow-brown or grayish-white deposit that cannot be removed by brushing or scraping with a fingernail. Its presence is not normal (see page 23). It can cause gum disease *(gingivitis, periodontitis)*,

57

accompanied by discomfort and halitosis (bad breath), and can eventually lead to loss of teeth. Many cats develop mouth disease and lose teeth. Most do not develop true cavities, but many develop extensive cavitylike erosions in the tooth enamel and cementum of the tooth root (*cervical line lesions, neck lesions, external odonto-clastic resorption lesions*). Many cats lose teeth because of these erosions and others because their owners miss the early stages of gum disease.

TARTAR PREVENTION Once tartar is present it can only be removed properly with special instruments—either tartar scrapers (tooth scalers) or an ultrasonic tooth cleaner. Tartar is best removed by a veterinarian, since anesthesia is usually necessary to do a really thorough cleaning job, followed by polishing to provide a smooth surface that discourages new tartar formation. Tartar originates in a soft white- to yellow-colored substance on teeth called *materia alba* or plaque, which is material left on the teeth after eating combined with saliva, bacteria, and bacterial by-products. You can remove this plaque and prevent tartar formation in the following ways:

1. Feed your cat a large quantity of dry cat food. Feeding a hard food diet will not absolutely prevent tartar in all cats, because its formation is dependent on the biochemical conditions in each cat's mouth. However, it has been shown experimentally that, in general, cats eating an all-dry-food diet accumulate substantially less tartar and have much less plaque than cats eating solely moist, soft food.

2. Encourage your cat to chew on (but not eat and swallow) large, hard bones. This will help remove plaque by abrasion. Although most cats will not chew on hard rubber or rawhide toys as dogs will, if you give them large hard bones with a little meat on them when they are young, cats will often develop the habit of bone chewing. Beef and lamb marrowbones are good. Keep in mind that bone chewing may cause broken teeth, and avoid bones that splinter, such as pork chop and chicken bones, to prevent stomach or intestinal perforation. Be sure to thoroughly cook any bones offered by roasting or boiling to avoid disease transmission. Some cats also enjoy chewing on freshly cooked corncobs.

3. Clean your cat's teeth yourself a few times a week. You can use a toothbrush, but a gauze pad, rough cloth, or cotton-tipped swab will also work. Moisten the cleaning tool with water, then scrub the teeth and gums vigorously. It's not usually necessary to do the inner tooth surfaces, because the motion of the tongue keeps the areas next to it relatively free from plaque. Dentifrices are not always necessary, but many products are available that provide additional abrasion (pastes containing calcium or silicates), an oxygenating effect (to inhibit bacteria), or antimicrobials (to inhibit bacteria). *Chlorhexidine gluconate* or *acetate* (0.1%) is an easy-to-find disinfectant that has been shown to inhibit plaque formation when brushed into the gum-tooth junction. Avoid toothpastes designed for humans as they foam excessively. If your cat's gums bleed even though they look healthy otherwise, it is not usually because you have scrubbed too hard, but because they are in the early stages of disease. Good tooth care should cause an early problem to correct itself. If you see loose teeth, gums that are red and pulling away from the teeth (receding), or if bleeding gums do not improve with good preventive care as suggested above, you will need the help of a veterinarian to clear up the condition. Loose teeth will need to be removed and dirty ones cleaned.

You can begin treatment at home with daily gum massage. Use a cotton-tipped swab to rub gently at the tooth-gum junction. This process will help a cat get used to the type of oral manipulation that will be needed to restore a diseased mouth to health. Tooth brushing on a regular basis will be necessary to achieve a healthy mouth in any cat who has been allowed to develop periodontal disease.

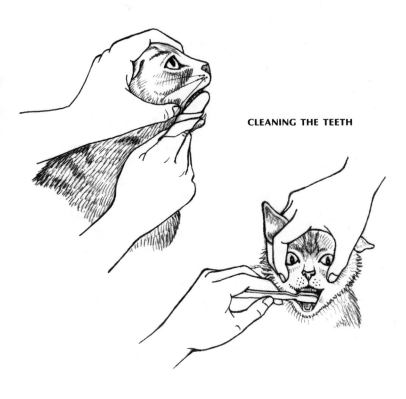

CLEANING THE TEETH

NUTRITION

For many years little was known about the domestic cat's nutritional requirements. Now, however, nutritional research has revealed that cats have distinctive nutrient needs that probably arose in concert with their development as true carnivores. Despite research efforts, minimum requirements for all the necessary food substances have not yet been well established for cats, so deciding exactly what is the most healthful diet for your cat's growth, adulthood, and old age can be challenging.

In selecting the right foods for your pet keep in mind that external manifestations of nutritional deprivation may not appear until months or even years of feeding an inadequate diet have passed. Once present, the physical effects of poor nutrition often can never be reversed. Use the information in this chapter and the following publication, which is revised periodically, to help you make the right feeding decisions for your cats:

National Research Council (U.S.), *Nutrient Requirement of Cats,* National Academy Press, Washington, D.C., 1986.

Nutrition is a complicated subject with specialized terminology. To help you understand it more fully, here are some terms that are used in the following pages.

TERMS USED TO EXPRESS NUTRIENT CONTENT OF FOODS AND/OR NUTRIENT REQUIREMENTS

1. "As-fed basis." This phrase refers to foods' nutrient and moisture contents expressed as percentages. Normally, the percentages used refer to the amounts found in a pet food product as it comes directly from the can, bag, or box. However, the values for moisture will increase if water is added to the food, thereby diluting the other nutrients on an as-fed basis. Since the moisture content of foods can vary considerably (from about 5% to about 80%) comparison of nutrients present to a nutritional chart or between products becomes difficult unless the differing moisture levels are taken into consideration (see "dry-matter basis"). However, when choosing among products of the same general moisture content (e.g., between canned foods) there will be no problems if they are compared with one another on an as-fed basis. When adding foods or

---

supplements to preformulated products, recommendations are often given on an as-fed basis in order to facilitate addition of the item (e.g., 1 teaspoonful per pound dry food as fed).

2. "Dry-matter basis." This phrase refers to the nutrient content of food expressed as a percentage of the food after all water is removed. For example, a food containing 20% protein and 50% water (moisture) on an as-fed basis will contain about 3 ounces (oz) (about 90 grams [g]) of protein in a pound (lb) (454 g). If all the water is removed, leaving ½ pound (227 g) dry matter, the amount of protein, 3 oz (90 g), per portion remains the same but the percentage expressed on a dry-matter basis increases to 40%. Expressing all nutrients on the same dry-matter basis (dry basis) makes comparison of different kinds of foods to one another and to charts of nutrient requirements easier. This is why requirements for certain vitamins, minerals, proteins, and fats are often expressed as a percentage of the dry matter of the food, i.e., on a dry basis (see chart, page 69). (To convert an amount of nutrient from an as-fed to a dry-matter basis, use the calculation on page 74).

3. "As a percentage of calories." The biological availability of certain nutrients, especially protein, is affected by calorie intake. In instances where the amount of a nutrient needed will be affected by the energy (calories) provided by the diet, nutrient content or requirements are often expressed as a percentage of calories provided by the diet. Although nutritionally correct, this concept is difficult for most people who are not professional nutritionists to apply, and information presented in this form is kept to a minimum in this book.

4. "Per pound (or kiligram) of body weight." The simpliest, but sometimes less technically correct means to express the amount of any nutrient needed is to give the requirement as a unit per pound (or kilogram) of body weight. By convention, nutrients are expressed in various units such as international units (IU), milligrams (mg), or micrograms (μg).

TERMS USED TO DESCRIBE NUTRIENT AVAILABILITY

1. "Digestibility." This is the relationship between the amount of a nutrient or food eaten and the amount absorbed expressed as a percentage. For example, a cat consuming a pound (454 g) of a food that is 80% digestible has only 12.8 oz (384 g) (16 oz, 454 g × 80%) available to the body for actual use. The difference in the two amounts represents the waste matter that is excreted.

2. "Utilization." This term expresses the relationship between the quantity of a nutrient or food eaten and the actual amount retained by the body. Like digestibility, the ratio is expressed as a percentage. Food utilization is the best overall way to determine the actual nutritional value of a food. Scientific analysis of food disposition in the body can provide this information. However, since food utilization figures are often not readily available to pet owners, food digestibility is often substituted for it in discussions of nutrition.

3. "Metabolizable energy" (ME). This term represents the number of calories available to the body from food. It is conventional among nutritionists to specify nutrient concentration requirements for pet foods as quantities needed per each 1,000 calories of metabolizable energy (Kcal ME) provided by the food, since some nutrient requirements change when the calories available from a given quantity of food increase or decrease. When comparing calories provided by food to calories required by the animal, it is important to be sure that both are expressed in the same energy units. Metabolizable energy units specify the actual energy available. Other units such as gross energy or digestible energy are less accurate measures of the actual calories provided by food.

PROTEINS Cats meet their nutritional requirements by ingesting proteins, fats, carbohydrates, vitamins, minerals, and water just as people do.

Proteins are essential substances for growth and repair of body tissues. They cannot be synthesized in the body from dietary constituents other than protein. Therefore, they are extremely important to nutrition. Cats also use protein for energy. When used in this way proteins supply about 3.5 calories for each gram consumed. Unlike dogs and humans who can adapt to using carbohydrates or fats in place of protein to supply calories, domestic cats must *always* use a portion of the protein they eat for energy. This is one important reason why cats must have diets high in protein. When well-balanced proteins supply at least 25% of the diet's calories most cats' needs will be met. The minimum needed can range from 15% to 29% of calories depending on protein source and life stage.

Proteins are composed of amino acids, and they vary widely in the kinds and proportions of amino acids present. *Essential* amino acids cannot be synthesized in the cat's body and must be supplied by the diet in special proportions for optimum use. Proteins that supply the essential amino acids in nearly optimum quantities are given a high *biological value* because they are used most completely and efficiently by the body. Proteins with a high biological value are the best ones to feed and provide the best bases for commercial cat foods. Examples of such proteins are eggs, muscle meat, fish meal, and soybeans. In general, the higher the biological value the lower the actual requirement for the protein in the diet. Cats, however, have requirements for certain amino acids that also influence exactly how much protein must be supplied.

Taurine is the most notable essential amino acid for cats. One important use for it is for detoxification in their livers. Unlike dogs and other less carnivorous mammals, cats cannot synthesize enough taurine from other sulfur-containing amino acids to meet detoxification needs and maintain adequate body reserves. Taurine is found only in proteins of animal origin. Cats fed diets deficient in taurine develop retinal degeneration (feline central retinal degeneration, FCR) that causes reduced vision and dilated pupils, and may progress to complete blindness. Taurine deficiency may also induce a fatal heart muscle disease (feline dilated cardiomyopathy), immune system dysfunction, and blood clotting disorder. Kittens from taurine-deficient mothers are undersized, may die or grow slowly, and have abnormal skeleton and brain development resulting in impaired locomotion. Taurine levels are not adequate in plant products such as soybeans, normally considered valuable in formulating pet foods. The increased dietary fiber provided by plant products used in many commercial foods requires increased taurine intake, and heat processing of the food also reduces taurine levels. To avoid deficiency, foods for cats must contain a good source of animal protein and/or be supplemented with pure taurine. Never feed cats foods designed for dogs. Cats have become taurine deficient when fed cereal-based dog foods, and cats need on average at least twice as much protein as dogs.

Eggs are an excellent source of protein (one egg = 7 g protein) of generally high biological value. They contain taurine, although less taurine than meat on an ounce-for-ounce basis. If you feed your cat eggs frequently, be sure they are cooked because raw egg white is not digested well. It also contains a substance called *avidin* that binds *biotin,* an important B vitamin, preventing its absorption from the gut. Additionally, raw eggs may contain *Salmonella* bacteria that may infect cats who eat raw eggs, causing illness and occasionally death.

Milk and milk products such as cottage cheese or yogurt are high in protein, calcium, and phosphorous, but cannot provide complete protein for cats without the addition of taurine or in combination with meat, eggs, or fish. Many cats develop diarrhea when fed any milk products; others develop diarrhea only when fed large amounts. Diarrhea associated with the ingestion of milk products occurs when the *lactose* (milk sugar) in them is not digested. Undigested lactose promotes bacterial fermentation and attracts water into the intestine, causing diarrhea. So provide milk and milk products as supplements to your cat's diet with care. If loose stools develop when milk is fed, stop it immediately and wait for the stool to return to normal before trying new milk products. Cats who cannot drink milk without developing diarrhea can often eat cottage cheese, which has a much lower lactose content.

FATS Fats provide the most concentrated source of energy (9 calories/g) of any of the necessary dietary components. They carry fat-soluble vitamins (D, E, A, K) and supply *linoleic acid* (linoleate) and *arachidonic acid* (arachidonate) that are essential to health in cats. Cats deficient in essential fatty acids grow poorly, have dry hair and dandruff, and may be listless and have increased susceptibility to infection. Diets lacking arachidonate will not support reproduction and adversely affect blood platelet function.

Unlike dogs, cats cannot convert linoleate to arachidonate, a characteristic they share with other strictly carnivorous animals. Therefore, both linoleic acid (found in plant oils and animal fats) and arachidonic acid (found *only* in animal tissues) must be supplied preformed in the diet of the cat. A diet that derives about 2.5% of its calories from linoleic acid and at least 0.04% of its calories from arachidonic acid will provide adequate levels of fatty acids and enough fat for absorption of the essential fat-soluble vitamins.

Although diets higher in fat are not essential to cats' health, cats are able to digest and metabolize fats extremely well, and very high-fat diets are not detrimental to them, providing proper levels of protein, vitamins, and minerals are also consumed. Moreover, fat (especially animal fat) increases the palatability of food to cats by affecting its texture (most important) and flavor. Cats generally prefer diets containing at least 15% fat as dry matter. Many commercial foods, especially dry and semimoist forms, provide lower fat levels. To improve palatability or supplement a diet you may think is fat deficient, add up to 1 tablespoon poultry fat, pork fat (lard), or corn oil for each 8-ounce (240 ml) measuring cup of dry or semimoist foods. Avoid hydrogenated coconut oils, as they can cause fatty liver disease in cats. Scaly skin and/or dry hair coat associated with inadequate levels of essential fatty acids should improve within one or two months after beginning supplementation.

A better approach to treating unhealthy skin resulting from dietary deficiencies is to switch to commercial foods known to be nutritionally adequate and to discuss the problem with your veterinarian, since skin and coat problems are often caused by diseases not related to diet (see p 133).

Carbohydrates (sugars, starches, and cellulose) are not required by cats in their diet. The digestible carbohydrates (sugars and starch), however, can be used as energy sources, providing 3.5 calories for each gram consumed. Cooking and/or fine grinding of carbohydrate sources (e.g., cereal grains, potatoes, vegetables) greatly improves their utilization and allows pet food manufacturers to formulate dry and semimoist foods based on these plant products that are not a major part of any cat's natural diet. Products containing as much as 35% carbohydrate on a dry-matter basis can be utilized well and still provide room for adequate levels of other nutrients. **CARBO- HYDRATES**

Cellulose, an indigestible carbohydrate, is a source of dietary fiber. Fiber is not considered essential for simple stomached carnivorous mammals like domestic cats. Fiber-containing foods are useful, however, in preventing constipation in older cats with reduced intestinal function (see page 171) and to reduce the caloric density of diets for cats who tend to become fat when allowed to eat without restriction (see page 175). Except for diets designed for special purposes such as weight reduction, diets for cats should contain no more than 5% fiber dry matter.

Cats require about 1 ounce (30 ml) of water per pound of body weight daily. They obtain this water in the food they eat and the liquids they drink. Water is also a by-product of metabolism; fat metabolism, in particular, is of great importance. The importance of foods in supplying the water requirements of cats is so great, in fact, that a cat on a moist food diet (which contains about 75% water) can easily be thought not to drink at all. Cats on other diets, however, do drink frequently, and the actual amount of liquid a cat must drink daily is influenced by many factors in addition to diet, among them exercise, environmental temperature, and the presence of fever, vomiting, or diarrhea. Lactation also increases the required water intake. So the best solution to the problem of water intake is to be sure that your cat has access to clean water at all times. (Milk may **WATER** be provided as an additional water source if it does not cause diarrhea.) Do not give your cat water considered unfit for human consumption, and, if for some reason you are unable to give your cat free water access, be sure to offer water at least three times a day.

A cat can go without food for days and lose 30% to 40% of his or her normal body weight without dying, but a water loss of 10% to 15% can be fatal. When cats stop eating (as they do frequently when sick) they must drink more water to make up for the decreased intake of food and in the amount provided by metabolism and for possible increases in need. Turn to page 247 to find out about providing water for your cat during illness.

VITAMINS

Although the required levels of all the essential vitamins that should be included in cats' diets have not been firmly established, many important facts about vitamins in the cat's diet are known and should be heeded when selecting a diet for your pet. The table on page 69 shows the currently recommended amounts of vitamins that should be fully available to a cat from his or her food. As with other nutrients, these levels will generally be lower than those actually present in commercial foods, since manufacturers must include higher levels when the food is formulated and first mixed to make up for nutrients that are not fully bioavailable from foods and losses caused by processing or storage.

VITAMIN A Cats cannot convert *beta carotene* (found in green vegetables) to vitamin A as can dogs and people, so you must be sure that other sources of fully formed vitamin A (found in animal tissues) are provided in the diet to prevent a deficiency that can result in skin, eye, and reproductive changes. On the other hand, too much vitamin A in the diet can result in proliferative gingivitis, skeletal deformities, and crippling. In order to prevent vitamin A deficiency or excess, use a complete commercial cat food with vitamin A added as a basis for feeding and use liver, which is high in vitamin A, only as a supplement to your cat's diet, not as a major part of it. Feed an average-sized adult cat no more than 1 ounce (30 g) of beef liver twice weekly. If necessary, balanced vitamin-mineral preparations may also be used as dietary supplements, but avoid giving unbalanced supplements such as cod liver oil to cats, since 1 teaspoonful can contain more than 5000 IU vitamin A. Use only balanced vitamin-mineral supplements recommended by your veterinarian and follow directions for their use carefully.

It is doubtful whether under normal feeding conditions vitamin E deficiency or excess will occur. There have been, however, many cases of vitamin E deficiency in cats because the need for vitamin E is significantly influenced by diet composition. Cases of vitamin E deficiency have resulted from an abnormal feeding practice considered normal by poorly informed owners: the feeding of excessive quantities of red meat tuna. It has also occasionally followed the feeding of other fish diets, fish oils (e.g., cod liver oil), or large quantities of liver.

Vitamin E deficiency results in oxidation of body fat and a generalized inflammation called *pansteatitis* (steatitis). Its signs include lack of appetite, fever, and pain accompanied by reluctance to move. It can eventually end in death. Vitamin E deficiency should be diagnosed and treated by a veterinarian, but, more important, you can prevent its occurrence. Use a complete commercial cat food as your cat's basic diet and avoid frequent feeding of red meat tuna. Any tuna fed should be clearly marked—supplemented with vitamin E. Do not use fish oils (e.g., cod liver oil) as dietary supplements and feed liver only as previously recommended.

Cats have relatively high requirements for B vitamins in their diets. Foods for cats must contain *at least* twice the amounts of many B vitamins found in diets adequate for dogs—another good reason not to feed cats dog food. Several B vitamins are destroyed by heating, a process used in making commercial cat foods, so all good processed foods must be supplemented with B vitamins. One heat-sensitive B vitamin, thiamine, is also destroyed by enzymes found in certain raw fish and in raw soybeans. Deficiency manifested by lack of appetite and neurologic disorders including seizures followed by weakness and death may develop in cats fed inadequately cooked fish or soy-based food and/or cooked products inadequately supplemented with thiamine.

Several B vitamins are synthesized by bacteria in the intestines of healthy cats. Intestinal problems, e.g., diarrhea, can eliminate this source, and antibiotics may also interfere with it. Vitamin supplementation is often necessary during prolonged illnesses involving the intestine or during prolonged antibiotic treatment.

Although few studies have been done that establish the mineral requirements of cats, it seems unlikely that a cat who eats a diet well balanced in other respects would become deficient in minerals. Unsuspecting cat owners can more easily provide improper rather than inadequate mineral supplies for their pets, since the relationship among the various minerals in the diet is as important as deficiency or excess. A good example of this problem is the interrelationship among the minerals calcium and phosphorus and vitamin D. These relationships are often upset by oversupplementation and/or by catering to a cat's food preferences instead of his or her needs.

CALCIUM, PHOSPHORUS, VITAMIN D Calcium and phosphorus should be present in the diet of cats in a ratio of about 1 to 1. If an adequate amount of each of these minerals is present but the ratio is incorrect, abnormal mineralization of bone occurs in the growing kitten and in the adult cat as well. If adequate amounts of calcium and phosphorus in the proper ratio are provided but without sufficient vitamin D, abnormalities of bone result again. Insufficient levels of vitamin D interfere with calcium absorption in the intestine. Excessive amounts of vitamin D in the presence of adequate levels of calcium and phosphorus may result in excessive mineralization of bone, abnormal teeth, and calcification of the soft tissues of the body. The delicacy of these relationships is remarkable.

Unthinking or uninformed owners most often distort the calcium-phosphorus balance of their cat's diet by feeding a diet consisting almost exclusively of muscle meat or organ meats such as liver, heart, or kidney. All of these meats contain phosphorus but are devoid of calcium, which results in a calcium-phosphorus ratio of 1 to 15 or greater. Prolonged feeding of such a diet results in severe demineralization of bones, pain, and sometimes fractures or paralysis, a condition called *nutritional secondary hyperparathyroidism.* An adult cat may exist on such a diet for years without showing signs of disease, but the body changes are occurring nevertheless. A cat's requirement for vitamin D is low, so that health problems relating to this nutrient are best avoided by preventing oversupplementation. Remember that the wild ancestors and living relatives of the domestic cat relied on a variety of foods. Follow the dietary recommendations set out previously and on the following pages and/or follow the advice of a knowledgeable veterinarian to prevent nutrition-induced disease in your cat.

MINIMUM REQUIREMENTS FOR GROWING KITTENS
(UNITS PER KILOGRAM OF DIET, DRY BASIS)[a]

NUTRIENT	UNIT	AMOUNT
Fat[b]		
Linoleic acid	g	5
Arachidonic acid	mg	200
Protein[c]	g	240
Arginine	g	10
Histidine	g	3
Isoleucine	g	5
Leucine	g	12
Lysine	g	8
Methionine plus cystine	g	7.5
(total sulfur amino acids)		
Methionine	g	4
Phenylalanine plus	g	8.5
tyrosine		
Phenylalanine	g	4
Taurine	mg	400
Threonine	g	7
Tryptophan	g	1.5
Valine	g	6
Minerals		
Calcium	g	8
Phosphorus	g	6
Magnesium	mg	400
Potassium	g	4
Sodium	mg	500
Chloride	g	1.9
Iron	mg	80
Copper	mg	5
Iodine	μg	350
Zinc	mg	50
Manganese	mg	5
Selenium	μg	100
Vitamins		
Vitamin A (retinol)	mg	1 (3333 IU)
Vitamin D (cholecalciferol)	μg	12.5 (500 IU)
Vitamin E	mg	30 (30 IU)
(alpha-tocopherol)		

NUTRIENT	UNIT	AMOUNT
Vitamin K[d] (phylloquinone)	μg	100
Thiamine	mg	5
Riboflavin	mg	4
Vitamin B$_6$ (pyridoxine)	mg	4
Niacin	mg	40
Pantothenic acid	mg	5
Folacin (folic acid[d])	μg	800
Biotin[d]	μg	70
Vitamin B$_{12}$ (cyanocobalamin)	μg	20
Choline[e]	g	2.4
Myo-inositol	mg	Requirement unknown; all experimental diets have included 150–200

[a]Based on a diet with a metabolizable energy concentration of 5.0 kcal/g dry matter. Since diet processing may destroy or impair the availability of some nutrients, and since some nutrients, especially the trace minerals, are less available from some natural feedstuffs than from purified diets, increased amounts of these nutrients should be included in commercial diets to ensure that the minimum requirements are met. The minimum requirements presented in this table assume availabilities similar to those present in purified experimental diets.

[b]No requirement for fat is known apart from the need for essential fatty acids and as a carrier of fat-soluble vitamins. Some fat normally enhances the palatability of the diet.

[c]Assuming that all the minimum essential amino acid requirements are met.

[d]These vitamins may not be required in the diet unless antimicrobial agents or antivitamin compounds are present in the diet.

[e]Choline is not essential in the diet but if this quantity of choline is not present the methionine requirement should be increased to provide the same quantity of methyl groups.

NOTE: The minimum requirements of all the nutrients are not known for the adult cat at maintenance. It is known that these levels of nutrients are adequate and that protein and methionine can be reduced to 140 and 3 g/kg diet, respectively. It is likely that the minimum requirements of all the other nutrients are also lower for maintenance than for the growing kitten.

The minimum requirements of all the nutrients are not known for reproduction for the adult male or female cat. It is probable that the minimum requirements for growing kittens in this table would satisfy all requirements for reproduction if the following were modified as shown: vitamin A, 6000 IU/kg diet, and taurine, 500 mg/kg diet.

Adapted with permission from: *Nutrient Requirements of Cats,* National Research Council (U.S.), Subcommittee on Cat Nutrition, National Academy Press, Washington, D.C., 1986

Commercial rations for cats are sold as dry foods, semimoist (soft-
moist) foods, and canned foods. Each type of product can provide
complete nutrition for your pet if it is formulated correctly.

In general it is most economical to use dry food (about 10% moisture
content) as a cat's basic diet. Its low moisture content allows it to be
left out for a cat to consume at will without its spoiling in all but the
most humid climates. Its crunchy texture helps keep a cat's teeth
clean, which is very important since many cats are subject to dental
disease (see page 57). However, dry foods, even well balanced,
cannot mimic the foods a cat would eat naturally. They contain
much larger amounts of vegetable material than a cat would naturally
consume, and some products contain artificial flavors, coloring
agents, and preservatives to which some cats are intolerant (see page
168). Cats also consume less total water (around 50% less) when
eating dry foods compared to canned food although they drink more.
This can become a health issue for older cats with kidney disease (see
page 234) and/or constipation (see page 234), or for cats who have
urinary tract disease (see page 177). Dry foods may become deficient in essential fatty acids when stored, especially when the
weather is warm and humid. Their physical composition allows less
fat to be incorporated initially, and contact with the oxygen in the
air makes the fat present turn rancid. Do not store dry foods at room
temperature for longer than six months; purchase them from dealers
who have a rapid food turnover.

Although many dry products provide excellent complete nutrition
and many cats do well eating dry foods alone, the most healthful diet
for a cat should include some other foods as well.

Semimoist cat foods are intermediate in moisture content (about
25% to 35%) and are usually designed to be nutritionally complete.
Semimoist foods are considerably more expensive than dry foods if
the additional water they contain is taken into consideration when
calculating the cost per feeding. Chemical humectants (e.g., propylene glycol), corn syrup, salts, sugar, and acids are used to hold water
in these products and keep them soft and free from spoilage. Also
semimoist products often contain artificial flavors and colors. They
are generally quite palatable to cats and convenient for their owners,
since such foods can be stored for months at room temperature if
unopened and they are often sold in single-feeding pouches.

Unfortunately, semimoist foods give none of the tooth-cleaning
benefit of dry foods, and they cannot begin to approach the more
natural quality of the best canned foods. Propylene glycol, a com-

mon preservative and energy source used in semimoist food for years causes oxidative damage to cats' red blood cells and will be required by law to be eliminated from cat foods sold in the United States by the end of 1993. Reserve semimoist foods for snacks.

CANNED FOOD   Canned products tend to be the most expensive way to feed cats since you pay for about 75% water. They are, however, safe to store for prolonged periods and highly palatable to cats. Their formulation allows the best manufacturers to include ingredients such as meat and liver and high levels of fat that mimic the components of a diet a cat might naturally prey upon. Complete canned foods are a desirable part of a cat's diet, but you must be careful to read package labels (see chart page 74) to be sure your cat is getting products intended to be fed as complete diets. Incomplete "gourmet" products should be fed only as dietary supplements. If the label does not make it clear that the food is intended to be complete in itself, use the product only in addition to a wide variety of other foods.

Heat processing destroys important vitamins (e.g., thiamine) and other nutrients (e.g., taurine), so all complete canned products will show evidence of supplementation in the list of ingredients on their labels. Some canned products contain artificial flavors, colors, and preservatives such as sodium nitrite. Like propylene glycol, sodium nitrite has been shown to induce oxidative damage to cats' red blood cells. To feed the most natural diet to your cat, avoid canned products that contain such additives.

Federal law requires that all cat foods in interstate commerce carry a listing of ingredients in decreasing order of predominance. Other regulations require a guaranteed analysis, listing minimum or maximum levels of certain nutrients present on an as-fed basis (i.e., not corrected for the amount of moisture present). Unfortunately, the required labels do not contain enough information to enable you to compare cat foods adequately with one another. The guaranteed analysis gives no indication of the *quality* of the nutrients present, nor does it give the exact quantities present. Companies are restricted from misrepresenting their products, however, and certain large manufacturers of cat foods have conducted extensive research and feeding trials in order to produce nutritious diets that need no supplementation. These foods carry labels that indicate their nutritional adequacy based on calculation, chemical analysis, or feeding trials (the best). The following rules of thumb will help you choose a cat food:

1. Look at the food. This is a fairly effective way of evaluating many canned foods. If you see pieces of bone, discolored meat, and poorly digestible items such as blood vessels and skin, it's a pretty good indication of poor quality food.

2. Consider the price. Cheap cat foods often contain cheap ingredients—poor quality protein and poorly digestible nutrients that pass through your cat unused. "Gourmet"-type cat foods, on the other hand, may contain high-quality ingredients but are often relatively overpriced.

3. Well-known manufacturers noted for their research generally produce good-quality cat foods you can trust.

4. See what kind of effect the food has when eaten. If your cat gets diarrhea or becomes flatulent on a food, it's not the diet you should continue to feed. Voluminous stools following feeding of certain brands of food often indicate excessive amounts of fiber or other indigestible substances. Good products are 75% to 80% absorbed by the gut unless specifically formulated to be therapeutic high-fiber foods.

5. Read the label and choose only products that have label claims of *complete* nutrition. Those that indicate they are adequate for *all life stages* based on *feeding* trials are the products that have stood up to the most rigorous testing. Calculation or chemical analysis cannot measure exactly how the product will be utilized by the cat.

6. Calculate the cost per feeding, since the price per bag, can, or box may be misleading. Record the cost per package and the purchase date. When empty, divide the price by the number of days it took to finish the product. The most "expensive" foods per package are often less expensive to feed per day than the apparently cheaper brands, as less volume is needed to provide proper nutrition.

7. Write or call the food manufacturer to obtain any additional information you might need. For example, the protein and dry-matter digestibility of good foods usually exceeds 80%. This information, however, is often not available on the food label. Reputable food manufacturers are happy to provide the customer with information and often provide toll-free numbers for this purpose.

PET FOOD LABELS

Pet food labels are legal documents that must include the following information unless they are intended to be used solely as treats or snacks and are labeled as such:

1. Name of product
2. Animal species for which it is to be used
3. Net weight of the product
4. Ingredient list in descending order of content of the ingredients
5. Guaranteed analysis listing protein, fat (minimum), and fiber and moisture (maximum) content
6. Manufacturer's name and address
7. Nutritional adequacy claim

An example: *Complete* (contains adequate levels of all required nutrients) and *balanced* (contains the proper proportions of required nutrients) for *all life stages* (will support kitten growth, pregnancy, and nursing, in addition to maintaining the adult cat).

Nutritionally incomplete products not labeled as snacks or treats must carry a statement that the "product is intended for intermittent or supplemental feeding only."

To understand lists of ingredients fully, consult another reference, since pet food manufacturers use a language of their own. For example: A beef-*flavored* product does not have to contain any actual beef muscle meat. The best reference is the *Manual of the Association of American Feed Control Officials* (AAFCO), which is published annually.

To compare foods adequately to one another, differences due to water content must be eliminated. To do this, first calculate the percentage of *dry matter:*

100% − moisture = percentage total dry matter

To calculate the amount of nutrient present on a dry basis (e.g., percent protein on a dry-matter basis):

$$\frac{\text{guaranteed percent of nutrient as fed}}{\text{percent dry matter}} \times 100 = \text{percent nutrient present on dry basis}$$

FEED A VARIED DIET

Once you have evaluated the commercial foods available as to their suitability as basic parts of your cat's diet, the next step is to actually formulate a diet for your cat. Complete foods that have undergone feeding trials should be adequate alone, but because expert nutritionists have not fully established the nutritional requirements of cats, it is probably best not to assume that any single commercial product will be adequate to fulfill all your cat's needs and best not to rely solely on cat food companies' honesty and expertise in evaluating feeding trials. Another reason not to use a single commercial food as the only means of feeding your cat is that cats develop narrow food preferences easily.

If you provide only one or a few kinds of food or always indulge your cat's food preferences he or she will often refuse to consume other nutritious foods and will tend to be reluctant to try new foods. This can easily lead to nutritional disease, since it has been scientifically proven that cats given free choice of foods will not always select a diet that fulfills their nutritional requirements. Contrary to what advertisements would lead us to believe, *cats are not naturally finicky eaters and palatability is not an indication of the nutritional adequacy of a food.* Avoid producing nutritional inadequacies, imbalances, and "picky eaters" by feeding a varied diet from the time your cat is very young. A nutritionally complete and adequately varied diet should resemble the following:

CATS ARE NOT NATURALLY FINICKY EATERS

Feed Daily	Complete and balanced commercial dry cat food. If needed, add cooking oil (e.g., corn oil) poultry fat, or lard. Use no more than 1 tablespoonful per 8 ounce (240 ml) cupful dry food. Feed once daily about ½ cup (53 g) per adult cat or allow free access. Complete and balanced canned foods—offer about one 6-ounce (180 g) can per 5 pounds body weight. Canned foods containing less than 5% fat as fed need fat added. Vary flavors frequently to avoid the development of food preferences and possible accompanying deficiencies.
Feed Twice a Week	Cooked beef liver—no more than 1 ounce (30 g) per adult cat. Excessive liver feeding can produce vitamin A

excess, diarrhea, and dark-colored stools. Organ meats (spleen, heart, kidney) can be substituted for liver, but fail to provide the high level of vitamins and minerals that liver does. Cooking meat products properly helps prevent parasite transmission (see page 106) without completely destroying important vitamins.

Feed Occasionally (Limit to less than 20% of the diet's calories)

Cheese, yogurt, sour cream, milk, cooked vegetables, cooked eggs, soups, cooked cereals, baby foods, brewer's yeast, cooked clams or fish. (Some raw fish contains thiaminase, an enzyme that destroys thiamine, and if fed to comprise more than 10% of the diet may cause thiamine deficiency.) Cats may also have other "people foods" such as fruits, uncooked vegetables, sweets, and condiments as treats if they do not cause digestive upsets; just remember that such foods do not contribute significantly to a cat's nutrition. Onions contain compounds (disulphides) that cause oxidative damage to cat red blood cells and may induce anema. Avoid feeding them. Chocolate (cocoa) may also cause poisoning (see page 218).

VITAMIN-MINERAL SUPPLEMENTS

If you feed your cat a varied diet with good quality complete rations at its base, vitamin-mineral supplements are probably not necessary on a daily basis. In fact, oversupplementation can lead to nutritional diseases every bit as serious as those resulting from nutritional deficiencies. There are, however, times when vitamin-mineral supplements that provide vitamins and minerals in proper amounts and proportions to meet known or estimated daily requirements can be beneficial to a cat's diet. Just remember to rely on balanced supplements available through your veterinarian or pet stores and to follow your veterinarian's or the package's instructions carefully. Avoid routine use of unbalanced dietary supplements such as bone meal, wheat germ, or cod liver oil. Not only can such products be expensive, on a cost-per-unit nutrient basis, but unbalanced products may easily result in oversupplementation. Cod liver oil, for example, is a substance that is frequently misused as a dietary supplement for cats.

One-half teaspoonful of NF (National Formulary) cod liver oil contains about 156 IU of vitamin D. A mere teaspoonful of cod liver oil daily could result in vitamin D excess for a cat, accompanied by bone and soft tissue abnormalities, since the cat's requirement for this vitamin is low. No more than 50 to 100 international units are recommended as a daily allowance.

Balanced vitamin-mineral preparations are probably best used to supplement the diet of sick (see page 249), pregnant or lactating (see page 280), or older cats (see page 229). They are also recommended for any cat (growing or adult) who is not fed a varied diet similar to the sample one provided here.

FEEDING A KITTEN

In order to meet a kitten's nutritional requirements for proper growth and development you not only have to provide all the nutrients necessary to maintain an adult cat, but also must provide about two to three times as many calories on a per-pound (per-kg) body-weight basis as for adults and about 50% more calories from protein as well. Frequent feedings will allow a kitten to meet the caloric requirement if the diet is energy dense (providing at least 4.5 calories for each gram dry matter). Protein requirements are most easily filled by selecting high-quality complete commercial rations containing 34% or more protein on a dry-weight basis. It is very important to provide the proper protein content, as kittens will not automatically select a diet that provides optimum quantities of protein.

High-quality protein foods can be used to supplement the basic diet. Although modern commercial foods make it unnecessary to supplement a kitten's diet for nutritional reasons, feeding tiny amounts of other foods as diet supplements to kittens is invaluable in avoiding the development of narrow food preferences later. Cats should eat a variety of novel foods after weaning but before six months of age, or they may never willingly eat new foods. Eggs, milk and milk products such as cottage cheese, sour cream, or yogurt are high-quality proteins that are useful as diet supplements for cats. Be sure, however, to avoid any milk product that causes diarrhea when fed. Small amounts of cooked fish, muscle meat, and beef liver [about 1 teaspoonful per pound body weight (about 3 g/kg) per week] are also good protein supplements that can be introduced.

CHANGING A KITTEN'S DIET

Be sure to find out what your kitten has been eating before you bring him or her home. If your kitten has not already been started on a well-balanced diet with quality complete foods as a basis, continue his or her original diet for a day or two, then gradually introduce the new foods that are to comprise the diet. Start with a single food, increasing the quantities of the new food gradually and decreasing the original until the kitten is consuming the new diet well. Then introduce other new foods in small portions one at a time to avoid digestive upsets. Kittens older than six weeks have all the teeth necessary to eat dry as well as canned products, and special dry foods sized just for kittens are sold in grocery and pet stores.

HOW OFTEN TO FEED

It is physically impossible for a small kitten to consume enough food (even of the highest quality) at one sitting to meet his or her daily caloric requirement. The most convenient method to assure yourself that your kitten is consuming enough to meet his or her caloric needs is to allow self-feeding. In this method food is left out where the kitten has free access to it, and the food is changed as necessary to keep it fresh. Most kittens do not overeat with this system. It may help prevent boredom, and it is more typical of natural feeding patterns. Experiments have shown that when given free access to food, cats prefer to eat ten to eighteen small meals randomly spaced in a twenty-four-hour period. Self-feeding must be abandoned or the portions reduced if the cat tends to become too fat.

Scheduled feeding (feeding by hand) is the system whereby you provide your kitten with several meals daily. It usually results in a cat who is anxious and ready to eat at mealtimes, making it easy for you to determine when his or her appetite is not normal. It can, however, result in a cat who is too attuned to food with a tendency to gorge at mealtime and a tendency to fatness. If you choose the scheduled-feeding method, provide your kitten with four or five meals a day until twelve weeks of age, three meals a day until six months of age, then offer food twice a day. Be sure to offer food warmed at least to room temperature, since cats find warm foods more palatable than chilled ones.

A combination of self- and scheduled feeding may be used. Many people successfully leave out a variety of commercial complete foods for their cat's free choice feeding and use supplementary foods as "treats" or scheduled meals.

You can use the caloric table as a rough guide to estimating your kitten's daily needs. Information on the cat food packages can also be used as feeding guides. But remember, each cat is an individual and as such has individualized caloric requirements that may vary as much as 20% more or less from the average. Your kitten's (or adult cat's) appearance can be used as a gauge of the adequacy of the diet fed. Look at and feel your kitten. A glossy coat, free of dandruff, a steady weight gain, and good health and activity are all signs that tend to indicate that an adequate diet is being fed. Poor growth, a poor coat, or frequent illness *could* mean that your kitten's diet is inadequate.

If you are using scheduled feeding, each meal should comfortably fill the kitten. If his or her stomach is distended and taut following a meal, or if he or she vomits shortly after eating, too much may be being eaten at one time. More frequent, smaller meals may be necessary.

Any dietary problems with kittens not quickly resolved at home (within twenty-four to thirty-six hours) should be discussed with a veterinarian. Because of their rapid growth, small size, and relatively high metabolic rate, what sometimes appears to be minor dietary problems can cause kittens to develop severe illnesses quickly.

AGE IN WEEKS	DAILY CALORIE REQUIREMENT PER POUND (KG) BODY WEIGHT
0–1	190 (418)
1–5	125 (275)
5–10	100 (220)
10–25	65 (143)
25–30	50 (110)
Adult (female or neutered male)	about 30–40 (65–85)*
Adult tomcat	50 (110)
Adult pregnant	50 (110)
Adult lactating	125 (275)

For calorie content of various types of foods see page 175 and 249.
*Depends on body size, activity level, and individual

FEEDING AN ADULT CAT

Although most adult cats require around 40 calories per pound body weight per day, each cat has his or her own individual requirements, and package information can be used only as a guide to feeding. Active cats require more calories than sedentary ones; uncastrated males, in particular, require more calories than neutered ones. Obesity in most cats, as in most people, usually indicates that you are feeding too much. Use whatever feeding method seems most convenient for you and your cat as long as you provide all the nutrients your cat needs. Most cats seem happiest if provided with at least two scheduled meals daily, free access to food, or a combination of free access and supplemental meals, since multiple meals are compatible with their natural tendencies. Of course, free access to food will have to be limited if you notice your cat becoming overweight. It has been proven that underfeeding does not encourage a cat's hunting tendencies, so cats kept for rodent control should be fed normally.

FEEDING AN OLDER CAT

Cats undergo aging changes as do humans and may require special diets for maximum health and activity in old age. In general, older animals require fewer calories per pound body weight than when they were young; the amount of food given must usually be decreased or the kind of food fed changed to one with lower calorie density to avoid obesity as a cat ages. Body changes can result in decreased utilization of nutrients, and, additionally, intestinal absorption of nutrients may be impaired. There is then a rationale for using balanced vitamin-mineral preparations to supplement the older cat's diet. Certain conditions, such as recurrent constipation (see page 234), or heart or kidney failure, which tend to occur more often in older animals, require special diets. The presence of such conditions should be determined by a veterinarian, however, before any special diet is used.

CATNIP

Although it is not necessary to a cat's diet, many cats enjoy eating catnip (*Nepeta cataria*), also called catmint, catswort, or nep. This member of the mint family contains a biologically active compound called nepetalactone that causes behavior changes in about two-thirds of all adult cats who eat it. (Cats younger than six to eight months usually don't respond to catnip but actively avoid it.) Usually the cat sniffs, then licks and chews the catnip. Headshaking and chin and cheek rubbing follow, and later total body rubbing and head-over-heels rolls are seen. The whole episode usually lasts less than fifteen minutes and will not be repeated before an hour or more passes even if more catnip is consumed immediately. Catnip provides a harmless entertainment for cats who are responders, and a pot-grown plant can be used to divert your cat's attention from houseplants. There is no evidence that catnip is toxic or addicting, and it can be offered freely since cats regulate their own indulgence in it.

If your cat does not care for catnip, you might try growing small pots of wheat, oat, or rye grass as substitutes. Although grasses do not provide the stimulation of catnip, many cats enjoy eating them, and they also help divert attention from houseplants.

For more information on feeding during pregnancy and lactation see page 280 and page 287.

For information on feeding orphan kittens see page 291.

For information on feeding sick animals see page 247.

TRAVELING WITH OR SHIPPING A CAT

Although cats do not travel in automobiles with their owners as frequently as dogs do, trips to the veterinarian, to vacation spots, or to new residences are frequent enough that real benefits are gained by accustoming your cat to travel when he or she is young. Not only are cats who become accustomed to car riding and to confinement when young more relaxed when traveling, they often come to enjoy it. Many cats have become seasoned travelers, and some have even learned to go car camping, because of their early training. **ACCUSTOM YOUR CAT TO TRAVEL EARLY**

Take your cat on frequent short rides at first, then gradually lengthen them. Confine your cat to a carrier (particularly at first) while riding. This gives the cat a secure place of his or her own in which to ride and a portable refuge in strange places (e.g., hotel rooms, veterinarian's offices). It also prevents the annoying and sometime dangerous movements of a cat who is uneasy about traveling. Although you may eventually become confident that your cat will cause no problems when traveling, it is best to continue to confine your cat to a carrier while riding to avoid problems that might arise unpredictably and to avoid injury to the cat in case of an accident. At the least, a cat loose in a car should be restrained by a harness and leash.

The following items may help you when traveling with or shipping your cat on commercial carriers:

1. Airlines require a health certificate signed by an accredited veterinarian for shipping, and other commercial carriers may also require one. Be sure to check with the shipper well before the departure date so you have time to obtain the necessary documents. Each state and foreign country has its own entry requirements for cats. Most states have no special requirements, but check with your veterinarian before traveling to be sure. Individual consulates are the best sources of current information for each foreign country.

2. Your veterinarian can prescribe safe tranquilizers for your cat if he or she seems particularly apprehensive about strange people and sounds. Some cats react unpredictably to tranquilizers, however, and become extremely wild and excitable. Cats accustomed to a carrier or traveling cage at home before the trip (preferably while young) usually travel well without tranquilization, and this is most desirable. Special arrangements may often be made for a cat to travel with you in the passenger area, so investigate this possibility if you think your cat will travel poorly in baggage.

3. A traveling crate should be strong, well-ventilated, and have enough room to enable your cat to stand up, turn around, and lie down comfortably. Federal regulations specify which crates are permissible for shipping with commercial carriers. Since they may change from time to time it is best to check with the shipper before purchasing a crate. A towel or other soft and absorbent bedding such as diapers can be placed inside. A small box containing litter and a few familiar toys can be provided but these items are not absolutely necessary and on short trips often result in more mess than they're worth.

4. Attach an identification tag to *both* the crate and the cat, stating the owner's name, the cat's name, the home address, and the destination. Also indicate the date and time of last food and water.

5. Do not feed your cat immediately prior to shipping.

6. Avoid giving water within about two hours of shipping time unless absolutely necessary (e.g., for health reasons or high environmental temperature).

7. Do not place food or water bowls loose in the crate. A *healthy* cat can go twenty-four hours without water, unless the environmental temperature is high, and much longer without food. If the trip is going to take longer than twenty-four hours, if the age and health of the cat or environmental temperature warrants it, be *sure* special arrangements are made for feeding, watering, and exercise. Cats can be trained to lick water from special bottles that can be attached to shipping crates to be sure water is available at all times.

MOVING A CAT TO A NEW HOME

Once a cat arrives at his or her destination special care is needed. Cats removed from their homes frequently try to return to them if they are allowed free access to the outdoors shortly after arrival. Confine your cat to a single room with food and water bowls, litter pan, and a bed until it is clear that he or she is calm. The more familiar the items you place in the room from your cat's old home the quicker the adjustment process will be. Open the door to the room and allow the cat to explore the rest of the new home on his or her own terms only after your cat seems completely at ease in the smaller space. Be sure free access to the original room is available in case your cat becomes frightened and agitated. Leaving the travel crate in the room with the door open provides a safe haven that many cats seem to appreciate while adapting to their new abodes.

Do not force introductions among cats already on the premises and the newcomer. Left to their own devices most cats work out appropriate territory sharing without engaging in serious battles despite many episodes of snarling, growling, hissing, spitting, and caterwauling. It is extremely important to provide each cat with his or her own litter pan and food and water bowl to avoid permanent and serious territory battles. If necessary, a veterinarian can provide both the newcomer and the previously resident cats with tranquilizers to calm them and help with the initial adjustment. However, tranquilizers are usually needed for a very few days, if at all, since most cats adapt well if handled with sensitivity.

Do not allow a newly moved cat to roam outdoors without close supervision. Keep your cat indoors for at least one to two weeks to discourage attempts to return to the previous home territory. Then allow outdoor access gradually and with caution. A cat must gradually become familiar with his or her new outdoor territory to avoid becoming lost if startled and to avoid battles with neighborhood cats. Some cats have traveled hundreds of miles in order to successfully return to their previous homes when they were lost in transit or were allowed outdoors before complete adaptation to the new environment. Most cats in this situation are lost forever.

For more information about traveling with a cat, consult:

American Society for the Prevention of Cruelty to Animals, *Traveling with Your Pet,* available for a fee from the ASPCA Education Department, 441 E. 92 Street, New York, N.Y. 10028.

Nicholas, Barbara, *The Portable Pet: How to Travel Anywhere with Your Dog or Cat,* Harvard Common Press, Boston, 1984.

BOARDING YOUR CAT

Although many owners would prefer to travel with their pets, cats unaccustomed to travel when young are best left at home. Should you anticipate frequent trips to places where your cat would be welcome, be sure to start taking your cat with you when he or she is a kitten to avoid adaptation problems later. It is often said that cats are very place oriented and resist change in environment. However, cats who are accustomed to being left for a few hours at the veterinary hospital or grooming parlor when young will soon learn to adapt to this situation without exhibiting signs of fear. Likewise, if you leave your cat overnight at the veterinary hospital or a boarding kennel while he or she is still young, the boarding situation becomes familiar. Adult cats will also usually learn to adapt, although the process may take longer. Should you anticipate frequent trips that will prevent you from leaving your cat at home, it is wise to arrange for a few overnight stays before boarding your cat for long periods of time. Once your cat is fully vaccinated many veterinarians are happy to provide this service, and it is a good way to help your pet learn that a night in the veterinary hospital need not be frightening. Should you anticipate frequent, long (five days or more) separations, be sure the veterinary hospital provides facilities separate from sick animals appropriate for healthy, active pets or select a boarding kennel that will provide adequate supervision and exercise for long stays.

Avoid any boarding operation (including veterinary hospitals) whose proprietors will not allow you to visit the animals' quarters at an appropriate time. Unscheduled visits are often disruptive to the kennel's schedule, but it is entirely reasonable to expect a request for a scheduled visit to be honored. Kennel employees should have good rapport with the animals. Good kennels look clean, smell fresh, are regularly disinfected, and provide safe and secure individual housing for each animal that prevents nose-to-nose contact with other boarders. Cats carry many infectious diseases that are easily transmitted from one cat to another unless the most strict procedures are followed. For health reasons it is often best to mix both cats and dogs in a kennel—a situation many cats unfamiliar with dogs find distressing at first. However, most adapt well if they cannot see or be seen by a dog. Proper housing is also adequately lighted, well ventilated, heated or cooled to avoid temperature extremes, and designed to protect boarders from exposure to the elements.

Owners of reputable boarding kennels will require certificates of vaccination against infectious diseases. They should also inquire about the pet's usual diet and be willing to feed your pet familiar foods. Drinking water, of course, should be provided at all times. It is also customary to administer medications normally given at home. Kennel policy about toys and bedding brought from home varies; so inquire about it should your cat need some comfort from home.

Another good sign is inspection of your pet for fleas before admission and the requirement that flea-infested pets be defleaed before entry to the kennel. This is an indication that the kennel makes every effort to keep the facility free from parasites.

Finally, the kennel operator should take note of your pet's veterinarian's name and telephone number, your instructions for care in case of an emergency, and where you or your legal representative can be reached should a problem arise.

Members of the American Boarding Kennels Association (ABKA), a nonprofit trade organization, pledge to operate their kennels in a manner that meets high standards. If the kennel you select is not only a member but accredited as well, it has had to pass an inspection.

Professional pet-sitting services have developed in many areas as an alternative to boarding kennels. Also many veterinary clinics have staff members who pet-sit part-time. When the cost is not prohibitive, use of these services is an excellent way to leave a pet at home when you must be away. Even if well adapted to boarding, many pets are happier in the familiar surroundings of home. Also, home stays avoid the ever-present danger of acquiring infection or parasites in a boarding kennel, even a well-run one. Ask your veterinarian for names of reputable pet-sitting services in your area.

PREVENTIVE VACCINATION PROCEDURES

There are several major infectious diseases for which safe and effective vaccines are available: among them rabies, feline panleukopenia (feline enteritis, feline "distemper"), and viral respiratory infections (rhinotracheitis, calicivirus). Each of these diseases can easily cause death in an unprotected cat. We are very fortunate to be able to prevent such serious illnesses with a procedure as technically simple as vaccination. (For more information on vaccines available for cats, see page 158).

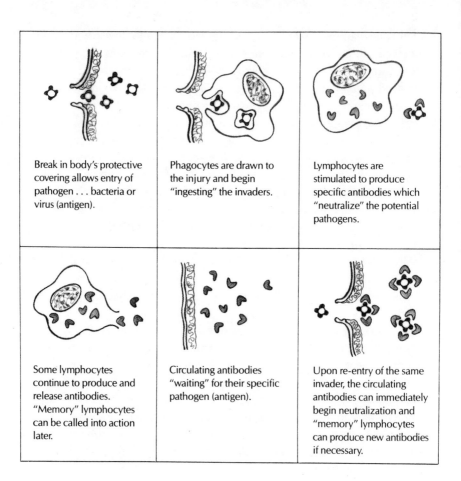

Break in body's protective covering allows entry of pathogen . . . bacteria or virus (antigen).	Phagocytes are drawn to the injury and begin "ingesting" the invaders.	Lymphocytes are stimulated to produce specific antibodies which "neutralize" the potential pathogens.
Some lymphocytes continue to produce and release antibodies. "Memory" lymphocytes can be called into action later.	Circulating antibodies "waiting" for their specific pathogen (antigen).	Upon re-entry of the same invader, the circulating antibodies can immediately begin neutralization and "memory" lymphocytes can produce new antibodies if necessary.

HOW VACCINES WORK

Antigens are molecules with particular areas on their surfaces that are recognized as foreign to the body. *Antibodies* are protein substances produced in the body that are responsible for recognizing these antigens. They are produced by cells called *lymphocytes* that originate in the bone marrow and multiply in the thymus, spleen, and lymph nodes. When lymphocytes recognize that a foreign substance (antigen), such as a virus or bacterium, has entered the body, they begin copious production of antibodies specific for the invader. Lymphocytes capable of antibody production against the invader multiply to produce progeny cells capable of producing the same antibodies. Some of these progeny cells immediately begin producing antibodies, while others become resting cells that serve as the body's "memory" of the invader. If the same (or a very similar) invader makes an appearance again later, these cells are able to respond quickly to its presence.

Vaccination introduces a modified disease agent into the body. Common methods of altering an organism's ability to produce disease are by chemical killing and by "breeding" to an innocuous state. Biotechnology can also produce vaccines that consist of harmless immunity-inducing portions of agents that cause disease when they enter the body intact. Modified viruses or bacteria are able to induce lymphocytes to produce antibodies capable of protecting the body against disease without actually producing illness. Frequently the body produces a higher (usually more protective) level of antibodies that are more specific to a disease agent on the second exposure to a vaccine, but different vaccines vary in their ability to produce a protective antibody level on first exposure. The duration of the body's immunological memory for different viruses and bacteria also varies. These are two reasons why the number of original vaccinations necessary for protection and the frequency of booster vaccinations vary with each disease.

Additional factors influence the vaccinations of a young animal. Cats and dogs receive a small amount of antibodies across the *placenta* (the organ that communicates between mother and fetus before birth). They receive a much greater amount in the *colostrum* (first milk) and milk when they are nursing. Kittens are capable of absorbing some antibodies through their gut for several days following birth, but the first twenty-four hours are most important. The amount of antibody received against each particular disease is dependent on the level of circulating antibody in the mother. The antibody received from the mother serves primarily to protect the kitten against disease for the first few weeks of life. Whether or not a nursing kitten receives a protective level of antibody depends on how recently the mother was exposed to the disease in question or how recently she was vaccinated. The antibody a cat receives can be a disadvantage as well as being useful since it can interfere with vaccination by tying up the vaccination-introduced antigen before it can stimulate the kitten's immune system. The protection kittens receive early in life against feline distemper is an example.

YOUNG ANIMALS ARE SPECIAL CASES

Some kittens lose their protective immunity against panleukopenia (feline "distemper") acquired in nursing as early as six weeks of age, others as late as four months after birth. Therefore, the ideal vaccination schedule is individualized for each cat, and the last vaccination is given after twelve to sixteen weeks of age. There are tests for determining the level of antibody against panleukopenia in each cat, but, in general, they are too expensive and time-consuming for routine use.

The techniques of vaccination are relatively simple. Knowledge of the proper handling of vaccines and of the physiology of the immune response is what makes it important to have your cat vaccinated by a veterinarian who is interested in each animal as an individual. Vaccination by a good veterinarian also insures that your cat gets a physical examination when he or she is young, and then also later, which may reveal important changes you have missed. Regular visits during the initial kitten vaccination series also provide a time to discuss any behavior or training problems you may have with your pet and allows a young animal to become well adjusted to visits to an animal hospital. If a veterinarian vaccinates your cat without taking a thorough history or performing a thorough physical examination and discussing your pet with you, something is amiss!

RABIES

RABIES AFFECTS THE NERVOUS SYSTEM The rabies virus can infect any warm-blooded animal, including humans. It causes a disease of the nervous system often manifested by changes in behavior followed by paralysis and death. The principal reservoirs of rabies in the United States are skunks, raccoons, bats, and foxes. Bats and skunks may shed (secrete) rabies virus in their saliva without exhibiting behavior that would arouse suspicion of infection. Any wild animal that allows you to get close enough to handle it should certainly be suspected of rabies and left alone. Cats should be supervised when outdoors to prevent exposure to rabid wildlife, especially during the night.

HOW RABIES IS SPREAD Rabies is usually spread when a rabid animal bites another, depositing virus from its saliva into the bite wound. However, the rabies virus can enter the body through any break in the skin, through the mucous membranes of the mouth, and probably those of the nose and eyes as well. After entering the body the rabies virus attaches to nervous tissue where it multiplies. Signs of rabies usually begin between about two to ten weeks following infection, but cases have developed more than one year after contact.

TWO FORMS OF RABIES Rabid cats usually first show changes in their temperament. At this time rabies can be particularly difficult to diagnose because the signs are so variable. A cat may become restless, apprehensive, overly affectionate, or shy. A cat will often have a tendency to hide at this stage. Some cats may be febrile (have a fever) and may have dilated pupils. Following these early signs the animal often becomes extremely ferocious, biting or clawing at objects without provocation.

This is often referred to as the *furious* form of rabies. These animals become insensible to pain, and, if confined, may bite or slash at the bars of their cages. Partial paralysis of the vocal cords results in a change in voice. Convulsions may be seen and may cause death.

The *dumb* form of rabies may follow the furious form or may be seen by itself. It is mainly characterized by paralysis. A cat's mouth may hang open and saliva may drip from it. Since rabid cats cannot ingest food or water they become quite dehydrated. More often, however, cats with the dumb form of rabies develop difficulty walking and then paralysis of the rear legs. Eventually total paralysis occurs.

Recovery from rabies is so extremely rare that animals suspected of being infected are usually euthanized and tested for infection after death. Protect your cat from rabies so you will never have to deal with the problem of owning a rabid animal. Cats should first be vaccinated against rabies when they are three to four months of age. There are several types of vaccine available. The most commonly used types contain inactivated virus. The vaccine is administered by *intramuscular* (in the muscle) injection into one of the hindlegs or *subcutaneously* (under the skin), usually near the shoulder blades. Protection against rabies is reached within one month after primary immunization. Vaccination against rabies is required by state law, and the same law regulates the frequency of booster vaccinations as well. The current recommendations of the Centers for Disease Control vary with the type of vaccine administered. In general, a booster shot is given one year following the original vaccination, then booster doses are given every one to three years depending on the product used.

RABIES VACCINATION

If you or your cat is exposed to a rabies suspect, that animal should be confined if possible and turned over to a public health officer for rabies quarantine or euthanasia. All bite wounds should be thoroughly washed with large quantities of soap and water and flushed with 70% ethyl alcohol, which kills rabies virus. Whether or not your cat will be quarantined following exposure to a rabies suspect will depend on state and local regulations. However, it is recommended that exposed, currently vaccinated cats be revaccinated immediately and confined for observation for ninety days.

Pseudorabies, a herpesvirus-induced disease of swine that is *fatal* when transmitted to cat or dogs, may be confused with rabies infection. Although aggressive behavior has not been reported, the fever, lack of appetite, restlessness, drooling, and self-mutilation that often

PSEUDORABIES MAY MIMIC RABIES

accompany this disease can look similar to signs of rabies. Since no treatment is successful, the affected animals must be euthanized. Prevent this infection by not feeding your cat raw pork.

FELINE PANLEUKOPENIA

Feline panleukopenia is an extremely common, very contagious, and often fatal viral disease that occurs in cats (both domestic and wild) and raccoons and other members of the raccoon family. The panleukopenia virus attacks rapidly growing body cells such as those in the bone marrow and the intestinal lining. As a result, the white blood count is lowered when the bone marrow is infected, the bowel becomes damaged, and the cat may die from secondary bacterial infection and/or dehydration. Although this disease is commonly called *distemper,* it is *not* at all related to *canine distemper* which often occurs in young dogs. Other common names for panleukopenia are feline infectious enteritis, cat or show fever, and cat plague.

SIGNS OF PANLEU-KOPENIA The *incubation period* (time from exposure to first signs of disease) for panleukopenia is usually about seven days, although it may vary from two to ten days. In young cats (under six months) in particular, the disease can be so severe and of such rapid onset that death occurs before an owner is truly aware that signs of illness are present. More often the first signs are fever (frequently 104 to 105°F), listlessness, lack of appetite, and vomiting usually accompanied by extreme dehydration. A cat may seem interested in drinking (some sit with their heads over or near their water bowls) but often will not drink or vomits soon after doing so. Diarrhea may accompany the first signs, but often seems to develop later. The stool is usually very watery and may contain pieces of intestinal lining and sometimes blood.

"PANLEUK" VIRUS RESISTS DISINFECTION The procedure for initial immunization against panleukopenia varies depending on, among other things, the immune status of your kitten and on your ability to isolate your cat from exposure to the virus before vaccination is complete. Every effort should be made to keep your kitten away from cats who might be shedding the virus and away from panleukopenia-contaminated environments until vaccination is complete. The "panleuk" virus is shed in all bodily secretions and excretions and can be transmitted from cat to cat easily without bodily contact with the infected carrier cat. It is one of the most resistant viruses and can remain alive and a source of infection for susceptible cats for several months even after premises have been cleaned thoroughly. Only 0.5% formalin or hypochlorite, a 1:32 dilution of household bleach in water, can kill this virus. The best policy to follow is not to introduce a susceptible cat into premises where a cat has had panleukopenia for three to four months following the episode even if the area has been disinfected. *Do not* allow an unvaccinated cat to associate with strange cats. Keep him or her indoors if necessary until vaccination is complete. Keep your kitten in your lap or in a carrier and out of contact with possibly sick cats while at your veterinarian's office.

Take your kitten to a veterinarian for his or her first vaccination at six to ten weeks of age. A good veterinarian will perform a complete physical examination before administering the vaccine. At this time he or she will also be able to answer any questions you may have about the care of your cat. Don't be afraid to ask questions; no question is "dumb" and you may learn something very important by asking.

VACCINES PROTECT AGAINST "PANLEUK"

The injection is usually given under the skin (subcutaneously) in the back between the shoulder blades and as with most vaccines, seems pretty painless; many kittens act as if they don't realize they are being vaccinated. Your veterinarian will ask you to bring your kitten back for a second vaccination in three weeks or more. In the meantime be sure to keep your kitten well isolated from exposure to disease. In general, two or three vaccinations are given before immunity is complete. Because there are various kinds of vaccines and variations in cats' ages at the time of first vaccination, fewer or more vaccinations may be necessary. The important thing to remember is that no matter how young when vaccination is begun, kittens should finish their vaccines *after* twelve to sixteen weeks of age. If you think the series is finished or have been told that the series is finished before your kitten is this age, bring him or her back to the veterinarian for another shot.

If your cat contracts panleukopenia, it is important to have immediate examination by a veterinarian and to get intensive treatment started early. A complete blood count is necessary to help confirm the disease (the virus causes a marked decrease in the number of white blood cells present), and hospitalization is often necessary for successful treatment. You may, however, be able to work with your veterinarian on treatment at home. Treatment consists of appropriate antibiotics, vitamins, and supportive care including fluids, hand-feeding, and antidiarrheal medication. Heroic measures such as blood transfusions have been necessary in some cases.

TREATMENT FOR PANLEU- KOPENIA

Although panleukopenia is often fatal, there is no reason to give up at the first sign of disease. Many cats have survived severe cases to live out normal, healthy lives.

INTERNAL AND EXTERNAL PARASITES

Parasites are creatures that at some point during their life cycle are dependent on a host (e.g., your cat). Not all parasites are harmful. In fact, in most well-cared-for small animals, owners overrate parasites as causes of illness. Under specific circumstances, certain parasites do cause disease; however, don't *assume* that because your cat is sick he or she has worms or that because he or she is scratching fleas must be present.

HOW TO USE THIS SECTION If you think your cat has a parasite problem, look for the signs in the Index of Signs (page 305). (Remember, though, not all animals with parasite infections show signs.) If you find the signs, turn to the appropriate pages and use the information there to help you decide whether or not you need to consult a veterinarian. In most cases of internal parasite infection you will need professional help (see the following pages). Many times you can correct an external parasite problem yourself.

If you don't think your cat has a parasite problem, it's a good idea to read or skim this section anyway to complete your knowledge of preventive medicine. The information is included here in the preventive medicine pages because the key to a successful fight against parasites is good prevention and control, which require good daily care. If you fail in your general daily care to take into account the life cycle of certain parasites, you may continue to have a problem even though you have administered treatment against the parasite to your cat. Learning about the different parasites discussed below will help you provide a healthy environment for your cat, thus preventing serious infection and reinfection of your pet as well as preventing human infection with certain parasites.

Internal parasites: Protozoans, flukes, tapeworms, and the following roundworms: ascarids, hookworms, whipworms, threadworms, stomach worms, eyeworms, lungworms, heartworms. *External parasites:* Fleas, ticks, lice, mites, flies.

Internal Parasites (Endoparasites)   The *endoparasites* consist of *protozoa, trematodes* (flukes), *cestodes* (tapeworms), and *nema-*

todes (roundworms). For the most part, the adults of these parasites live in the intestines. *They may be present with or without causing illness, and you may or may not see them in your cat's stools.* Only if your cat is infected with one of the larger forms *may* you be able actually to see the parasites. If you think your cat has intestinal parasites but can't be sure because you have not seen them or if you have a new cat, take a fecal sample to your veterinarian. (A table-spoonful is plenty.) It should be as fresh as possible, in any case not more than twenty-four hours old even if kept under refrigeration. Veterinarians use special procedures to separate the parasites and/or their eggs from the stool and look for evidence of infection micro-scopically. A variety of drugs is used to treat internal parasites. Most can be administered orally by you at home. The products mentioned here are generally designated by their chemical generic name.

PROTOZOANS

There are few intestinal protozoans that cause illness in cats. Signs of infection, if present, are variable but often include diarrhea not responsive to home treatment. There is no method to diagnose or treat these parasites at home, so you as an owner must rely on the help of a veterinarian, who can diagnose their presence microscopi-cally or with special lab tests and prescribe proper medication.

The most common intestinal protozoal infections of cats are by *coccidia* or *Giardia* organisms, and most are self-limiting and asymp-tomatic. However, kittens that are raised in dirty environments highly contaminated by parasites may become ill and develop diarrhea (sometimes bloody) when infected with coccidia or *Giardia*.

One coccidia of special interest is *Toxoplasma gondii*. This micro-scopic organism is found in all parts of the world. Like other members of its class it is able to produce signs of intestinal disease (e.g., diarrhea) in cats, but it also has a tissue phase that can produce serious generalized disease. At times it can become a human health hazard.

TOXOPLASMA INFECTION

Cats and other mammals, including humans, may acquire *Toxo-plasma* before birth when the mother becomes newly infected dur-ing pregnancy or when a previously acquired but quiescent infection becomes reactivated. The more likely sources of infection for a pet cat are the consumption of undercooked or raw meat (including wild caught rodents or birds) containing the infective tissue stages of the disease. These oocysts can contaminate soil where they can be picked up by the feet or fur of a passing cat or other mammal and

HOW TOXOPLASMA IS ACQUIRED

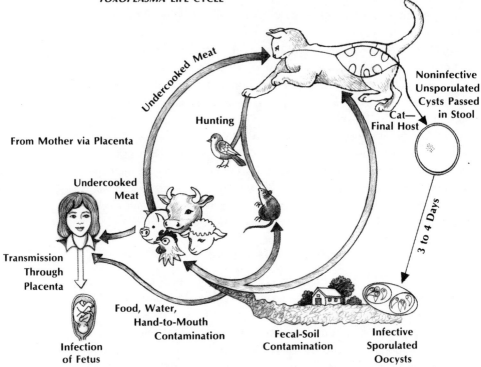

TOXOPLASMA LIFE CYCLE

Undercooked Meat

Hunting

From Mother via Placenta

Cat—Final Host

Noninfective Unsporulated Cysts Passed in Stool

3 to 4 Days

Undercooked Meat

Transmission Through Placenta

Infection of Fetus

Food, Water, Hand-to-Mouth Contamination

Fecal-Soil Contamination

Infective Sporulated Oocysts

later ingested while grooming. Infected soil can contaminate food products such as milk or vegetables, and oocysts can be transported by flies and cockroaches from contaminated soil or oocyst-infected cat stool to surfaces where they may be accidentally ingested.

SIGNS OF TOXO-PLASMOSIS After infection, signs of disease may or may not be seen depending on many factors including age, the presence of concurrent infections (e.g., feline leukemia virus [see page 191], feline immunodeficiency virus [see page 195]) and general state of health. In general, signs of illness are most likely to develop in kittens, very old cats, or others who have weakened immune systems. If signs do develop, they may be as simple as diarrhea or so complex as to mimic many other diseases. Signs that have been seen include fever, lack of appetite, lethargy, enlarged lymph nodes, weight loss, coughing and difficulty breathing, signs of pancreas and/or bowel inflammation (e.g., vomiting, diarrhea), signs of liver disease including vomiting and yellowish gums, and eye or nervous system problems. Nervous system signs can result in almost any disorder including personality changes, seizures, loss of bowel and/or bladder control to difficulty walking or even heightened sensitivity to touch. Pregnant cats may abort. Because of the many possibilities involved, diagnosis must be made with the help of a veterinarian who will use laboratory tests to confirm the infection.

Alarmist articles concerning toxoplasmosis in people and in cats have appeared in newspapers and popular magazines. They have often emphasized the congenital type of transmission from pregnant women to their unborn children, which can result in severe birth defects and infant death, and they have often dwelt on the possibility of acquiring infection from cat stool. In fact, birth defects due to *Toxoplasma* infection are relatively rare, and the disease in healthy adult humans is commonly so mild that it passes undiagnosed. Research indicates that 30 to 60% of adults in the United States have had toxoplasmosis; in other countries the incidence is much higher. It is now known that toxoplasmosis in humans is a common infection but a rare cause of disease. (The exception is the individual with a weakened immune system such as the AIDS patient or transplant recipient.) Although human infection can be acquired from material contaminated with infected cat feces, adults are more likely to contract toxoplasmosis from eating raw or undercooked meat than by contact with cats. (Infection rates of more than 80% have been found in people who eat raw meat, especially those eating undercooked lamb and pork.) Children, on the other hand, are most likely to become infected by coming into contact with soil that has been contaminated with cat feces containing *Toxoplasma*. This is because children are more likely to put contaminated soil or other dirty objects in their mouths, and they are much less likely than adults to wash their hands and fingernails after playing in the dirt.

Since cats (both wild and domestic) are the only animals that shed the infective stages of *Toxoplasma* in their stools, it is important to control toxoplasmosis in cats to break the cycle of transmission to other animals and to people.

Toxoplasmosis can be easily prevented in your cat by observing the folowing rules:

1. Feed only pasteurized dairy products, commercial cat foods that have been subjected to heat during processing, or thoroughly cooked meat (heat through to 140°F, [60°C]). (Meat frozen to temperatures below −68°F (−20°C) and thawed before feeding is safe, but most home freezers cannot meet these requirements, and it is, therefore, unsafe to feed any uncooked meat to your cat.)

2. Confine your cat to prevent capture and consumption of *Toxo-*

TOXOPLASMA INFECTION IN HUMANS IS NOT USUALLY SERIOUS

TOXO-PLASMOSIS PREVENTION

plasma-infected birds or rodents and to prevent contact with the feces of infected carrier animals. Bell cats who cannot be confined indoors to limit any successful hunting.

Blood tests are available through physicians for individuals who would like to find out whether they have been previously infected by *Toxoplasma* and are, therefore, immune to further infection. Human infections can be minimized by strictly following the recommendations listed below. Pregnant women or women contemplating pregnancy who have not been previously infected with *toxoplasma* should be particularly careful to follow these guidelines.

1. Avoid eating unpasteurized dairy products or raw or undercooked meat of any type (heat through to 140°F, [60°C]). Wash your hands after handling raw meat.

2. Take cats showing signs of illness to be examined by a veterinarian who can perform a fecal examination for *Toxoplasma* organisms. Cats shedding oocysts should be hospitalized or isolated in some other manner until the shedding stops (in about ten to fourteen days) to prevent further transmission of the organism.

3. Follow the rules for preventing *Toxoplasma* infection of cats.

4. Avoid careless handling of stools of cats that are allowed to contact sources of *Toxoplasma* infection. In rural areas, cats should not be allowed to defecate in hay racks, feeding troughs, or other areas where farm animals may eat. Provide litter boxes for them which will encourage defecation in relatively controlled sites. Remove stool from the litter box daily (organisms in stool take two to four days at average room temperatures to become infective), and use disposable pan liners or disposable cat boxes if possible. Nondisposable cat litter pans should be scalded with water heated to 131°F, (50°C) or disinfected with 10% ammonia solution whenever the litter is replaced. Dispose of cat litter and stool by flushing it down the toilet or burning it. Wear disposable gloves while cleaning the litter pan.

5. Wear gloves while gardening to prevent contact with *Toxoplasma*-contaminated soil.

6. Cover children's sandboxes when not in use to prevent fecal contamination.

7. Control cockroaches, flies, rodents, and stray cats, which can act as transport hosts and carriers of the *Toxoplasma* organism.

8. Avoid handling or holding free-roaming cats close to your mouth in order to prevent contact with feet or fur that could have touched infected soil. Keep free-roaming cats off bedding, tables, and counter tops.

9. Wash all uncooked, possibly soil-contaminated vegetables thoroughly before eating.

10. Make thorough handwashing and nail scrubbing a part of each child's and adult's daily routine, especially following contact with free-roaming cats, farm animals, soil, unpasteurized dairy products, and uncooked meat or vegetables.

FLUKES (TREMATODES)

Like protozoans, trematode parasites are uncommon causes of disease in cats. One fluke, *Paragonimus,* can cause cysts in the lungs of both cats and dogs, leading to a chronic cough and pneumonia. Infection can be prevented by keeping your pet from eating raw crayfish or from drinking water contaminated with infective stages of the fluke. Infection can be diagnosed by finding the microscopic fluke eggs in the stool or lung secretions. Treatment is with praziquantel or fenbendazole. There are several other kinds of these flatworms which parasitize different parts of the body including the lungs, liver, and small intestine. Signs of infection vary greatly and diagnosis must be made by a veterinarian. You can prevent infection of your cat by restricting hunting since infection is usually acquired by ingesting prey, including raw fish, certain crayfish or crabs, frogs, reptiles, or snails, and rats.

TAPEWORMS (CESTODES)

Cats acquire tapeworms by eating any of three types of infected materials: 1) prey, offal (discarded animal parts), or uncooked meat; 2) raw, freshwater fish; or 3) infected fleas or biting lice. The common tapeworms (*Taenia* species and *Dipylidium caninum*) are acquired by ingesting prey or infected fleas and have similar life cycles.

The adult tapeworm has a head with hooks and suckers that attach to the host's intestinal wall and a body consisting of a series of reproductive segments. It obtains nourishment by absorbing the nutrients in the host's digestive tract directly through the cuticle that covers each body segment of the worm. Eggs produced by the adult tapeworm pass out with the cat's feces and are eaten by an intermediate host (such as a rabbit, rodent for *Taenia* species, or flea for *Dipylidiuim caninum*) in whom they grow into an infective stage commonly called a bladderworm. When the cat eats an intermediate host, this immature form completes its life cycle by becoming an adult tapeworm in the cat. The life cycle of tapeworms acquired from fish is more complex.

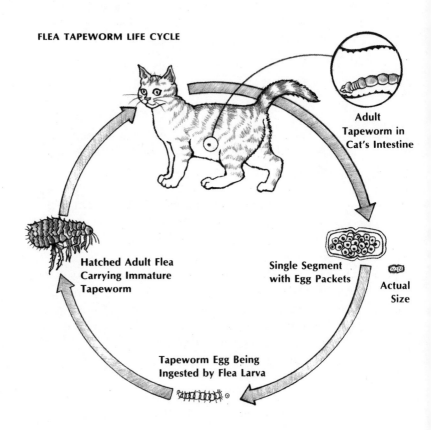

FLEA TAPEWORM LIFE CYCLE

Adult
Tapeworm in
Cat's Intestine

Single Segment
with Egg Packets

Actual
Size

Hatched Adult Flea
Carrying Immature
Tapeworm

Tapeworm Egg Being
Ingested by Flea Larva

DIAGNOSING TAPEWORMS   Although heavy tapeworm infestation can cause poor growth, coat changes, variable appetite, or gastrointestinal disturbances, in general you will have no reason to suspect infection until you see tapeworm segments clinging to the hair or skin around the anus or in a fresh bowel movement. Fresh tapeworm segments are opaque white or pinkish white, flat, and somewhat rectangularly shaped. They often move with a stretching out and shrinking back motion. When dry, the segments become yellow or off-white, translucent, and shaped somewhat like grains of rice. Tapeworm segments are not always present with tapeworm infection. When absent, diagnosis may possibly be made through microscopic fecal examination.

In most cases it is easy to rid a cat of tapeworms. If you demonstrate
that your cat has tapeworms, most veterinarians will supply you with
safe, tapeworm-killing medication that can be administered at home
without unpleasant side effects such as vomiting or diarrhea. Praziquantel or epsiprantel are common veterinary prescribed antitapeworm drugs. Sometimes, however, the deworming must be
done in the veterinary hospital.

Avoid using antitapeworm drugs available in pet stores. Most are
ineffective. Effective over-the-counter drugs containing arecoline
can be dangerous. They may cause excessive vomiting, severe diarrhea, and sometimes convulsions followed by death; they are not
recommended for use in cats. After deworming with a product recommended by your veterinarian, make an effort to prevent your cat
from re-exposure to sources of tapeworm infection (e.g., flea control
is very important). If you don't, deworming may have to be repeated
several times a year.

Can people get tapeworms from their cats? In general, the answer is
no, but in certain cases tapeworms can pose a health hazard. Small
children have sometimes gotten a tapeworm following accidental
ingestion of a flea. The tapeworm *Echinococcus multilocularis,*
which is mainly an intestinal parasite of coyotes, wolves, and foxes
but may also affect domestic dogs, can also pose a health hazard.
Cats can acquire *Echinococcus* infection by eating infected raw
meat. Sheep, cows, horses, pigs, deer, moose, and rodents may all
carry the infective stages, so these tapeworms are a problem mainly
in rural areas. The tapeworms mature in infected cats and dogs, and
their eggs are passed out in the stool, where they contaminate the
soil and infect intermediate hosts such as sheep or humans. Humans
may be infected by direct contact with the eggs whether they are on
the dog or cat, the stool or soil, or on unwashed vegetables contaminated with infective soil. When the bladderworm forms in human
body tissues, severe disease can occur. If you live in a rural area, it
is important to have your cat's stool examined periodically by a
veterinarian; do not allow your cats to scavenge raw meat or hunt.
Practice good hygiene to prevent infection: Hands, utensils, or food
that may have come into contact with infective eggs on the cat or
in the soil should always be washed before contact with your mouth.
If your cat must be used for rodent control in areas where *Echinococcus multilocularis* is a problem, he or she should be dewormed
monthly with antitapeworm medications (e.g., praziquantel), and
you should keep in mind the risk of toxoplasmosis.

ROUNDWORMS (NEMATODES)

Although most people are aware that roundworm infections occur in cats, many are unaware that, like the other classes of internal parasites, there are several kinds of roundworms. Common ones are covered in the following pages.

ASCARIDS

Ascarids are the type of roundworms commonly seen in the stool of kittens. They are white, cylindrical, and pointed at both ends. They may be relatively small and threadlike in appearance or as long as 3 or 4 inches (around 7 to 10 cm), somewhat resembling small white earthworms. Adult ascarids live in the small intestine and get their nourishment by absorbing nutrients in the digestive juices through their cuticle (outer covering). Mature ascarids produce eggs that pass out in the cat's stool. After about one to four weeks the eggs become infective and contain larval worms. If the infective eggs are ingested by an appropriate host, they complete their life cycle, eventually becoming adult worms in the host's intestine. If they are eaten by an inappropriate host, such as a rodent or cockroach, the larval worms encyst in the tissues of the host where they remain unless a cat or other animal eats the abnormal host and through digestion releases the larvae.

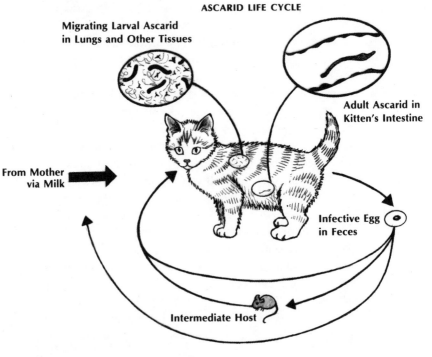

ASCARID LIFE CYCLE

Migrating Larval Ascarid in Lungs and Other Tissues

Adult Ascarid in Kitten's Intestine

From Mother via Milk

Infective Egg in Feces

Intermediate Host

Larvae of the common cat roundworm, *Toxocara cati,* can be transmitted from an adult female cat through her milk to nursing kittens, so infection may be found in very young cats. It is impossible to prevent this early infection by deworming the female before she gives birth. Therefore, it is probably easiest and best in terms of possible effects on human health to assume that all kittens have ascarid infections and to deworm them routinely.

Ascarids do not usually cause apparent disease in adult cats, however, heavy infections with *Toxocara cati* in kittens in particular, can lead to death. This roundworm migrates through the lungs en route to the intestine and can cause a cough or even pneumonia. More commonly, vomiting (of worms, sometimes), diarrhea, and progressive weakness are seen. Severely infected kittens may have dull coats and potbellies on a thin frame, and some may even develop bowel obstruction or rupture from impaction with ascarid roundworms.

The drugs *piperazine* (at a dose of 50 mg/lb body weight base, 110 mg/kg body weight base) and *pyrantel pamoate* (9 mg/lb, 20 mg/kg) are used to remove adult ascarids from the intestines. Both are very safe and effective drugs that you can obtain from your veterinarian or a pet shop; both drugs can be administered at home. There is no need to make your cat fast before administering the dewormers, and they do not usually cause vomiting or diarrhea. Avoid over-the-counter products containing dichlorophene and/or toluene since these have been associated with toxicity. Other drugs used to kill ascarids may be available only with a prescription from a veterinarian. These include febantel, fenbendazole, dichlorvos, and ivermectin. Kittens can be dewormed as early as four weeks after birth in order to remove ascarids before they start shedding eggs into the stool, resulting in environmental contamination. Public health authorities strongly recommend this procedure. Deworming should be repeated *at least* once two to four weeks later to remove any adult worms that were immature and not killed at the first dosing. For extremely heavy infections, deworming may have to be repeated several times before all worms present are killed. Therefore, it is common to deworm kittens every two to three weeks until they are three months of age.

Ascarid eggs are very resistant to environmental stresses. They can remain alive and infective for months or years once they have contaminated soil. These factors make it very important to practice good sanitation to prevent reinfection of your cat as well as infection of other cats and humans. Roundworm eggs cannot survive on surfaces that dry completely and that are exposed to sunlight as much as possible. Surfaces should be thoroughly cleaned with iodine-based disinfectants containing 120 parts per million free iodine. A 1% sodium hypochlorite solution (3 cups liquid chlorine laundry bleach to 1 gallon water) will damage but not kill roundworm eggs as an aid to removal. Rodents and cockroaches, which may serve as intermediate hosts for the worms, should be controlled.

ASCARIDS ARE A HUMAN HEALTH HAZARD Although feline ascarids do not occur in human intestines, their larve *may* cause *visceral larva migrans,* a rare condition in which roundworm larvae migrate throughout the body. *Visceral larva migrans* may cause anything from no signs of illness to severe signs, including blindness. The condition occurs most often in young children who play in soil infested with the eggs of the common *dog* roundworm, *Toxocara canis,* and put their contaminated hands in their mouths. But *Toxocara cati* has been incriminated in some cases. Although complete recovery is the rule, the possibility of human infection is a significant reason for good ascarid control and for good general hygiene.

HOOKWORMS

POSSIBLE SIGNS OF HOOKWORMS Hookworms (*Ancylostoma* and *Uncinaria* species) are small intestinal parasites (about one-fourth to one-half inch long, 0.6 to 1.25 cm) that attach to the wall of the small intestine and suck blood. Cats may become infected by ingesting infective larval worms off the ground, eating a transport host such as a mouse, or by penetration of their skin by infective larvae. Kittens may become infected before birth by larvae migrating through the mother's body tissues and shortly after birth by larvae passed in colostrum and milk.

Migration of hookworm larvae through the skin can cause itching reflected by scratching, redness, and sometimes bumps and scabs on the skin. Hookworms living in the intestine can cause diarrhea, severe anemia, weakness, and emaciation leading to death. Infection in young animals sometimes causes anemia and death even before hookworm eggs are detectable in the stool.

DIAGNOSIS AND TREATMENT Hookworms cannot be diagnosed and treated effectively without the aid of a veterinarian. Hookworms are small enough to be overlooked even when they are passed in the stool. Signs of illness caused by hookworm infection can be caused by other diseases as well. The safest and most effective compounds for treatment are available only through veterinarians. If your cat has to be treated for hookworms your veterinarian will probably use a drug called pyrantel pamoate (9 mg/lb, 20 mg/kg) that you may be able to administer at home. Other kinds of effective drugs include febantel, disophenol, dichlorvos, and ivermectin.

Hookworms are a problem only in areas that provide an environment suitable for the development of infective larvae. The preinfective stages require moderate temperatures (between about 73°F and 86°F, [22.8° to 30°C]) and moisture for development. Prevent reinfection or spread of hookworms by keeping your cat indoors and having him or her use a litter pan that is thoroughly cleaned *at least* weekly (preferably daily) until your cat is diagnosed as hookworm free. Cage areas should be washed daily and allowed to dry, and outdoor areas where stool may have been deposited must be kept dry for three weeks to kill larvae. In areas of gravel, dirt, sand, or bark, concentrated sodium chloride solution (irritating to cat's feet) or sodium borate (borax, 10 pounds per 100 square feet, broadcast dry, raked lightly, and moistened) must be applied to kill the larvae. Repeat the application monthly.

HOW TO PREVENT HOOKWORM INFECTION

STOMACH WORMS

Stomach worms infect both cats and dogs and occur mainly in the southeastern United States. They frequently cause vomiting and cannot be differentiated from other causes of vomiting without examination of a fecal sample and the aid of a veterinarian. You can prevent infection of your cat by preventing the ingestion of cockroaches, crickets, and beetles, which serve as intermediate hosts for the development of one type of stomach worm (*Physaloptera*), as well as the ingestion of vomitus from other infected animals, which may carry a worm called *Ollulanus tricuspis*. Piperazine salts, pyrantel pamoate, dichlorvos, or fenbendazole is used for treatment.

THREADWORMS

The threadworms, *Strongyloides stercoralis,* is a roundworm parasite of cats, dogs, and humans. Infection with this species and other kinds of threadworms is acquired most commonly when infective larvae penetrate the skin. This can cause red lumps, crusts, and scratching. And during their migration through the body the larvae can produce signs of respiratory disease, such as a cough. Cats can also become infected by ingestion of infective larvae. Threadworms are very small worms and will not be seen in the stool. When diagnosis is established by a veterinarian, thiabendazole is often used for treatment. Prevent *Strongyloides* infection by providing your cat with a clean, dry environment since the infective larvae cannot survive without a moist environment.

LUNGWORMS

Lungworms, as their name implies, are small (about one-fourth-inch, 0.6 cm long) roundworms who as adults live in the lungs of cats. The more common lungworm, *Aelurostrongylus abstrusus,* infects cats who have eaten snails, slugs, rodents, frogs, lizards, or birds carrying infective larvae of the worm. These intermediate and transfer hosts become infected when they ingest larvae that have been coughed up and then swallowed and passed in the stool of affected cats. Although infection is uncommon, lungworms do occur in many areas all over the United States and Europe, so an informed cat owner should be aware of their occurrence.

SIGNS OF LUNGWORM INFECTION The first sign of lungworm infection is usually a persistant cough, often accompanied by a gradual weight loss. Other signs in addition to cough can be fever, loss of appetite, nasal discharge, and sneezing. Therefore, it is easy to confuse this disease with other causes of respiratory distress.

LUNGWORM DIAGNOSIS AND TREATMENT Diagnosis and treatment of lungworm disease may be difficult and must be done by a veterinarian. Veterinarians look for lungworm larvae (or eggs, in certain cases) in the stool (or sputum) of infected cats, so it can be helpful to bring a stool sample when you take your cat to be examined. There are few effective drug treatments; they include ivermectin and fenbendazole. Prevent infection with the common lungworm by restricting your cat from hunting.

WHIPWORMS

Whipworms (*Trichuris* species) are intestinal roundworms that are known to occur in the *cecum* (part of the large intestine) and sometimes cause diarrhea and weight loss. Although once thought not to occur in cats, whipworms have been rarely diagnosed in them. Infection is acquired directly by ingesting infective larvae from contaminated soil. Diagnosis must usually be made by a veterinarian since infection is often symptomless. Ask your veterinarian if you live in an area where whipworms are found. If you do, consider having a stool sample examined semi-annually for evidence of whipworm infection.

EYEWORMS

Eyeworms are small roundworms (less than one half inch [1.25 cm] long) that live in the conjunctival sac of the infected cat. They cause reddening and irritation of the conjuctiva, discharge from the eye, and, sometimes, damage to the eyeball itself. Eyeworms occur in North America (especially the western United States) and Asia and are transmitted through the mouthparts of flies that feed on secretions from the eye. You or your veterinarian can eliminate infection with these worms if you find them by removing them with a pair of fine forceps or tweezers.

HEARTWORMS

Heartworms (*Dirofilaria immitis*) are roundworm parasites ranging from 6 to 12 inches long (15 to 30 cm) that are found in the hearts, pulmonary arteries, and venae cavae of infected *dogs*. They can cause serious, even life-threatening disease in dogs, and they may also cause health problems in cats, although much more rarely. These worms are transmitted by mosquitoes that feed on infected animals and ingest immature forms (larvae) of the heartworm along with their blood meal. After a period in which the larvae mature the mosquito transmits the larvae that cause infection to a new host when it takes another blood meal.

There are areas all over the world where heartworm infection is likely to occur. In the United States, infection in dogs is particularly common along the Atlantic and Gulf Coasts, in the Mississippi Valley, and in Hawaii. However, heartworm infection is also found in the Midwest, Pacific far west, and Alaska. If you live in an endemic area and your cat spends a great deal of time outdoors, he or she is at risk of heartworm infection.

Cats are more resistant to heartworm infection than dogs. When infection does occur there are fewer worms, they do not grow as large, and they usually die spontaneously in about two years. Since cats are not the normal host for the heartworm, larvae may often travel to other areas of the body such as the brain, spinal cord, and tissues under the skin instead of the heart. Signs of heartworms in infected cats may not be visible at all, or they may be very nonspecific such as loss of appetite, lethargy, and weight loss. On the other hand, the course of illness can be rapid, resulting in a sudden, unexpected death due to obstruction of the arteries of the lung (pulmonary embolization). More chronic cases may be marked by sporadic coughing or difficulty breathing and thereby be confused with feline asthma (see page 159). Sometimes the main sign of infection is bouts of vomiting; in areas of high heartworm incidence, infection must always be considered as a possible cause of unexplained vomiting by cats who may have been exposed to infected mosquitoes.

Adult heartworms in cats do not readily produce the young larval forms that are usually found in the blood of infected dogs and that are most often used to diagnose infection in them. This fact coupled with the fact that heartworm infection in cats can mimic many other diseases often makes diagnosis difficult. A veterinarian who suspects heartworm infection in your cat can perform blood tests, chest radiographs (X-ray pictures), heart and blood vessel evaluation, and other specialized tests as needed to determine the presence and severity of heartworm-induced disease. When diagnosis is confirmed, he or she can give you the best advice as to whether treatment is advisable, since the drugs used for treatment may be associated with serious, even life-threatening, side effects themselves.

Prevent heartworm infection in your cat by keeping your pet indoors during mosquito season. Consult your veterinarian about prevention in high-risk areas.

PINWORMS

In answer to a common question: cats, like dogs, do not get or spread pinworms. The human pinworm, *Enterobius vermicularis,* occurs only in humans and higher primates such as chimpanzees.

TRICHINOSIS

Trichinosis is a roundworm infection that occurs when larval forms of *Trichinella spiralis* are eaten and encyst in the muscle tissue. This disease affects humans, pigs, and other mammals, including cats, dogs, and rats. Vomiting, diarrhea (bloody), and signs of muscle involvement including stiffness and weakness, and signs of pain have occurred in affected cats. Although cats are among the animals most susceptible to trichinosis, infection is not frequently recognized. Prevent trichinosis by not feeding raw or undercooked pork and by restricting hunting (to prevent cat's preying on possibly infected rodents). This will also prevent pseudorabies infection (see page 89).

External Parasites   External parasites of cats are *arthropods* (hard-coated insects and insectlike animals) that live on cat skin, feeding on blood, tissue fluid, or the skin itself.

FLEAS

Fleas are probably the most prevalent external parasite of cats. Fleas are wingless, small dark brown insects capable of jumping great distances relative to their body size. They obtain nourishment by sucking blood. Fleas are not very host-specific. In spite of the fact that there are several flea species, cat fleas (*Ctenocephalides felis*) can be found on dogs, dog fleas (*Ctenocephalides canis*) can be found on cats, and cat and dog fleas will feed on humans. Human fleas (*Pulex irritans*) also feed on dogs and occasionally on cats. The important thing is not the kind of flea present, but that a cat should not have fleas at all. A *single* flea on a pet is a cause for concern. Flea infestation should not be considered a normal or natural condition, and just a few fleas can sometimes be responsible for significant loss of blood in kittens, old animals, or any weakened cat. This blood loss *(anemia)* can result in death, particularly in young cats. Fleas are carriers of disease, including the organism that causes human bubonic plague and also tapeworms (see page 97). Allergic dermatitis is also commonly caused by fleas.

ADULT FLEA FEEDING ON CAT

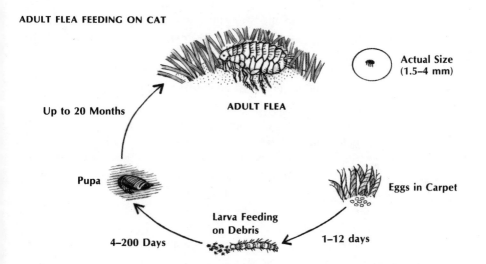

Actual Size (1.5–4 mm)

ADULT FLEA

Up to 20 Months

Pupa

Eggs in Carpet

Larva Feeding on Debris

4–200 Days

1–12 days

Optimum Environmental Conditions for Development 65–85°F (18–27°C) 75–85% Humidity

Female fleas lay their eggs only after consuming a blood meal. They may lay them directly on the host, but because the eggs aren't sticky, they usually drop off. Flea eggs are white and about the size of a small grain of salt. If a cat is heavily infested with fleas, eggs may be found in his or her coat mixed with flea feces (partially digested blood), which are about the same size but colored black. (Moistening suspected flea excreta should produce a blood red spot.) The eggs hatch into larvae anytime from two days to two weeks after being laid.

FLEA LIFE CYCLE— IMPORTANT IN CONTROL

Mature flea larvae resemble very small fly maggots. They are about one-quarter (about 6 mm) inch long and white to creamy yellow in color. They are usually found in cracks in floors, under carpets, in pet bedding, and other similar places. The larvae feed only a little, eating adult flea excreta or other organic debris in the environment. Then they spin cocoons in which they develop into adult fleas. Depending on environmental conditions, larvae may take from about ten days to several months to become adult fleas. They are very sensitive to drying; therefore, they prefer an environment that is uniformly moist but not wet, a condition that is often found in sandy areas outdoors. Once larval fleas enter their cocoons, they are called *pupae.* Pupae are extremely resistant to any chemical or physical means of destruction and may survive for up to twenty months before emerging as adult fleas. After hatching, adult fleas can live up to twelve months without feeding, just waiting to jump on your pet.

Since a major part of the flea life cycle takes place off the cat, flea control on a single host is not sufficient to get rid of fleas completely. Fastidious housekeeping is essential, and flea control must be practiced on all pets living in a single house. Existing fleas must be removed from the premises (including from vehicles in which flea-infested pets have been transported) so that the pet can be used as a sentinel to alert you to any potential reinfestations.

Washing or burning infested bedding and thorough vacuuming can be sufficient to get rid of small numbers of fleas providing the cleaning routine is kept up weekly year-round and providing that all pets in the household are kept scrupulously clean. In the case of a moderate to heavy infestation, houses, yards, and catteries must be sprayed or fumigated with commercial insecticides, or the services of professional exterminators must be obtained.

HOW TO DETECT FLEAS AT HOME Two ways to detect fleas in your environment are the white handkerchief and white sock techniques. In the first, a white linen handkerchief is inserted between the end of the vacuum cleaner hose and its coupling to the power source. After vacuuming the pet's sleeping area, the carpet, and other areas (even the cat), remove the handkerchief and place it quickly and carefully into a plastic bag. Then seal it. With a magnifying glass, it is easy to detect flea eggs, larvae, pupae, and even adult fleas trapped in the handkerchief.

The white sock technique detects adult fleas in a suspected area. Put on a pair of white knee socks and walk briskly around the suspected area for five minutes. Fleas respond to vibrations in the environment, body heat, and exhaled carbon dioxide and often jump onto the socks, where they can be seen. *Any* flea observed is significant, as one adult female flea can lay up to forty eggs per day and a breeding pair of fleas can easily produce 600 offspring in a month!

Products for treating premises that have fleas include a variety of insecticides, insect growth regulators, and a few noninsecticidal products. Insecticides are available as liquids to be sprayed in- or outdoors or as indoor foggers (antiflea "bombs") that release a fine mist into the air when activated. Any good veterinary clinic should be able to help you select a product, but be sure to read the labels on any products you choose and ask any questions that may come to mind. It is very important to select insecticidal products that have the lowest possible toxicity to species other than the flea and that are *nonpersistent* in the environment (see chart, page 113). Most products that meet these requirements need *repeated application* to the infested area (usually every two weeks for at least three or four applications) to eliminate adult fleas, which will continue to emerge from the pesticide-resistant cocoon stage as the previously applied pesticide degrades.

HOW TO SELECT FLEA CONTROL PRODUCTS

Insect growth regulators (e.g., methoprene, fenoxycarb) are biochemicals that mimic the insect hormone necessary for proper flea development, thus disrupting the early flea life stages and causing them to die. These products can provide about two to five months of persistent flea control when applied to areas harboring only flea eggs and larvae. They cannot kill pupae or adult fleas. Although these relatively environmentally safe chemicals cannot by themselves provide full flea control, when used appropriately they can lessen the amount of pesticide that has to be applied to the environment over time in order to kill adult fleas by providing a way to eliminate fleas in the earlier life stages. Insect growth regulators are included in various premise sprays, foggers, and pet sprays in combination with a variety of insecticides. Read the labels and, if necessary, ask your veterinarian for advice on how to find the best product for your circumstances, as more than 300 products are available for the control of fleas on pets and premises.

Nonchemical methods of flea control are important to the success of any program using chemicals and for continuing good flea control once fleas are eliminated from the premises. Before using flea-control products, thorough cleaning of washable floor surfaces and vacuuming of carpets (a vacuum equipped with a beater bar is best) and furniture is critical. Special attention should be given to baseboards, sheltered areas under furniture, and the spaces around and under furniture cushions. Burn the vacuum cleaner bags after use. Pieces of flea collars, or flea powders placed in vacuum cleaner bags will also kill emerging adult fleas. However, they may also result in additional aerosol environmental contamination by pesticides, and this is not an approved use of insecticides by the Environmental Protection Agency. Also avoid using napthalene moth crystals (moth balls) in vacuum cleaner bags to kill fleas since they can generate explosive gas. Area rugs should be washed regularly, and steam cleaning of wall-to-wall carpets will kill all flea life stages if done properly. Various insecticides and larvacidal products can be applied in carpet-washing solutions if necessary, and drying products that kill fleas by dessication can be sprinkled on carpets. The major key to good flea control is absolute cleanliness in the environment and on the pet.

START PET FLEA CONTROL WITH A BATH If your cat has fleas, the first thing to do is to give him or her a good bath. You can use a gentle human shampoo or a commercial shampoo containing insecticides to kill fleas. If you use a regular shampoo, remember that you are only removing fleas mechanically. If you don't rinse your cat's coat well, fleas stunned by the water will wake up as the coat dries and still be around to cause trouble. Insecticidal shampoos have no significant residual action, but they do help kill fleas during the bath. A bath once a week followed by a cream rinse can be sufficient for flea control in low-flea-density areas. (Certain bath oils and cream rinses designed for people seem to have flea-repelling effects. Ask your veterinarian for instructions for using a specific product on your cat.) Once your cat is clean, use any of the following for continued flea control.

FLEA DIPS Dips are insecticides that are applied to the cat's coat as a liquid and allowed to dry. It is easiest to sponge on a dip while the cat is still wet following a bath. It is not necessary to immerse a cat in the dipping liquid. Avoid applying insecticides around the cat's eyes, nose, and mouth (even if directed to do so by the label). Dips containing pyrethrins or synthetic pyrethrins (see chart, page 113) are generally less toxic and less environmentally persistent than those containing other insecticides, and they can provide very effective flea control if applied regularly. In areas with a major flea problem, it is desirable to switch between product categories periodically to avoid the possible emergence of a strain of flea resistant to any single insecticide group.

FLEA SPRAYS, ROLL-ONS, AND POWDERS Flea sprays, roll-ons, and powders (dust) are made from a large variety of insecticides, insecticide potentiators, and sometimes insect growth inhibitors in an alcohol or water carrier (sprays, roll-ons) or a diatomaceous earth or silica carrier (powders). In general, the same considerations about toxicity, environmental persistence, and flea resistance apply to the selection of a spray or powder as to a dip. You may want to ask your veterinarian what is currently recommended in your area. In general, powders, sprays, and roll-ons must be applied frequently—often daily—to provide good flea control. Many animals and owners object to this process. It is important to apply most powders and sprays moderately and regularly, rather than infrequently and heavily, if good flea control is to be achieved. The legs, back, tail, and rump of the cat are the most important areas to cover, and it is essential to apply these products near the skin by pushing the hair against its direction of growth and rubbing the product in. It is often helpful to apply sprays or powders just before a pet is allowed outdoors. This allows any fleas that jump on during outdoor activity to be killed immediately (and not brought back indoors!), as well as allowing sprays to dry and excess powder to fall out of the fur.

Avoid applying sprays or powders to irritated or raw skin. Insecticides are more readily absorbed systemically from areas where the skin has been broken. Alcohol can be irritating to sensitive skin, and the drying action of the carriers in flea powders—which itself helps kill fleas—can also be irritating to both normal and abnormal skin.

FLEA COLLARS

The most effective flea collars contain organophosphate or carbamate insecticides (see chart, page 113) incorporated into a plastic base that allows their slow release. These chemicals act directly on the flea, causing its death. Their action in flea collars is not due to absorption by the cat and ingestion by the parasite with a blood meal. A false sense of security may arise when a pet wears a flea collar, and this can result in infested premises if early evidence of collar failure is not noticed. Collars should be replaced on a regular schedule *well before the stated expiration date on the package.* Pets wearing flea collars should be bathed frequently and examined often for fleas. Any evidence of fleas on a pet who is wearing a flea collar is grounds for reevaluation of the full flea control program with special attention to the premises.

Flea collars can be used safely on *healthy* cats as young as two months of age, but package directions to the contrary should be heeded. Flea collars should be applied loosely (you should be able to insert two fingers held side by side between the cat's neck and collar) and wetting should be avoided to prevent premature loss of the antiflea effect. Other insecticides should not be applied in the presence of a flea collar unless advised by a veterinarian.

FLEA COLLARS CAN CAUSE CONTACT DERMATITIS A few cats are sensitive to insecticides and develop *contact dermatitis* when a flea collar is applied. The dermatitis often first appears as hair loss and reddening of the neck skin under the flea collar. If the collar is not removed, the skin condition can progress to large raw areas, sometimes secondarily infected with bacteria, that can be difficult to clear up and need the attention of a veterinarian. Flea collar dermatitis can sometimes be prevented by airing the collar for two or three days before putting it on the cat. Cats who cannot wear flea collars should *not* have similar insecticides applied to their skin in the form of dips, sprays, or powders.

MANUAL FLEA REMOVAL Removal of fleas by hand or with a flea comb is an extremely inefficient method of flea control. To ensure a flea-free animal, the entire coat must be combed by hand for at least forty-five minutes daily, a process few people will routinely undertake. Of course, if you see a flea, you should remove it, but don't rely on this as a means of routine control if other methods can be used. If they cannot be, be sure to combine combing with regular bathing and extremely fastidious housekeeping. And consider purchasing a flea-comb unit that can attach to your vacuum cleaner. Suction increases the effectiveness of the combing process.

HOME REMEDIES Scientific experiments have been unable to substantiate the effectiveness of home remedies against fleas, such as applying ultrasonic collars or eucalyptus bud- or pennyroyal oil–impregnated collars or feeding cats garlic or brewer's yeast. Flea traps that consist of a light source suspended over sticky paper have been shown by scientific experiment to catch no more than 2% of fleas released into a controlled environment. If you want to stick to such remedies, examine your cat *thoroughly* and *frequently* for evidence of fleas. If *any* are present, immediately reevaluate your means of flea control.

SYSTEMIC FLEA CONTROL Organophosphate insecticides have been developed that are designed to kill fleas only after they have taken a blood meal from a pet. These products were developed for dogs and can be *extremely dangerous* to cats. They have a potent ability to lower an animal's blood level of *cholinesterase,* an enzyme that is important to normal nervous system function. They can result in significant drug interactions when other drugs with similar effects are administered in the course of anesthesia or disease treatment and are readily toxic themselves to cats, causing vomiting, muscle tremors, hyperexcitability, drooling, diarrhea, and death. Common names of systemic flea control drugs are *cythionate* and *fenthion.* Avoid them in cats.

The sticktight flea *Echidnophaga gallinacea* is mainly a parasite of poultry, but it can attack cats. You can recognize sticktight fleas easily because the adults stick tightly to the cat's skin and don't run off when approached. They are voracious blood suckers and, if found, should be removed by the use of a flea dip followed by routine means of environmental flea control.

In the Middle Ages it was common for humans, dogs, and cats to be infested with fleas. Modern standards of cleanliness have made human infestation with fleas rare and unacceptable in normal, clean environments. This state is maintained without antiflea dips, sprays, and powders as part of one's daily toilette. A similar state exists for cats who are kept clean and who live in clean households surrounded by neighbors who set the same high standards for their pets. Flea infestation could be a thing of the past for pets if all cats and dogs had owners who gave them good care.

COMMON INSECTICIDES

CHEMICAL CLASSIFICATION	INSECTICIDE	ADVANTAGES/ DISADVANTAGES
Botanicals	d-limonene† linalool† pyrethrin (Sectrol*)† rotenone	Rapid kill; usually safe; degrade rapidly after application; short residual action
Carbamates	aldicarb (Temik*) bendiocarb (Fibam*) carbaryl (Sevin*)† carbofuran (Furandan*, Bay70142*) methiocarb (Mesurol*) methomyl (Lannate*) propoxpur (Sendran*, Baygon*)†	Slow environmental degradation; more potentially toxic than pyrethroids, less so than organophosphates; longer residual activity; flea resistance reported in certain geographic areas

CHEMICAL CLASSIFICATION	INSECTICIDE	ADVANTAGES/ DISADVANTAGES
Growth regulators	fenoxycarb (Tenocide*, Torus*)† methoprene (Precor*, Siphotrol*)†	Usually very safe; target immature insect stages; do not kill adult fleas
Organochlorides	aldrin chlordane chlordecone (Kepone*) DDT dieldrin endosulfan (Thiodan*) endrin lindane methoxychlor TDE toxaphene	Good residual action; persist in the environment; toxic to wildlife
Organophosphates	chlorpyrifos (Dursban*)† coumaphos (Co-ral*) cruformate (Ruelene*) cythionate (Proban*)† diazinon (Spectracide*)† dichlorvos (DDVP*, Vapona*, Task*)† dimethoate (Cygon*) disulfoton (Di-Syston*)	Potent nerve toxins (cholinesterase inhibitors) with high potential for acute toxicity, suspected chronic toxicity for some products; good residual activity; broad spectrum of external and internal parasite- and "pest"-killing activity

CHEMICAL CLASSIFICATION	INSECTICIDE	ADVANTAGES/ DISADVANTAGES
	famphur (Warbex*) fenthion (Pro-Spot*, Spotton*) fonofos (Dyfonate*) malathion (Malamar*, MLT* Zithiol*, Cython*)† naled (Dibrom*) parathion (Baldan*) phorate (Thimet*) phosmet (Prolate*, Kemolate*, Imidan*) propetamphos (Safrotin*) ronnel (Korlan*, Nankor*, Ectoral*, Etrolene*, Trolene*), temephos, (Abate*) tetrachlorvinphos (Rabon*, Gardona*) trichlorfon (Dipterex*, Neguvon*)	
Pyrethroids (Synthetic pyrethrins)	allethrin (Pynamin*) d-trans allethrin cypermethrin fenvalerate (Ectrin*) permethrin (Expar*)† d-phenothrin resmethrin (SBP-1382*) tetramethrin (Neo-pynamin*)	Rapid kill; usually safe; moderately rapid degradation in environment and on animal; longer residual activity

*Trade name
†Common ingredient in flea control products

TICKS

Ticks are not commonly found on cats, probably because cats habitually groom themselves thoroughly. If you live in a woodsy or rural area and your cat goes outside, you may occasionally find a tick. Adult female ticks look different before and after they have taken a blood meal (see illustration); male ticks don't swell with feeding. The most serious damage ticks usually do is cause an area of skin inflammation at the site of attachment, but their presence should never be ignored. Heavy tick infestation can cause anemia in kittens or weakened adult cats; ticks can transmit diseases and can sometimes cause paralysis by releasing substances toxic to nerves while feeding. *Borrelia burgdorferi,* the bacteria responsible for Lyme disease* can be transmitted by ticks to humans, cats, and dogs.

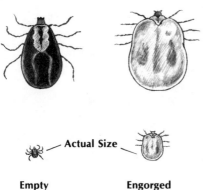

FEMALE TICKS

Actual Size

Empty   Engorged

HOW TO REMOVE TICKS Since cats rarely have more than one or two ticks on their bodies, the easiest way to remove them is by hand. Using forceps, tweezers, or your thumb and index finger protected by tissue or disposable gloves, grasp the tick as close as possible to where its mouthparts insert into the cat's skin. Then exert a firm but gentle, constant pull. (There's no need to twist.) If you've pulled just right and gotten the tick at the optimum time after attachment, the entire tick will detach. If the mouthparts are left embedded, don't worry. The tick never

*There is no clear relationship between evidence of exposure to *Borrelia burgdorferi* (blood tests positive for antibody to the bacterium) and signs of any disease in cats. Signs of Lyme disease in humans or dogs may include fever, swollen lymph nodes, heart conditions, neurologic abnormalities, eye inflammation, arthritis and/or kidney inflammation. When other diseases are ruled out, suspected infections with Lyme bacteria can be treated with antibiotics (usually a penicillin- or tetracycline-family drug). Since any relationship between tick exposure and Lyme disease in cats is unclear, the best way to prevent problems is to keep your cat away from brushy areas, which may be tick infested, apply tick-killing insecticides to the cat's fur frequently, and/or remove ticks daily. Infection of humans or dogs does not occur until the tick has been attached and feeding for several hours, and this is probably true for any transmission to cats as well.

grows back, the mouthparts fall out naturally, and only rarely does a tick bite become infected. The site of the tick bite usually becomes red and thickened in reaction to a substance secreted in the tick's saliva, but it usually heals in about two weeks. *Do not* try to burn off ticks with a match, or apply kerosene, gasoline, or other similar petroleum products. If you feel you must apply something to the tick, use a drop of concentrated flea or tick dip or alcohol, apply it only to the tick, not to the surrounding skin or hair. Wait for a few minutes, then pull the tick out. Always avoid contact with the body fluids of ticks to avoid infection of yourself by disease-causing organisms (the Lyme disease spirochete bacterium can penetrate the skin directly), and always wash your hands with soap and water after removing a tick.

LICE

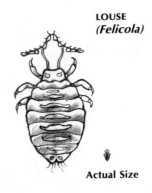

**LOUSE
*(Felicola)***

Lice are much less commonly seen than fleas or ticks on well-cared-for cats. Adult lice are pale colored and about one tenth inch (2.5 mm) or less in length. They spend their entire life on one host and attach their tiny white eggs to the hair. Cat lice (*Felicola subrostratus*) eat skin scales and hair. They can cause signs of itching, dandruff, and a rough hair coat.

Actual Size

Some cats develop tiny scabs all over their skin. Lice can also carry certain tapeworm larvae. Kill lice with a thorough bath followed by a spray or dip for cats effective against ticks and fleas. Repeat the treatment weekly for three to four weeks and include all cats living with or exposed to the infested cat.

MITES (MANGE)

Mange is a general term for infestation with mites. It is not any single disease in itself. The mites discussed here are ear mites, *Cheyletiella* mites, head mites, and trombiculid mites. Other mite infestations of cats (e.g., *Demodex* and *Sarcoptes*) are rare.

EAR MITES

Ear mites, *Otodectes cynotis,* live in the ear canal of cats and dogs and feed on skin debris, blood, and tissue fluids. They are the most common mites that infest cats. Ear mites cause the formation of large amounts of dark black to reddish brown wax in the ear. An infected cat may hold his or her ears in an abnormally flat-tened manner and shake his or her head or scratch his or her ears with unusual vigor.

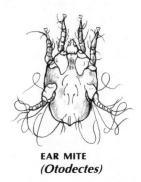

EAR MITE
(Otodectes)

If you think your cat has ear mites, remove some of the discharge from the ear canal with a cotton swab. You may be able to see the mites by examining the waxy material in a bright light or by putting it on a piece of black paper. (A magnifying glass may help you.) Live ear mites look like moving white specks about the size of the point of a dressmaker's pin.

If you have seen mites and there is not much ear discharge, you may be able to treat the condition at home. *Do not* attempt home treatment unless you have seen the mites. Other ear problems can cause similar discharges and may be complicated by the use of an ear mite preparation. Treatment consists of cleaning out the ears and instilling insecticide liquid with an eyedropper or dropper bottle. How often this must be done depends on the product used. However, no matter which topical product is selected, the full treatment period must extend over a total of thirty days in order to kill all stages in the mite life cycle. It is also advisable to clean the premises thoroughly and to bathe the cat and apply topical insecticides to the cat's coat, as ear mites are occasionally found in the fur or in the environment, where they may survive for months. It is important to treat all cats and dogs in the household to avoid reinfestation. Bathe, spray, and/or dip the animals in antiflea preparations once a week for three to four weeks to kill any mites that may be found in the fur. Whether or not you will need to see a veterinarian to obtain an effective ear mite preparation depends on the area in which you live, as some states control over-the-counter sale of insecticides more closely than others. Effective preparations often contain one or more of the following: *rotenone, pyrethrins, piperonyl butoxide, thiabendazole, dichlorophene, methoxychlor, or ivermectin.* Veterinarians may also administer some injectable drugs to kill the mites.

CHEYLETIELLA MITES (WALKING DANDRUFF)

Cheyletiella are off-white or yellowish large mites that most commonly infest young kittens brought up in dirty environments. They cause a dandrufflike condition and mild signs of itching. This mite can be seen with the naked eye if an infested cat is carefully examined. Control is easily achieved by cleansing with insecticidal shampoo or using insecticidal dips, sprays, or powders (e.g., pyrethrins, carbaryl, lime-sulfur) once a week for three weeks on *all* animals on the premises. *Cheyletiella* mites are capable of infesting dogs, foxes, rabbits, and humans as well as cats. Infection of people with the common "walking dandruff" mite of cats (*Cheyletiella blakei*) is usually only transient and, if necessary, can be treated with insecticidal shampoos. Premises should be treated with insecticides (see flea control, page 109) as a few female mites may live off the host for as long as ten days. If topical treatment is not possible, some veterinarians may administer antimite drugs by injection.

HEAD MITES

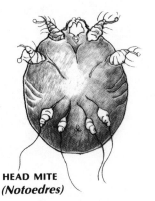

HEAD MITE
(Notoedres)

Head mites, *Notoedres cati,* are microscopic mites that infest cats and that can transiently infest human beings and dogs. These mites burrow beneath the horny layers of the skin causing intense signs of itching followed by hair loss. Because these mites seem to prefer the skin of the head and ears, thickened, wrinkled skin and gray crusts and scales are usually first seen in these areas and on the back of the neck. In neglected cases lesions of this appearance may be found on the feet and under the tail. *Notoedres* infestation is easily spread from cat to cat. **SIGNS OF HEAD MANGE**

If you suspect that your cat has head mange, infection can only be confirmed by microscopic examination of a skin scraping. Therefore, it is advisable to have your cat examined by a veterinarian before beginning treatment for the mites. Not only can he or she confirm the presence of mites and give you detailed information on the use of a proper insecticide to prevent toxicity to your cat, but a veterinarian can also administer *corticosteroid* drugs (see page 262), if necessary, to help relieve the itching until the mites are completely gone, and antibiotics in cases of secondary bacterial infection. **DIAGNOSIS OF HEAD MANGE**

119

If you cannot obtain the services of a veterinarian and choose to begin treatment yourself, be sure to pick an insecticide marked clearly as safe for cats and follow the directions on it carefully. Treatment must include all cats in contact with the infected one. It consists of clipping hair on affected areas on long-haired cats, bathing, and applying a dip which kills *Notoedres* at least twice at 7- to 10-day intervals. Dips reported effective against *Notoredres* and safe for cats include 2.5% dilution of lime sulfur (orchard spray available at garden stores), and 0.2% malathion. Dipping must often continue for four to eight treatments. Veterinarians may treat cases of head mite infestation with antimite drugs administered by injection.

TROMBICULID MITES (CHIGGERS)

Trombiculid mites (chiggers, harvest mites) are red, orange, or yellowish mites that have larvae that feed on the tissue fluids of cats and other mammals. (The nymphs and adults feed on plants or invertebrates.) The larvae are often found on the head and neck, particularly in and around the ears, but can infest any part of the body, causing scratching which is sometimes very severe. Look for red, orange, or yellowish specks about the size of the point of a dressmaker's pin in affected areas. Use a magnifying glass if necessary. If you cannot find the mites, diagnosis may have to be made by an examination of a skin scraping performed by a veterinarian. Mites found solely in the ear can be eliminated by the treatments for ear mites (see page 118). Mites on other body areas can be controlled with dips or other preparations effective against head mites. Prevent reinfestation by keeping your cat indoors, away from woodsy semiwild areas where the mites are found most often.

FLIES

Adult flies are not normally parasitic on cats. Some types of adult flies lay their eggs in raw or infected wounds. When the eggs hatch, the maggots feed on the tissue present, producing a condition called *myiasis*. Maggots are frequently found in infected ears as well as in neglected skin wounds and under matted hair. To treat myiasis, all the maggots must be removed manually, the areas washed with an antibacterial soap (e.g., povidone-iodine), and a topical antibiotic cream or ointment applied to treat any secondary bacterial infection that may be present. It is extremely important to treat the predisposing condition or myiasis is likely to recur.

A particular kind of bot fly of the *Cuterebra* species, whose maggot (larva) is a natural parasite of rodents, may occasionally infest cats that snoop around rodent burrows. These larvae penetrate the skin, then become surrounded by thickened tissue and are connected to the skin surface by a breathing pore. These areas are often found on the head and neck and sometimes they become infected, causing an abscess to form. Removing the maggot from the pocket will cure the problem. This can be done by gently enlarging the pore with tweezers and carefully removing the whole larva. Crushing the larva can cause a serious allergic reaction, so if you suspect *Cuterebra* infections in your cat, you should consider contacting your veterinarian for help.

THE VALUE OF PREVENTIVE MEDICINE

Begin to practice preventive medicine as soon as you take a new cat into your home. In a short time the proper way to care for a healthy cat will become second nature to you. The effects of poor preventive medicine early in a cat's life can sometimes never be reversed. On the other hand, a cat that is fed well, groomed regularly, and kept in a clean and parasite-free environment will have a good start on a long and healthy life. Combine these things with love and proper training and a yearly visit to a veterinarian for booster shots and examination, and you should find that living with your cat is a simple, enjoyable, and rewarding experience.

PARASITES SHARED BY CATS AND DOGS

Cat   Dog

External parasites

Fleas ⟶ Fleas
⟵

Ear mites ⟶ Ear mites
⟵

Cheyletiella mites ⟶ *Cheyletiella* mites
⟵

Internal parasites

Protozoa: Protozoa:
Toxoplasma ⟶ *Toxoplasma*
         via environmental contamination by stool

Flukes ⟶ Flukes
         via ingested crayfish or contaminated water
⟵

Tapeworms   Tapeworms
(Dipylidium) ⟶ *(Dipylidium)*
                via ingested fleas
⟵

Ascarids   Ascarids
(Toxascaris leonina only) ⟶ *(Toxascaris leonina* only)
         via environmental contamination by stool
⟵

Heartworms ⟶ Heartworms
         via mosquito infection only
⟵

Hookworms ⟶ Hookworms
(certain   via environmental infection by stool   (certain
species only) ⟵ species only)

Lungworms   Lungworms
(Capillaria aerophyla only) ⟶ *(Capillaria aerophyla* only)
         via environmental contamination with
           stool or ingestion of indirect host
⟵

Stomach worms ⟶ Stomach worms
         indirectly via ingested beetles, etc., or
         directly via ingestion of infected vomitus
⟵

3

DIAGNOSTIC MEDICINE:

~~~~~

What to Do When Your Cat Is Sick

SKIN (INTEGUMENTARY SYSTEM)

HEAD

RESPIRATORY SYSTEM

**MUSCLE AND BONE
(MUSCULOSKELETAL SYSTEM)**

**DIGESTIVE SYSTEM
(GASTROINTESTINAL SYSTEM)**

**REPRODUCTIVE AND URINARY
ORGANS (GENITOURINARY SYSTEM)**

**HEART AND BLOOD
(CARDIOVASCULAR SYSTEM)**

MULTISYSTEM DISEASES

EMERGENCY MEDICINE

GERIATRIC MEDICINE

TIMES WHEN A VETERINARIAN'S HELP IS NEEDED

Any emergency
Whenever you fail to diagnose the problem
Whenever home treatment fails
For any problem that requires X-ray pictures, ultrasound, or other specialized medical equipment, laboratory analysis, or anesthesia
For any problem requiring prescription drugs, including antibiotics
For yearly physical examination and booster vaccination

If you have been giving your cat the kind of good care you have learned about in the first part of this book, but illness occurs, you are not necessarily at fault. Even the best cared for cat may become sick or injured. The following pages and the sections on emergency medicine and geriatric medicine are here to help you in such situations. The best way to use these three sections, as with the rest of the book, is to read them through completely and become familiar with the contents. In this way when a problem occurs you will not have to waste time attempting to digest the new material. You will already know how to deal with the problem, or a quick review will be all that is necessary. Knowing the contents ahead of time will also help to prevent certain problems, (see, for example, "Wound Infection and Abscesses," page 129, and "Poisoning," page 210). If your cat is already sick, you can start with the Index of Signs of illness and the General Index for the book.

The Index of Signs is an alphabetical listing of changes that may occur when your cat is sick. *Symptoms* are subjective indicators of disease. Because your cat cannot describe his or her feelings in words, he or she technically has no symptoms, only *signs,* which are any objective evidence of disease or injury you can detect. To use the index, first determine what your cat's signs are; for example, you *see* scratching (not itching, your cat *feels* the itching) and you *see* red bumps on your cat's skin. Then look up these changes in the Index of Signs and turn to the page listed to find out about the problem and what to do. If you can't find the signs you see or you can't put the signs into words, look in the index under the part that is involved, for example, "Skin." Use the General Index whenever you want to read about a general subject (e.g., breeding) or a particular disease (e.g., rabies). Some signs are included in the General Index in addition to the Index of Signs. Remember, only *common* problems are discussed here in terms of home treatment. If you cannot find what you are looking for in either index, consult a veterinarian. The prob-

HOW TO USE THE INDEXES

125

lem may or may not be serious but is not one I've considered run-of-the-mill for the general cat population.

You should watch carefully for signs of illness. Sometimes a cat is very sick before signs of illness are obvious (even to a practiced eye). Because cats can't talk, the practice of veterinary medicine is often more difficult than that of human medicine. Since you are closest to your cat you may be able to notice signs of illness before your veterinarian can find any abnormalities on a simple physical examination. Anything you can tell your veterinarian about signs may be *very* important.

THE VALUE OF SPECIALIZED TESTS   A relatively few signs signal the presence of many diseases. Very different diseases cause the same signs and can sometimes be differentiated from one another only by specialized diagnostic aids, such as X rays, blood tests, and urinalysis. Keep this in mind if you think your cat has all the signs of a particular illness but fails to respond to the suggested treatment. Also, keep in mind the value of *intuition* in recognizing that your cat is ill or injured. You know your cat best. If "something just doesn't seem right," sit down with your cat, take his or her temperature (see page 242), and perform a physical examination (see page 2). Often you will turn up specific signs that you can read about and deal with at home. If you don't, don't assume that you are wrong and that your cat is okay. Rely on your intuition and get your cat examined by a veterinarian. The doctor may find something wrong on physical examination or can perform specialized tests if necessary.

Three common general signs of illness in cats are *change in behavior, change in appetite,* and *fever.* Two other general signs you may see are *shivering* and *dehydration.*

CHANGE IN BEHAVIOR   Don't take any change in behavior lightly. Although most cats become less active and more quiet when they are sick or injured *(depression of activity),* any behavioral change can indicate a medical problem. Many cats lessen or stop self-grooming behaviors when they are ill, so unkempt fur may signal a behavior change. Cats can have "emotional" problems as well, but they are much less common than illness-associated behavior changes, and you will need to consult other books to deal with such problems at home (see page 42).

CHANGE OF APPETITE OR WATER INTAKE   Cats may lose their appetites completely when they are sick (*anorexia*). More often, however, you will notice a *change* in appetite. The sick cat may eat more or less. One day's change, though, is not usually important. Watch your cat's food intake carefully. Once a cat is grown, food intake should be fairly constant from day to day (see page 80). Changes that persist longer than five days with no other signs of illness should be discussed with your veterinarian. Changes accompanied by other signs should not be allowed to continue longer than twenty-four hours before you or your veterinarian investigates the problem.

The normal resting cat maintains his or her rectal temperature within the range of 101.0°F to 102.5°F (38.3° to 39.2°C). (For how to take a cat's temperature, see page 242.) An elevated body temperature *(fever)* usually indicates disease, but keep in mind that factors such as exercise, excitement, and high environmental temperature can elevate a cat's temperature as well. Many kinds of bacteria produce toxins (called *exogenous pyrogens*) that cause the body to release chemical substances called *endogenous pyrogens,* which produce fever. Other agents such as viruses, fungi, antibody-antigen complexes, and tumors produce fever in a similar manner. These exogenous pyrogens induce white blood cells to produce endogenous pyrogens, which pass into the brain and cause the hypothalamus to raise its body temperature set point.

FEVER

It is important to remember that fever is a *sign* of disease, not a disease in itself. Drugs may be used to lower an extremely high fever (greater than 106°F [41.1°C]), but aspirin, the most common drug used for this purpose, must be used with great caution in cats. The important thing is to find the cause of the fever and treat it. In fact, there are indications that the presence of fever may even be beneficial in some diseases.

Except in kittens less than four weeks of age, lowered body temperature (less than 100°F [37.8°C]), is usually indicative of overwhelming disease, and the affected animal needs immediate care.

Shivering may or may not be a sign of illness. Many cats shiver when frightened, excited, or otherwise emotionally upset. Cats also shiver when they are cold. Unless they are accustomed to being outside in cool weather without protection, cats, like people, get cold and shiver in an attempt to increase body heat.

SHIVERING

Shivering may also be a sign of pain. It is often seen with the kind of pain that is difficult to localize, such as abdominal or spinal pain. During the early part of *febrile disease* (illness with fever), shivering sometimes occurs. The heat it produces contributes to the rising body temperature. If your cat is shivering, try to eliminate emotional causes and take his or her temperature before concluding that this sign is due to pain.

127

All body tissues are bathed in fluids consisting primarily of water, ions, proteins, and some other chemical substances such as nutrients and waste products. Normal tissue fluids are extremely important in maintaining normal cellular functions. Changes in the body's water composition are always accompanied by changes in other constituents of tissue fluids. Small changes can have important consequences!

The most common tissue fluid alteration seen in sick animals is depletion of body water, or *dehydration.* Dehydration occurs whenever the body's output of water exceeds its intake. One common cause of dehydration during illness is not taking in enough water to meet the body's fixed daily requirements. Water is continually lost in urine, feces, respiratory gases, and evaporation from some body surfaces (minor in cats). Dehydration also occurs in conditions that cause excessive water and/or *electrolyte* (ion) loss, such as vomiting and diarrhea. Fever also increases the body's water needs.

Although dehydration begins as soon as water output exceeds intake, the signs of dehydration are usually undetectable until a water deficit of about 4% of total body weight has occurred. If your cat has visible signs of dehydration, he or she may have been sick longer than you realize and may need professional veterinary care.

SIGNS OF DEHYDRATION IN ORDER OF INCREASING SEVERITY

1. *Decreased elasticity of the skin.* The tissues beneath the skin contain a large portion of the total body water. Because this water compartment is one of the least important to the body, it is drawn upon first in a situation of dehydration. To test for dehydration, pick up a fold of skin along the middle of the cat's back and let it drop. In a well-hydrated, normally fleshed cat the skin will immediately spring back into place. In a moderately dehydrated cat skin will move into place slowly. In cases of severe dehydration the skin may form a tent that remains in the skin (fat animals tend to have more elastic skin than thin ones, which can obscure signs of dehydration). The normal cat must be at least 5% dehydrated before any change in skin elasticity is detected.

2. *Dryness of the mucous membranes of the mouth and eyes.* This may be difficult to evaluate until dehydration becomes severe, as panting may also dry the mucous membranes. Normal mucous membranes have a glistening, slightly moist appearance.

3. *Sunken eyes.* This condition can also be due to severe weight loss, but in any case it's serious.

4. *Circulatory collapse (shock).* See page 202. Capillary refill time (see page 202) is usually two to three seconds with 7% dehydration and more than three seconds at 10% dehydration. Shock occurs with 12% to 15% dehydration.

Mild dehydration and its accompanying ion imbalance can be prevented and/or corrected by administering water and nutrients orally. With more severe dehydration, or with disease that prevents oral intake, fluids must be administered by other routes. In such cases veterinarians administer fluids *subcutaneously* (under the skin) or *intravenously* (directly into the bloodstream), if necessary. Fluids given via these routes are sterile and of varied composition. The fluid your veterinarian chooses will depend on the route of administration and the cause of dehydration. Good fluid therapy is an important part of the care of almost all animals sick enough to require hospitalization.

When you determine the signs your cat has and have read about what they indicate, you will need to begin treatment. (If you do not already know how to proceed with the treatment involved or need more information on the care of a sick cat see the section "Nursing at Home," page 241).

SKIN (INTEGUMENTARY SYSTEM)

In addition to the information in this section, other causes of skin disease will be found in the sections on external parasites (see page 106) and nutrition (see page 60).

WOUNDS, WOUND INFECTION, AND ABSCESSES

Wounds and their frequent sequelae, *abscesses,* are the most common skin problems seen in cats who are allowed outdoors. Whether or not your cat needs to see a veterinarian for wound care depends a lot on the kind of wound it is. Short, clean *lacerations* (cuts) or cuts that do not completely penetrate the skin and most *abrasions* (scrapes) usually need only to be washed thoroughly with mild soap and rinsed with large volumes of warm, clean water. After thorough washing these injuries should be examined daily for signs of infection. Larger cuts (about one-half-inch long or longer) and punctures usually need veterinary attention.

Wound healing is essentially the same process whether it occurs by **HOW WOUNDS** *primary* or *secondary* intention. The wound fills with a clot. The **HEAL** wound edges contract, reducing the wound in size. White blood cells called *macrophages* enter the wound and remove dead tissue and foreign material. Blood vessels and connective tissue cells enter the wound, followed by nerve fibers and lymphatic cells. At the same time this is happening, skin cells move in to close the surface opening, and finally the wound is healed. Wounds that are allowed to heal without apposing (bringing together) their edges heal by *secondary intention.* Healing by *primary intention* is more rapid. Your veterinarian tries to achieve primary intention healing by suturing larger wounds closed. Suturing clean wounds closed also helps prevent them from becoming infected while they are healing. Wounds, however, which are likely to become infected cannot be sutured closed or must be sutured only with special care. Puncture wounds—most commonly bite wounds or claw wounds—are among the most frequently seen wounds on cats that fall into this category.

PUNCTURE WOUNDS NEED SPECIAL ATTENTION Bite wounds and claw wounds require special attention not only because they are likely to become infected (which interferes with healing), but also because if the body's defenses (white blood cells and lymph nodes) are unable to overcome the bacteria, infection may spread from the original wound to the bloodstream. This may result in a *septicemia* (bacterial toxins in the blood) or a *bacteremia* (actual bacteria in the blood) and can sometimes eventually lead to death. Although puncture wounds are difficult to wash, you should make an attempt to clean them thoroughly whenever you notice any on your cat. Flushing a mild disinfectant into the wound under light pressure (with a eyedropper, turkey baster, or syringe) is one of the best home remedies because this action tends to wash debris out of the wound. Disinfectants that are used in veterinary hospitals and that you can buy there or in drugstores include 0.001% to 1% povidone-iodine (the more dilute solutions are actually more potent disinfectants and less damaging to healthy tissue), 0.55% chlorhexidine, and 0.125% to 0.5% sodium hypochlorite (one fourth to full strength Dakin's solution), which can be made by diluting household bleach 1:10 to 1:40 with water. Flushing with hydrogen peroxide, once thought to be an effective wound treatment, has fallen into disfavor due to its weak antibacterial properties. Its foaming action is impressive but is best reserved for flushing debris or blood clots from a wound. If used, the concentration of hydrogen peroxide should never be more than 3%. Do not instill oil-based antibiotic wound ointments or those containing the local anesthetic *benzocaine* into the wound cavity as oily products may interfere with healing. Any benzocaine absorbed through the skin is toxic to red blood cells. If possible, antibiotics should be administered by a veterinarian from the start of treatment (within twenty-four hours of the bite) since bite wounds are so prone to infection. The biting cat (or other animal) should be investigated regarding the status of its rabies immunization.

ABSCESSES

An *abscess* is a localized collection of pus in a cavity caused by the death and destruction of body tissues. Abscesses are the most common type of infection occurring in improperly treated bite or claw wounds. They usually cause swelling under the skin at the wound site and sometimes signs of pain, but often go unnoticed until they begin to drain sticky white, yellow to yellow-green, or blood-tinged pus. Abscesses are frequently found on the head (cheeks, ears), legs and feet, and on the tail (near its base). They occur much less frequently in the tissues behind the eye (retrobulbar abscess) caus-

ABSCESS

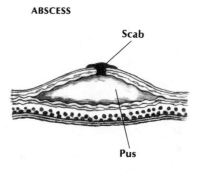

Scab

Pus

ing swelling, protrusion of the eye, and signs of pain particularly when attempts are made to open the mouth. Veterinarians treat abscesses by opening them surgically under anesthesia and by removing all visibly dead and infected tissue (*débridement*). Antibiotics are administered, and you are usually instructed to clean the wound daily at home. You can often tell when an abscess that is not draining is formed and ready to open by feeling it with your finger. If you can feel a soft spot or if the swelling feels fluid filled under the skin, it is ready to lance. Sometimes your veterinarian will advise you to put warm packs on an inflamed and infected area that is not yet abscessed. This helps localize the infection so effective drainage can be provided. By transiently increasing the blood supply to the area, hot packs may help antibiotics get into the infection, preventing abscessation in some instances. You may want to try this without a veterinarian's advice on an infected, diffuse swelling *(cellulitis)* that has not yet abscessed if your cat does not have a fever and seems fairly normal except for the signs of inflammation.

HOME TREATMENT FOR ABSCESSES

If your cat has a well-localized abscess that has burst or is covered by a scab that can be removed and has *no fever,* you may be able to get the abscess to heal with home treatment alone. You must pull off the scab if the abscess is not yet draining, then determine how extensive the abscess is. Any abscess in which you can't reach to the full extent of the pocket probably won't heal but will spread or recur and need a veterinarian's attention. Determine the extent of the pocket by wrapping your gloved finger in a sterile gauze pad and probing the wound thoroughly. Be gentle, but be sure to clean out all pus and loose tissue and to probe to the wound's farthest reaches. A small abscess can be cleaned and probed with a cotton-tipped swab. Clean the abscess thoroughly with a disinfectant once or twice a day (see page 256). If the opening of the wound is large enough,

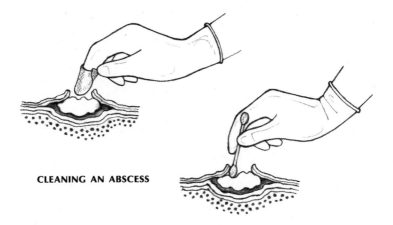

CLEANING AN ABSCESS

you can pour the disinfectant solution directly into it. A syringe (bulb or hypodermic type) or eye dropper can be used to flush the solution into smaller wounds. The disinfectant can be applied to a gauze pad which is used to wipe the wound or to a cotton-tipped swab which can be inserted into very small wounds.

Some cats find these procedures uncomfortable, so be alert to avoid injury to yourself if the cat bites or scratches to show his or her displeasure. Clean the wound until visible tissue is free of debris and/or until the solution runs clear. Repeat the cleaning once or twice a day until debris no longer accumulates in the wound.

TIMES TO SEEK VETERINARY HELP WITH ABSCESSES   If your cat has a fever or any other signs of illness accompanying an abscess or wound, *do not* attempt home treatment without the help of a veterinarian. Fever and/or other general signs of illness indicate that the problem is a more serious infection that the body's defenses have not been able to localize. Improperly treated wounds can be responsible for serious and expensive complications—among them bone infections, recurrent abscesses, and bacterial infections of internal organs such as liver, heart, and lungs.

Another type of abscess in cats is the *tooth root* abscess caused by an infected tooth, usually found in a neglected mouth. This kind of infection may cause swelling on the face; the swelling may come and go. Treatment usually requires that the infected tooth be removed to prevent recurrent abscessation. So see your veterinarian if you suspect this problem. *Foreign bodies* not removed from a wound can also cause a recurring abscess. Plant awns (wild barley "foxtails") often cause this type of abscess between the toes or in the genital area of dogs. They are much less common in cats, but these abscesses must be probed by an expert until the foreign object is found and removed or they will not heal. If you are lucky at home, a foreign body abscess will open and, by *expressing* (squeezing out) the contents, you will be able to pop out the foreign body. Infected anal glands frequently abscess (see page 173).

Tetanus is mentioned here with wounds because this disease is usually contracted following a wound that allows entry of the bacteria that cause it. Cats are much more resistant to infection with *Clostridium tetani,* the bacterium that causes tetanus, than humans are. In fact, tetanus infection in cats is rare, so veterinarians don't normally vaccinate cats against it. The tetanus-causing organism is commonly found in manure and manure-contaminated soil. Tetanus antitoxin and/or penicillin (which kills the tetanus bacteria) can be given by a veterinarian when a cat gets a manure-contaminated wound or acquires a wound in filthy surroundings. Signs of tetanus include progressive stiffness and hyperactivity, difficulty opening the mouth and swallowing, and rigid extension of all limbs and the tail. Cats with tetanus need a veterinarian's care.

ALLERGIC DERMATITIS

Some cats, like some people, are born with a predisposition to develop reactions when exposed to certain substances in their environment. Cats with allergic dermatitis usually develop skin disease characterized by signs of itching, such as biting and scratching the skin, when exposed to the material to which they have become allergic. In some cases there is no evidence of itching, but other skin abnormalities occur (see page 139). Exposure to the substance may be by inhalation (this route of sensitization is common in a form of allergy called *atopy*), ingestion (e.g., food allergies), inoculation (flea bites, drugs), or direct contact of the skin with the offending substance. You will usually see reddening of the skin, small bumps, oozing and possibly sticky areas and scabs, and sometimes dandrufflike scales. The reddened skin may feel abnormally warm to the touch. In neglected cases there is hair loss, large areas of raw skin may develop, and the skin may even become thickened. If these changes go untreated long enough, they can become permanent. Areas where scratching is severe may become infected. Cats with allergic dermatitis may lick at their flanks, abdomen, and the inside of their rear legs excessively when grooming, causing a characteristic symmetrical hair loss unaccompanied by any actual skin changes. Cats with this form of allergic dermatitis must be differentiated from those with other (e.g., hormonal) causes of hair loss that take a similar pattern. In addition to skin signs, cats with allergic dermatitis may have more general signs of allergy such as a watery nasal discharge and sneezing, tearing, and conjunctivitis. Some may even have vomiting or diarrhea.

ALLERGIC DERMATITIS HAS MANY CAUSES Fleas are probably the most common cause of allergic dermatitis. If you practice good flea control (see page 109), you may be able to prevent the dermatitis from developing or relieve a case that has already developed. Be careful, however, about putting flea sprays or dips on an irritated skin; they sometimes make the irritation worse. If you think you are controlling fleas but your cat continues to scratch, there can be several possibilities. For example:

1. The bite of a single flea (which you may not see) can cause extreme itching in an allergic animal.

2. Cats can be allergic to many things *other than or in addition to* fleas—among them pollens, house dust, molds, trees, wool, foods, cigarette smoke.

3. The condition may not be allergic dermatitis (for an example, see page 136).

BATHING IS PART OF THE HOME TREATMENT Frequent bathing (every one to two weeks) helps to control the signs in many cats and also helps prevent secondary bacterial infection. It removes allergens from the coat and seems to relieve some of the skin inflammation associated with allergic dermatitis. Use a gentle hypoallergenic shampoo (for example, castile shampoo, baby shampoo, or a veterinarian-prescribed shampoo, not bar soap or dishwashing detergent) to avoid additional damage to a sensitive skin. If your cat's skin and hair become too dry with bathing, an emollient oil diluted with sufficient water to avoid leaving the fur excessively greasy can be used as a final rinse. Hypoallergenic bath oils for people are satisfactory, or a veterinarian can prescribe a product. If you find that bathing makes your cat's signs worse, don't, of course, continue to use it as a treatment.

Often, once the itching has begun it continues even if you remove the original cause of the irritation. This may be due to scratching, which releases itch-causing substances from the damaged cells. When such a cycle occurs, a veterinarian must administer and/or prescribe drugs such as antihistamines, antiinflammatory fatty acids, or corticosteroids to control the problem. In many allergic cats drug treatment must be repeated intermittently or administered continuously.

Skin testing, blood testing, and hyposensitization (induction of immune tolerance by the injection of small amounts of allergen) as used in people with certain allergies have been helpful in some cats with allergic dermatitis induced by environmental allergens such as pollen, molds, and house dust. Special elimination diets, often based on rice or potatoes and lamb, turkey, or rabbit, are useful to diagnose and treat allergy signs related to food sensitivities. A *minimum* of four weeks' diet restriction is needed to rule out food-induced allergy. Many veterinarians have a special interest in skin disease and can make an effort to find out what allergies affect your cat. Cats with very difficult allergy problems can be diagnosed and treated by a veterinary dermatologist. For persistent problems, ask your veterinarian for a referral to a specialist.

CONTACT IRRITANT DERMATITIS

Contact irritant dermatitis can occur in *any* cat whose skin comes into contact with an irritating substance such as certain soaps, detergents, plants, paints, insect sprays, or other chemicals. The reaction can look similar to that described for allergic dermatitis, but tends to be limited to the areas that have been in contact with the substance and is more common in sparsely haired skin areas. If left untreated, the affected areas often become moist and sticky.

Contact irritant dermatitis is treated much like allergic dermatitis, but long-term success is more likely since it is usually easier to find the offending substance and remove it permanently. The first thing to do is to remove the cause. If the contact dermatitis is due to a flea collar (see page 111), remove the flea collar. Bathe your cat and rinse his or her coat thoroughly. If these methods are insufficient to relieve the signs, have a veterinarian examine your cat. Corticosteroids will probably be given, and a soothing antibiotic-corticosteroid cream dispensed, if necessary, for home use. Since cats often lick off any topically applied medications an Elizabethan collar (see page 259) may be suggested as a way to prevent licking of an affected skin area.

PODODERMATITIS

Pododermatitis is an inflammation of the skin of the foot. When it involves the foot pads, it can be a sign of a systemic immune problem, but it is frequently due to local causes (e.g., a wound between the toes, contact with a irritant substance) and may also be due to infection with bacteria or fungi (e.g., ringworm).

The web of the foot in the affected areas is reddened and usually moist from *exudation* (leakage of fluid from tissue) and licking. It may be swollen. This condition can be painful enough to cause lameness on the affected foot.

EXAMINE THE FOOT BEFORE BEGINNING TREATMENT Examine the foot carefully in a bright light. Look closely for evidence of foreign bodies or wounds. Probe gently for areas of soreness. If you find an invader and can remove it, the pododermatitis may improve quickly. Often the original cause is gone but the problem persists because the cat continues to lick the irritated area. Washing the foot with a gentle antiseptic soap (e.g., chlorhexidine, povidone-iodine), drying, and soaking it in warm water for fifteen minutes twice a day followed by thorough drying is often helpful. Try to prevent your cat from licking the affected area. In addition, the application of a soothing hydrocortisone cream usually helps clear up simple irritation-associated conditions quickly if you can keep the cat from licking the medication off. These products are sold over the counter in drugstores. If the inflammation and/or soreness persists longer than forty-eight hours without signs of improvement, a veterinarian will have to diagnose and administer treatment. Prolonged use of corticosteroid ointments in any but the most simple condition confounds diagnosis, aggravates certain conditions (e.g., ringworm), and interferes with healing.

RINGWORM (DERMATOPHYTOSIS, DERMATOMYCOSIS)

Ringworm is an infection of the hair, toenails, or skin caused by special types of fungi that may be transmitted to cats from other animals, people, or the soil. Cats under one year of age are more often affected than other animals, and infection is most severe in animals weakened by other infections, parasites, or stress. The "classic" sign of ringworm is a rapidly growing, circular area of hair loss, but ringworm can appear in many other ways—scaly patches, irregular hair loss, crusts, and discolored, deformed toenails. Areas of reddened or darkened skin or small scabby bumps usually considered more typical of allergic reactions may also indicate ringworm.

x

A ringworm infection can be present with no evidence of skin disease at all!

Certain kinds of ringworm can be transmitted from cats to humans. Adult humans are relatively resistant to ringworm, however, and are unlikely to become infected if normal hygiene habits are followed. Children should avoid handling animals infected with ringworm because they are more likely to become infected and tend to be less hygiene conscious. Infected cats should also be isolated from other uninfected pets to avoid spread of infection. Veterinarians can diagnose certain cases of ringworm with the use of an ultraviolet light alone (the most common type of ringworm, *Microsporum canis,* may fluoresce green). In other cases microscopic examination of skin scrapings and/or a fungal culture may be necessary. An inexperienced person may confuse ringworm with other skin conditions such as allergies or mite infestation, and when cats show *any* signs of skin disease ringworm must be considered. If you are in doubt, see your veterinarian.

Many uncomplicated cases of ringworm heal spontaneously in one to three months, so isolated infected areas may be cleared with simple home care. The affected area should be clipped free of hair and washed daily in a povidone-iodine (e.g., Betadine) or chlorhexidine shampoo (e.g., Nolvasan), followed by application of an antifungal cream or drops. Products containing 2% miconazole nitrate or 1% clotrimazole, which inhibit the growth of ringworm, can be purchased in a drugstore without a prescription. They have been shown to be more effective than over-the-counter products containing tolnaftate. A 0.05% solution of liquid chlorine bleach applied once a day can be effective on localized lesions if more sophisticated products are unavailable. Ringworm cases that do not respond to this simple regime, that have secondary bacterial infections, or that involve the toenails or several body areas need to have more extensive topical treatment as well as a prolonged treatment with systemic antifungal drugs. Topical treatments include dips of 2.5% lime sulfur, captan (1:200 dilution of 45% technical captan), 0.2% enilconazole, or 0.05% chlorhexidine. *Griseofulvin* is a common systemic drug used for treatment of more serious ringworm cases; it is incorporated into new hair growth to prevent recurrence of the fungus. Other antifungal drugs (e.g., ketoconazole) are also available on prescription by a veterinarian once an appropriate diagnosis is made.

PREMISES MUST BE CLEANED TO PREVENT REPEAT INFECTIONS If your cat is diagnosed as having ringworm, clean your house thoroughly and change any air filters in your heating-ventilation system. Wash and disinfect or discard your cat's bedding, collar, harness and/or leash, and grooming equipment. Products containing iodophors, chlorhexidine, or 0.5% chlorine bleach (5.25% solution of liquid chlorine bleach, mixed one part to ten parts water) are effective disinfectants that can be mopped or sprayed onto surfaces or used to soak certain washable materials. Cleaning should be repeated weekly until the cat is fully cured. The ringworm fungus forms spores (something like bread mold does), and thorough cleaning helps remove them and thus prevents reinfection. Untreated ringworm spores may survive in dry environments as long as four years!

FELINE ACNE

Feline acne is a skin condition that occurs on the chin and edges of the lips in affected cats. In its mildest form you will see blackheads that may form in the skin because the cat does not wash the chin thoroughly and/or because of abnormal oil (sebum) secretion of the skin glands in the area. When infection occurs, swelling of the chin may be seen, and in severe cases actual pustules (pus-containing bumps) or small abscesses form. Although mild cases of feline acne respond readily to treatment, you can expect recurrences when treatment is stopped since the underlying cause usually remains.

Home treatment consists of washing the chin of affected cats daily. Use a shampoo containing 2.5% to 3% benzoyl peroxide and rinse thoroughly. An alternative is to scrub affected areas gently with a cotton ball moistened with rubbing alcohol once a day (no need to rinse). After improvement, cleaning can be reduced to twice a week

to help prevent recurrences. Cases that don't respond to home treatment or chins that have become very infected will need to be treated with the help of a veterinarian who can shave your cat's chin and prescribe antibiotics and/or prescription drugs that modify oil gland secretions if necessary. Some persistent or recurrent cases of feline acne associated with abnormal sebum formation respond to fatty acid supplementation in the diet. Veterinarians can dispense commercial fatty acid supplements or you can try giving your cat 1 teaspoonful (5 ml) poultry fat daily. Lessening of blackhead formation should occur within six weeks if supplementaton is effective.

EOSINOPHILIC GRANULOMA COMPLEX (EGC)

The eosinophilic granuloma complex (EGC) consists of three different-looking skin abnormalities that have been traditionally grouped together by veterinarians as if they represented different manifestations of a single disease. In fact, these skin lesions, *feline indolent ulcer* (rodent ulcer, eosinophilic ulcer), *eosinophilic plaque,* and *eosinophilic granuloma* (linear granuloma) do not represent a single disease but the way a cat's skin reacts to a variety of different primary problems. Each abnormality may appear alone or in any combination with the others depending on the individual cat's response to the initiating factor(s). For the most part, the skin problems seen with EGC seem to be related to allergy-induced or parasite- (e.g., flea or mosquito bite) induced skin disease. In some cases viruses such as feline leukemia virus (see page 191) or bacteria have been associated with forms of EGC. Factors that affect general immune system function such as genetic background and stress may also play a role, since all of the different skin problems grouped under EGC show evidence of immune system activation when a skin biopsy (surgical removal of a small piece of skin for a pathologist's evaluation) is taken and examined under a microscope.

Indolent ulcers are usually found on the upper edges of one or both lips, most often in the area that overlies the canine (cuspid teeth). They can, however, occur anywhere on the body. Indolent ulcers are usually oval shaped with a depressed area in the center and a raised edge. The surface is raw and bright pink to red but may look brownish if a crust (scab) has formed on the surface. Although the surface looks eroded, the skin in the affected area often feels thickened. These ulcers do not normally seem to cause the affected cat any discomfort. Both young and old cats of either sex or any breed may develop indolent ulcers, but most are seen in middle-aged fe-

FELINE INDOLENT ULCERS

139

RODENT ULCER

male cats. It is not unusual for cats with indolent ulcers to also have eosinophilic plaques and/or linear granulomas.

Eosinophilic ulcers alone are sometimes no more than a cosmetic problem for the affected cat, and small areas that are unaccompanied by other signs and do not seem to enlarge may be left untreated. Most indolent ulcers slowly enlarge and deepen if left untreated, and, in rare cases, they can undergo malignant transformation and become cancerous. So diagnosis of the cause and treatment of the ulcer is always best for the cat.

FELINE EOSINOPHILIC PLAQUES Eosinophilic plaques are raised, well-defined, reddened areas with a raw surface that may ooze tissue fluids. They may occur anywhere on the body or in the mouth of the affected cat, and they range in size from about one-quarter inch (about 6 mm) to several inches in diameter. Cats lick and scratch at eosinophilic plaques as they seem to be associated with intense itching. Most affected cats are at least two years old, and there is no breed or sex predilection for developing this skin abnormality. In areas where fleas are prevalent, eosinophilic plaques found on the abdomen, rump, and groin are often associated with flea bite allergy.

FELINE EOSINOPHILIC GRANULOMAS Eosinophilic (linear) granulomas are well-defined reddish to yellow colored, raised skin areas that may appear anywhere on the body or in the mouth of affected cats. Although the abnormal areas may be linear in shape, they also often form firm bumps in the skin. Most linear granulomas are found on the posterior surface of the hindlegs.

Another common site is the chin. They are often found incidentally during physical examination, since eosinophilic granulomas are rarely associated with discomfort, and they often seem to wax and wane in size even if untreated.

As with other skin conditions of cats, treatment for EGC is most successful when the cause of the problem is found and removed. Since all of the skin abnormalities in this group have been associated with allergy, attempts should be made to rule out fleas and other skin parasites, foods, and inhaled allergens as triggers for the skin reaction or repeated problems will be likely. Keep your cat clean and practice good flea control. If you or your veterinarian suspect food allergy, you will need to feed a restricted diet for at *least* four weeks to discern any positive response (see page 135).

TREATMENT OF EGC

Most cases of EGC will not respond to simple home care, since the skin abnormalities represent a reaction to long-standing stimulation of the immune system. Your veterinarian may prescribe corticosteroid drugs (e.g., prednisone), fatty acid supplements, and/or antibiotics to treat certain cases. For some difficult cases, immunomodulating drugs other than corticosteroids are used, but most good veterinarians prefer to avoid them due to their potential for serious side effects. To this end most veterinarians will perform diagnostic tests such as complete blood counts (CBCs), skin biopsies, and skin testing in addition to physical examination in an attempt to choose the best treatment and rule out conditions involving the skin which may mimic EGC, such as cancer. Treatment for complicated cases include hyposensitization, surgery, radiation, and laser therapy. Consult a veterinarian specializing in dermatology if your cat has skin abnormalities typical of EGC that do not respond to standard treatment.

BROKEN CLAWS (TOENAILS)

In general, cats have few problems with their claws because they keep them retracted when not in use and maintain them by self-grooming and claw-conditioning behaviors. Occasionally cats' claws become frayed and/or broken during a fight or when they are running and/or climbing to avoid pursuit. Frayed claws need no special attention since the frayed nail layer will be removed in the cat's normal claw-sharpening routine, revealing the undamaged nail beneath. For broken claws, on the other hand, any weakened pieces, which still remain partially attached at the base, may need to be removed.

Before removing the claw, guard yourself against injury from your cat by using appropriate restraint (see page 251). If you don't feel entirely safe, enlist a veterinarian to help you. To remove the broken nail extend the claw (see page 9), grasp it with your fingertips, a pair of tweezers, or small needle-nosed pliers and give a quick, hard jerk. The broken part usually comes off readily, and any pain associated with its removal is of very short duration when you use this technique. Bleeding is usually minimal and stops entirely within five minutes. If any bleeding is so severe as to require a pressure bandage (see page 203), your cat could have a blood-clotting disorder, and you should consult your veterinarian. If the claw doesn't come off, you will have to leave it in place until it drops off or have your veterinarian remove it. Broken claws that are dirty and/or expose a lot of raw tissue at the nail base occasionally become infected. Should you suspect your cat's claw injury is serious or if you see signs of infection such as reddening of the skin at the base of the nail and/or sticky discharge in the area, consult your veterinarian for more advice. Broken nails followed by nail bed infections (*paronychia*) need treatment which may include systemic antibiotics and disinfectant soaks.

FOOT PAD INJURIES

The most common problems affecting cats' foot pads are small cuts (lacerations) and punctures acquired during fights with other cats. As with other wounds the potential for infection always exists, so even if the foot pad injury seems minor your cat should be kept indoors and observed for several days to see if signs of infection develop (see page 143).

FOOT PAD
CUTS

Deep cuts on foot pads often cause profuse bleeding, requiring application of a pressure bandage (see page 203) to avoid serious blood loss. Any cut severe enough to require a pressure bandage will probably need stitches to achieve rapid, satisfactory healing and avoid repeated bleeding. Leave a pressure bandage on until a veterinarian's advice can be obtained but no longer than twenty-four hours without reinspection of the wound and rebandaging.

Once bleeding has stopped, minor cuts should be inspected for foreign material, then gently washed with disinfectant soap, rinsed, and gently dried. The affected foot should be bandaged to protect the wound from dirt and recurrent bleeding. Change the bandage whenever it becomes wet and at least every third day in order to inspect the wound for signs of infection and proper healing. Rebandaging can be stopped once the wound is well healed (not just sealed closed). This could take as long as three weeks; weight bearing puts a lot of stress on cut pads, thereby interfering with healing.

Any puncture of the foot pad should be inspected for evidence of a **FOOT PAD** foreign object such as a small thorn or glass shard. Although bleeding **PUNCTURES** is usually minimal, lameness can be severe and persistent, and puncture wounds are followed by infection more often than cuts are. Anytime your cat is limping you should perform a thorough inspection of the foot pads. Be sure to do this in bright light and use a magnifying glass if necessary. If you see a protruding foreign body, you can carefully try to tease it loose with a sterilized sewing needle. (To sterilize a needle, heat the tip in a flame until it is glowing red, then allow it to cool, or immerse it in rubbing alcohol for ten minutes.) Once the foreign object is loose enough to be firmly grasped with tweezers or needle-nosed pliers, extract it carefully but quickly from the wound. Do not attempt this on an uncooperative cat (see page 253) unless you are willing to risk being bitten. Success is indicated by immediate improvement of the lameness. If you have any doubt that the object has been fully removed, if the lameness persists after home treatment, or if signs of infection such as swelling around or drainage from the wound occur, consult your veterinarian. Cats who have received puncture wounds rarely acquire tetanus (see page 133).

FELINE SOLAR DERMATITIS (SUN DAMAGE)

Feline solar dermatitis can occur in any skin area that has received excessive sun exposure. The ear edges are the most commonly affected sites, but any area with thin hair can be damaged, such as the areas in front of the ears, the eyelids, nose, and lips. White cats and cats that have patches of white fur and light-colored skin are most susceptible to feline solar dermatitis especially if they live in a warm and sunny area.

Inflammation and irritation follow excessive skin exposure to the **SIGNS OF** sun's burning rays. The first change you might notice is a slight **SOLAR** reddening of the affected area. Changes like this have been seen in **DERMATITIS** kittens as young as three months of age. The reddening (sunburn) does not seem to cause significant pain, but it is often followed by hair loss in the area, making it even more susceptible to future sun damage. With repeated sun exposures the reddening becomes more pronounced, skin flaking and peeling occur, and crusts (scabs) may form. If the ear margins (edges) are the site of the most damage, they will eventually begin to curl as well as to develop more scabs and bleeding. At this stage the ears often seem to be painful or itchy. Crusted feline solar dermatitis affecting the nose and ears is often mistaken for fight wounds despite the fact that the scabs never resolve but only become worse without treatment. If sun exposure is allowed to continue once skin changes are seen, many cases of feline solar dermatitis transform into skin cancer, most often squamous cell carcinoma.

HOW TO PREVENT SOLAR DERMATITIS If your cat has light coloring, it is very important to prevent sun damage to his or her skin. Keep the cat indoors between 10:00 A.M. and 4:00 P.M. when the ultraviolet rays from the sun are most damaging. Discourage sunbathing in windows as well, since the damaging rays are not blocked by regular plate glass. Hypoallergenic sunscreen lotions containing PABA (para-aminobenzoic acid) designed for people can also be applied to light-colored cats' skin (ears especially) for sun protection. Supervise your cat for a few minutes after application to prevent immediate grooming, which may remove the product before it sinks into the skin.

TREATMENT OF SOLAR DERMATITIS Early cases of feline solar dermatitis improve quickly when sun exposure is removed. Very early skin cancers caused by sun exposure can sometimes be eliminated by special, locally applied heat, laser or radiation treatments followed by measures to prevent further sun exposure. Active carotenoids given orally (25 mg betacarotene once a day) also have helped some cats. Once advanced cancer has developed the only treatment is surgical removal of the affected tissues. Surgery on the nose is often deforming but effective. Amputation of the ear margins usually has a very cosmetically acceptable result. Ask your veterinarian for an evaluation of your cat's skin if you think he or she is developing solar dermatitis and prevent further sun exposure. Do not delay seeking advice about scabbed and/or bleeding areas, since early treatment of skin cancers associated with solar dermatitis is the easiest, most effective method and has the best cosmetic result.

MASTITIS

Mastitis is an inflammation of one or more of the *mammary glands* (breasts) in female cats. While it may be due to abnormal drainage of milk from the gland or to trauma, it is usually caused by bacterial infection. Affected glands look enlarged, may be discolored (red, purplish, or blue), and often feel hard and warm. They are often painful, making the female reluctant to let her kittens nurse. If you express some milk from the affected gland, it may be blood streaked, pink, gray, or brown. Often, however, the milk does not look unusual to the unaided eye. If left untreated, the gland may abscess or the female may develop more generalized signs of illness such as depression, loss of appetite, and/or fever.

In order to prevent sick kittens, do not allow them to nurse from infected glands. Placing a piece of adhesive tape over the nipple of the gland will usually effectively prevent nursing. Affected glands should be milked out three to four times a day. Ask your veterinarian to show you how to do this properly. Warm packs applied to the gland seem to relieve discomfort and speed localization of infection. Infected glands must be treated with antibiotics. Your veterinarian can culture the milk so the offending bacteria can be identified and will prescribe the appropriate antibiotic.

TUMORS (CANCER)

Tumors are often noticed as growths in, on, or under a cat's skin. Skin cancers are the second most common type of tumors in cats. For more information turn to pages 233 and 234.

UMBILICAL HERNIA

An *umbilical hernia* is a defect involving the body wall that is usually first noticed in young kittens as a lump under the abdominal skin. Its diagnosis and treatment are covered on page 294.

HEAD

Eyes   The eyes are very important and delicate organs. Mild and unobtrusive conditions can rapidly become severe, and many untreated conditions can cause irreversible damage. *Don't ignore even minor evidence of irritation.* Unless you are sure of the diagnosis and treatment, any minor eye problem that doesn't clear quickly (within twenty-four hours) as well as any obvious change you see in the eye should be brought to the attention of an expert. *Do not* use anything in the eye not specifically labeled for ophthalmic use, and do not use a preparation in the eye just because you had it left over from an eye problem you or your cat had in the past. Ophthalmic drugs have very specific uses, and the use of a drug in a condition for which it was not specifically intended can cause serious injury or complication.

EPIPHORA (TEARING)

Epiphora is the abnormal overflow of tears from the eye. It has *many* causes because tearing is the eye's response to irritation. Among the causes are allergy, infections, *conjunctivitis,* corneal injuries, and plugged tear ducts. In cats, excessive tearing unaccompanied by other signs of illness is sometimes associated with mild respiratory infections (see page 153). In Persian cats, in particular, epiphora is mainly a cosmetic problem caused by the abnormal, extreme facial shortening of some individuals and the shallow tear pool created by the protruding eyes. If you can eliminate other causes of tearing in these cats, staining of the fur can be controlled by frequent washing of the affected area and, if necessary, by clipping away stained hair.

CONJUNCTIVITIS

Conjunctivitis is an inflammation, sometimes caused by or accompanied by infection of the membranes (conjunctiva) that line the lids and cover part of the eye. It is probably the most common eye problem of cats because it occurs in association with several of the common respiratory infections (see page 152) and also because the conjunctiva is exposed to trauma and many irritants. Conjunctivitis may affect one eye alone or both simultaneously. The first sign of conjunctivitis may only be an increase in tearing with no other signs of irritation or illness. In many instances this type of conjunctival irritation will clear spontaneously in three to seven days. In other cases, the tearing changes or the first sign you notice is an excessive amount of sticky yellowish discharge that accumulates at the medial corners of the eye. Conjunctivitis accompanied by this kind of discharge is often associated with bacterial infection.

There are many degrees of inflammation. In mild cases the conjunctiva itself may look only slightly swollen or wrinkled. In more severe cases the conjunctiva is more pink than normal, sometimes very swollen, and the vessels of the sclera (see page 18) are very prominent. Although mild conjunctivitis may clear without treatment, cases that are persistent, cause inflammation of the lids and/or discomfort, or are accompanied by other signs of illness must be treated by a veterinarian to avoid permanent damage to the eye.

In mild cases, the first step in treatment at home is to examine your cat thoroughly for other signs of illness and to examine the eyes looking for a local cause of conjunctivitis to be removed if found. If there are no general signs of illness, if the eyes themselves look normal, and if the discharge is of the clear, watery type, you may choose to postpone treatment for a few days. Cats with mild conjunctivitis that persists beyond seventy-two hours or that includes a persistent sticky discharge, as well as those with conjunctivitis accompanied by other signs of illness should be examined by a veterinarian who can determine whether antibiotics are necessary or who may find causes not obvious to you.

Conjunctivitis occurs frequently in kittens less than six weeks old. For more information see page 295.

For another cause of conjunctivitis, see Eyeworms, page 105.

TRAUMA TO OR FOREIGN OBJECT IN THE EYE

Epiphora and conjunctivitis may be signs of a foreign body in the eye or eye injury due to trauma. So it's a good idea to examine your cat's eye thoroughly whenever there are such signs. If epiphora and/or conjunctivitis are *unilateral* (on one side) only, are accompanied by squinting, pawing at the eye, or other signs of pain, a thorough examination for a foreign body or eye injury *must* be made.

The first thing to do when examining your cat's eye is to get in a good light. Slight but extremely important changes in the eye are easily overlooked in dim light. Place the thumb of one hand just below the edge of the lower lid of the affected eye and the thumb of the opposite hand just above the edge of the upper lid. This rolls the lids away from the eyeball, allowing examination of the conjunctiva and most of the cornea. The surface of the cornea should look smooth and completely transparent. (If in doubt, compare it to the opposite, probably uninjured, eye.) Be sure to look along the edge of the third eyelid to see if there is anything protruding from behind it. It is a good idea to look under the third eyelid, but most cats with a painful eye will not allow you to lift this eyelid without some form of anesthesia. You can, however, moisten a cotton-tipped swab and move it *gently* along the inner surface of the lids and under the third eyelid. Occasionally a foreign body will cling to the swab and be removed, or the swab will sometimes bring a hidden foreign body into view. This must be done

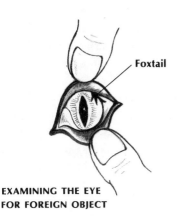

Foxtail

EXAMINING THE EYE
FOR FOREIGN OBJECT

with *extreme* care to avoid injury to the cornea and should be attempted at home with only the most cooperative cat to avoid damage to both you and the pet. If you see a large object (e.g., foxtail), you can grasp it with your fingertips or a pair of tweezers and remove it. Small foreign bodies are most easily removed with a moistened cotton swab or a piece of tissue. Any foreign object not easily removed should be entrusted to a veterinarian, and *any* sign of irritation that persists more than a few hours following foreign body removal is reason to have the eye examined by an expert.

In most cases of foreign body in the eye or trauma to the eye examination is best performed by a veterinarian. Since a cat can't tell you when there is eye irritation, it is often easy to overlook small but significant eye damage. Veterinarians use special eye stains to color the surface of the cornea. These stains show the presence of corneal damage not otherwise evident. Veterinarians also can give local or general anesthetic to relieve pain during examination, allowing a more thorough search.

PROLAPSED THIRD EYELID

The third eyelid (nictitating membrane, haw, see Anatomy, page 17) often moves from its normal position near the medial corners of the eyes to partially obscure the eye. When this occurs on one side only and intermittently as if blinking, it is often a sign of local irritation to that eye, such as a foreign body or damage to the cornea. When it occurs in both eyes (often described by owners as a "film over the eye") and for prolonged periods of time (several hours to several days), it sometimes interferes with vision and can have many causes.

The most common cause of this second type of third eyelid elevation (third eyelid prolapse, *haws* syndrome) in a cat who seems relatively healthy is a gastrointestinal upset. Signs that often accompany this kind of third eyelid prolapse are a change in appetite, a loose stool, or transient vomiting. When the gastrointestinal disturbance is corrected, the third eyelids will return to their normal positions. Third eyelid elevation accompanied by more serious signs of illness (fever, weight loss, complete absence of appetite) should prompt you to have your cat examined by a veterinarian, since serious systemic illness such as autonomic polyganglionopathy (Key-Gaskell syndrome), a nervous system disorder, may be accompanied by third eyelid prolapse.

Third eyelid prolapse that occurs in an apparently healthy cat displaying no signs of illness (not even mild intestinal disturbance) is frequently without apparent cause. It usually disappears spontaneously. If, after performing a physical examination, you feel confident that your cat is healthy you may then choose to wait and watch your cat for a few days in hopes that the problem will quickly correct itself. If prolapse is severe enough to interfere with vision, your veterinarian can supply you with a prescription for eye drops that will provide temporary symptomatic relief, if no evidence of general illness is found when he or she examines your cat.

EARS

EXTERNAL EAR INFLAMMATION (OTITIS EXTERNA)

Otitis externa is a term used to describe an inflammation of the external ear (outside of the eardrum). It has many causes, but the signs are usually the same. Head shaking and scratching at the ears are probably the most common. In some cases the cat will tilt the head slightly toward the side of the irritated ear; touching the ear may cause signs of pain. Large amounts of waxy discharge are often present; in severe cases there may be actual pus. The inside of the pinna is sometimes abnormally pink, and there may be swelling. (See Anatomy, page 18, if you are not familiar with a normal cat ear.) The normal smell of a healthy cat ear becomes fetid as the inflammation gets worse.

The most common cause of otitis externa of cats is probably ear mites (see page 118). If you cannot be sure that ear inflammation in your cat is caused by mites or if you are not *sure* you can treat the problem at home, enlist the aid of a veterinarian. Ear inflammation not treated promptly and vigorously can result in ear conditions that could have been easily cured at first but are now difficult or impossible to treat successfully, and the infection can progress to include the middle and inner ear. If you are unable to obtain the services of a veterinarian and don't think the ear problem is caused by ear mites or a foreign object in the ear (rare in cats) and choose to attempt home treatment, try using 70% isopropyl alcohol (rubbing alcohol), 10% povidone-iodine solution, or 0.5% chlorhexidine solution. First clean out the affected ear (see page 53). Then twice a day, after a more minor ear cleaning, instill several drops of the disinfectant into the ear canal and massage the base of the ear to spread the medication all the way down the canal (see page 250). If you see improvement within three or four days continue treatment for two weeks. If there is no improvement or if the treatment seems too irritating to

EAR MITES OFTEN CAUSE OTITIS

your cat's ear, be sure to seek professional help, since there is risk of permanent damage to the middle ear if home care is inappropriate.

YEAST INFECTIONS ARE FOUND IN CATS A yeast, *Malassezia pachydermatis,* is found in as many as one-third of cat ear infections. Signs of discomfort that may range from mild to severe are often associated with a brown, waxy discharge when excessive numbers of these organisms are present. Usually an increase in ear scratching is seen. This yeast thrives in a warm, moist environment. A microscopic examination of debris associated with this type of ear inflammation is needed to be sure the yeast is present and significant. Ears that are kept clean, dry, and slightly acid in pH are less likely to develop excessive numbers of yeast; so predisposed cats often need a routine of home ear care to prevent repetitive problems. Commercial products containing alcohol and boric acid, instilled into the ears once or twice a week, can prevent yeast-associated otitis externa. Home remedies for prevention are white vinegar (5% acetic acid) diluted 1:1 with water or 70% isopropyl alcohol instilled once or twice a week and after bathing.

The skin of cats' ears may be damaged by sun exposure. For more information see Feline Solar Dermatitis, page 143.

EAR SWELLINGS

Swellings on cats' ears are usually abscesses (see page 131). In a few cases they are *hematomas* (accumulations of blood under the skin) caused by trauma to the ear—such as excessive ear scratching and head shaking accompanying untreated otitis externa, or by fights. If there is no fever and the swelling is not draining, an abscess may be indistinguishable from a hematoma without examination of the contents by a veterinarian. Hematomas must be treated surgically by drainage and suturing to prevent deformity of the ear. Untreated hematomas often result in folding of the pinna. If deformity is of no concern to you, you can allow a hematoma to heal on its own. Just be sure underlying problems such as ear infection are corrected.

Nose Important conditions involving only the nose in cats are rare. A watery or sticky, opaque white to yellow discharge from one or both nostrils is usually accompanied by sneezing and is often a sign of more generalized illness, most often respiratory infection (see page 153). Feline solar dermatitis can cause damage to the nasal skin. For more information see page 143.

MOUTH

FOREIGN OBJECT IN MOUTH

Cats who have gotten foreign objects stuck in their mouths usually paw at their mouths and make unusual movements with their lips and tongues. They may make gagging motions and drool, but do not always do so. Try not to get excited if you think your cat has something stuck in his or her mouth. Try to reassure and calm your cat, then perform a thorough mouth examination in good light (see page 24). Be sure to examine the area of the mouth around the molars thoroughly; look under the tongue, at the soft and hard palates, and far into the back of the mouth to the pharynx. The most common objects you may find are sewing needles and thread, pieces of string wrapped around the tongue or teeth, and small pieces of bone (e.g., splintered chicken bones). If you see the foreign body, grasp it with your fingertips or tweezers and remove it quickly and cautiously to avoid injury to yourself. If your cat is uncooperative or if you can't find anything but the signs persist, you will have to have your cat examined by a veterinarian. (If your cat is choking see 226.)

BROKEN TOOTH

A broken tooth can become the cause of serious medical problems in a cat if it is neglected. When the inside chamber of the tooth (*pulp cavity, chamber*), which contains the blood supply and nerve, is exposed by breakage, the tooth dies and may develop an abscess (localized infection) around its root. Such localized infections may be associated with facial swelling, pain, and reluctance to eat, chew, or pick up hard objects. However, many cats show no specific signs of discomfort and the broken tooth is found only incidentally on physical examination. Some cats develop serious systemic bacterial infections from infected broken teeth, so it is important always to examine the mouth for evidence of infected teeth whenever the presence of any kind of bacterial infection is diagnosed.

Some tooth fractures are very minor and do not expose the pulp chamber or kill the tooth. They require no special veterinary care unless there are sharp edges on the break that need to be smoothed. The more usual type of break is severe enough to expose the pulp cavity. If this type of break has been present for some time, a dark gray-black spot is seen in the area normally occupied by the pulp. The surrounding part of the tooth may be the normal creamy white color, or it may also be discolored pinkish brown or gray. Should you notice a broken tooth at this stage, a veterinarian's examination is indicated but not urgent. A freshly broken tooth with pulp exposure has a bright, reddish-pink pulp area that may bleed if touched. This type of tooth injury calls for a veterinarian's examination within a few hours if an attempt to preserve the tooth's vitality is desired. Veterinarians with special training in dentistry will take steps to seal the freshly exposed pulp chamber in the hope that the broken tooth will survive without abscessation.

Since it is relatively rare for a cat owner to discover a freshly broken tooth, the more usual treatments administered are extraction or root canal therapy. Cats tolerate tooth extraction well since, unlike humans, their teeth have little tendency to migrate out of their normal position when an opposing tooth is removed. Root canal therapy is performed when tooth preservation is important for cosmetic or functional reasons. Ask your veterinarian for more information if you think your cat may require treatment for a broken tooth.

DENTAL TARTAR

Dental tartar is hard, white, yellow, or brown material on your cat's teeth. For more information, see pages 23 and 57.

GINGIVITIS

Red or bleeding gums may be signs of gingivitis. See pages 22 and 57 for more information. Gingivitis not responding to home treatment as discussed in these sections needs to be examined by a veterinarian. Some cats seem abnormally prone to gingivitis, and some cases are difficult (sometimes impossible) to treat successfully even with expert veterinary help.

RESPIRATORY SYSTEM

FELINE RESPIRATORY DISEASE COMPLEX (FRDC)

Respiratory infections of cats are caused by numerous organisms. The most common are several different viruses and a bacteriumlike organism (see chart) that infect the tissues of the nasal cavity, respiratory passages and lungs, eyes, and sometimes the mouth. These respiratory infections can range from mild to very severe illnesses. All are contagious from cat to cat, some more extremely so than others. They are often spread by licking and grooming between cats and sharing food and water dishes. Some are also spread by sneezing and coughing although this may occur only over short distances.

They are probably the most frequently seen infectious diseases of cats. The important thing for you as a cat owner to know is not how to distinguish among the various respiratory infections (veterinarians often can't without refined laboratory tests), but how to prevent them, how to recognize that an infection is present, and how to determine when veterinary care is necessary.

The most common signs of feline respiratory disease complex are sneezing, fever, watery to sticky puslike discharges from the nose and eyes, lack of appetite, and listlessness. Sometimes drooling is seen, and in these instances raw areas (*ulcers*) can often be found on the tongue or hard palate. Some very mild infections are marked only by evidence of a mild eye irritation (conjunctivitis) accompanied by a small amount of watery eye discharge and no other signs. In severe cases the eyes can be swollen and crusted shut from discharges, the nasal passages clogged, the nose raw, and the cat most uncooperative with any efforts to give aid.

SIGNS OF INFECTION

Whether a respiratory infection is mild, moderate, or severe is dependent upon many factors—among them, the age of the cat, his or her general health, the acquired resistance from previous exposure or vaccination, and the strain of the infective organism.

Respiratory infection in which the signs are mild—small amounts of watery eye and/or nose discharge and a few sneezes unaccompanied by fever—usually do not require veterinary care if the cat is eating normally (or near normally) and does not seem unduly depressed. Cases accompanied by any of the following signs should alert you to have your cat examined by a veterinarian: persistent fever, lack of appetite, marked listlessness, dehydration, puslike eye or nose discharges, or cough (a sign that the infection may include the lower air passages or that pneumonia may be present). Prompt and intensive treatment is necessary to avoid undesirable aftereffects of respiratory infections.

WHEN TO SEEK VETERINARY HELP FOR FRDC

AGENTS CAUSING RESPIRATORY INFECTION IN CATS

DISEASE	DISEASE AGENT	PRINCIPAL SIGNS	COMMENTS
Feline viral rhinotracheitis (FVR, "rhino")	herpesvirus type 1	Sneezing, coughing, eye and nose discharge, fever, drooling, lack of appetite, termination of pregnancy (miscarriage)	Usually, severe infection of longer than one week's duration. Can be fatal. Infected newborns usually weaken and die. Remains infective 1 to 2 days in the environment. Most recovered cats remain carriers.
Feline calicivirus (FCV, formerly feline influenza)	calicivirus	Most often, transient fever and lameness lasting up to 4 days; tongue and mouth ulcers, drooling; less often, sneezing, watery eye and nose discharges. Symptoms vary; probably most severe in combination with other infections.	More than fifteen different virus strains; vaccines may not provide full protection against all strains. Remains infective up to 10 days in the environment. Recovered cats may become carriers and may have severe chronic mouth disease.

DISEASE	DISEASE AGENT	PRINCIPAL SIGNS	COMMENTS
Chlamydia psittaci infection (formerly feline pneumonitis)	*Chlamydia psittaci* variety *felis*	In juvenile and adult cats conjunctivitis, often unilateral, squinting, watery eye discharge; infrequently sneezing. In newborns *ophthalmia neonatorum* (see page 295), fatal pneumonia.	Usually mild infection acquired by intimate exposure. Signs may last 4 to 6 weeks. Responds to antibiotics. May occasionally cause human conjunctivitis. Recovered cat may become carriers.
Feline reovirus infection	reovirus	Watery eye discharge.	Usually very mild infection. Often no treatment needed.

In most instances you will be responsible for the major portion of treatment of respiratory illnesses in your cat. Veterinarians are reluctant to hospitalize cases of viral respiratory infection unless absolutely necessary because these diseases are contagious to other cats and can contaminate the hospital. The first step in home treatment of respiratory infection (even the most mild) is to keep your cat indoors. This protects the cat from the stress of temperature changes, prevents the cat from disappearing while sick, and also helps prevent transmission of the infection to other cats in the neighborhood. If possible, make an attempt to isolate your sick cat from any other cats to prevent spread of the infection. Change your outer clothes and wash your hands each time you medicate or handle the sick cat; provide separate food and water bowls and litter pan for the affected cat. These precautions are difficult in most household situations and

TREATMENT OF RESPIRATORY INFECTION

in some instances impossible. If you own a cattery, such precautions are a must; ask your veterinarian for additional help. Further nursing care consists of keeping a daily temperature record (see page 242) and the administration of antibiotics (in most cases to control secondary bacterial infection that occurs after the cat is weakened by the original infection), decongestants, eye medications, and vitamins as directed by your veterinarian, and hand-feeding as necessary (see page 247). Since most sick cats do not groom themselves well, gentle removal of eye and nose crusts with a soft tissue or cotton ball moistened with warm water and daily bushing go a long way in making a sick cat look and feel better. Cats who have extreme congestion of the nasal passages may benefit by the twice daily (no more) administration of 0.025% oxymetazoline or 0.25% aqueous phenylephrine nose drops (one drop into each nostril twice a day for no longer than three days) and by the use of a vaporizer for fifteen to thirty minutes about three times a day. (If you don't have access to a vaporizer you can run a hot shower until the bathroom is steamy and place your cat in the bathroom for fifteen to thirty minutes). In respiratory infections treated at home it is often necessary to work closely with your veterinarian on an outpatient basis. Injections of fluids to control dehydration and of antibiotics can be given as necessary, and periodic evaluation of your cat's progress can be made by an expert. Sometimes close cooperation between you and your veterinarian is not sufficient, and hospitalization is necessary.

AFTEREFFECTS OF FRDC Although prolonged treatment is necessary in severe cases of respiratory infection (more than two weeks in some), complete recovery usually occurs. Some cats (usually neglected cases, or kittens or cats suffering from other concurrent infections) suffer permanent damage to the tissues lining the eye, sinuses, or nasal passages. These cats may have a constant clear discharge from the nose and/or eye. Some with sinus damage have a recurrent or persistent cloudy discharge from the nose accompanied by sneezing and signs of nasal congestion. Cats left with such problems following respiratory infection are not always disabled but need examination and treatment by a veterinarian to determine whether the problem can be cured. Another aftereffect of respiratory disease is that many recovered cats remain carriers of the disease. Although apparently healthy, they can spread the infection to susceptible cats, and when stressed (e.g., boarded away from home) or treated with corticosteroid drugs (e.g., prednisone) may have milder recurrences of signs of infection.

The most severe respiratory infection problems in cats are found where large numbers of cats are kept together with inadequate sanitary precautions, as is often the case in substandard breeding operations, boarding kennels, pet shops, and grooming parlors. Infections can be acquired in veterinary hospitals as well, but the problem occurs there less often because most veterinarians know how to use all sanitary precautions available to avoid exposure of uninfected cats. The average pet owner can prevent feline upper respiratory infection by keeping his or her cat indoors, by avoiding handling stray cats, by avoiding boarding the cat whenever possible, and by isolating new cats until they are free of signs of disease for at least one month and are fully vaccinated. Catteries and other multicat households must follow special precautions to avoid contamination of the premises and repeated problems with respiratory infection. These include:

1. House only small groups of cats (less than ten) together and give each cat his or her separate pen. Enclosures for individuals should be constructed and placed so that it is impossible for one cat to sneeze on another or to engage in mutual grooming that will allow the exchange of salivary or respiratory secretions. Cats should not be moved from pen to pen before the new pen is thoroughly disinfected.

2. Keep cats in well-ventilated areas with a minimum of ten air exchanges occurring per hour. The temperature and humidity should be kept constant. Uncontrolled and extreme temperature fluctuations are stressful, and high humidity encourages the survival of organisms associated with respiratory infection.

3. Provide isolation and quarantine facilities. Sick cats should be removed from the cattery at the first sign of any illness and quarantined for *at least* two weeks (preferably for one month) after recovery. All new cats to be introduced to the colony and all cats taken off the premises to places where they are likely to be exposed to disease should be quarantined for a minimum of one month before introduction to the other group members. During this time they can be observed for any signs of illness and tested for disease. Cats suspected of carrying respiratory disease-causing organisms should ideally never be introduced to the group. Kittens should be kept only with their own littermates and mother and be completely isolated from exposure to other cats. Where there are preexisting problems with carrier cats, kittens will have to be weaned at four to five weeks of age and vaccinated early to avoid infection by their own mother as their nursing-derived immunity wanes.

A properly managed multicat household or cattery will need at least five distinct areas for housing cats—a common area where healthy adult cats are housed, a maternity ward for pregnant and/or nursing females and their kittens, a nursery for kittens that are weaned, a quarantine room for apparently healthy incoming cats, and an isolation room for obviously sick cats. Most individuals experienced in raising cats find it necessary to have a separate facility for unneutered males and a separate nursery for each litter. Ideally each cat in quarantine or isolation should be housed there alone.

4. Follow good sanitary practices to prevent the spread of disease-causing organisms that can travel from cat to cat via inanimate objects such as clothing, grooming tools, and by hand. Thoroughly wash and disinfect all food and water pans and thoroughly disinfect all cage surfaces before transferring a new cat to a previously occupied pen. Good disinfectants are liquid household bleach (5.25% sodium hypochlorite, mixed 1 part bleach to 30 parts water, 4 oz/gallon (30 ml/liter), and quaternary ammonium compounds.

Objects need to be soaked in disinfectants for *at least* 5 minutes after washing to be disinfected, then rinsed in clear, clean water before use. Do not provide bedding, rugs, or furniture that cannot be washed and adequately disinfected. Your outer clothing should be changed and your hands should be thoroughly washed before you feed or handle healthy cats, after treating sick cats or following exposure to cats not members of the group. In many cases your footwear will have to be changed and/or disinfected to stop the spread of infections.

5. Vaccinate cats against feline viral rhinotracheitis, feline calicivirus infection, and *Chlamydia psittaci* infection. Although the vaccines were once thought to be extremely effective, the nature of immunity to these infectious agents results in some occasional, but inevitable vaccination difficulties. Vaccination cannot prevent some cats from carrying these agents, even though it may prevent them from showing outward signs of illness.

Vaccination for feline viral rhinotracheitis is highly effective in preventing signs of infection in individual pet cats, but it is less effective in multiple cat households, especially those that do not follow strict guidelines for disease prevention. The crowding and stress found in such environments favor the development of signs of respiratory infection despite vaccination and increase the frequency of virus shedding by cats who become virus carriers.

Both feline calicivirus and feline *Chlamydia* vaccines have been found to be less effective against strains of the organisms found naturally than those that were used in the laboratory to develop the vaccines. This means that vaccinated cats may still develop signs of infection caused by these organisms. Usually, however, the signs are much less severe and less prolonged than those in unvaccinated cats. Even if no signs of infection occur, vaccination may not prevent the development of a carrier state. Nevertheless, it is customary to control signs of calicivirus infection by vaccination. Vaccination against *Chlamydia* infection is often limited to cats who reside in multicat environments that have been proven to have a problem with this infection. In general, vaccines for this infection provide limited immunity of short duration and are thought to increase the incidence of adverse vaccine reactions when combined with other vaccines. You and your veterinarian will have to decide which vaccine products are needed based on your cat's age, likelihood of exposure, and the vaccine products currently available. Multicat households may have success in eliminating *Chlamydia* infection by antibiotic treatment of all cats at once whether or not they show signs of infection.

Normally, vaccination against agents of respiratory infection is given concurrent with panleukopenia immunization starting at six to ten weeks of age. Kittens born into multiple cat households may need to start vaccination earlier when problems with respiratory infection exist. Vaccines are repeated at two- to four-week intervals until the kitten is twelve to sixteen weeks of age.

For more information about the control of respiratory and other diseases in multiple cat environments see:

Pedersen, Niels C., *Feline Husbandry, Diseases and Management in the Multiple-Cat Environment,* American Veterinary Publications, Inc., Goleta, Ca., 1991.

ALLERGIC BRONCHITIS (ASTHMA)

Inflammation of the airways in the lung (*bronchitis*) can follow or accompany most respiratory diseases of cats. It is also a response to inhaled infectious organisms and irritant materials such as litter dust or wood smoke. One common cause of bronchitis of cats is allergic reaction to inhaled allergens that may worsen with repeated exposure to them. Over time the chronic airway inflammation can result in permanent lung damage (e.g., emphysema) that causes persistent signs even when the original cause is removed.

Cats with allergic bronchitis usually seem healthy (no fever, eating well) but have intermittent bouts of deep, low-pitched, moist-sounding coughs. The affected cat usually sits with his or her shoulders hunched up, coughs several times, and sometimes gags up foamy mucuslike material or swallows hard following each coughing bout. Coughing is sometimes accompanied by mild sneezing and shortness of breath. Often the problem is more severe at certain times of the year than others. This is usually an indication of allergy to pollens and/or mold spores. Cats with allergies to cigarette smoke, perfumes, or other air pollutants may have signs year-round. If left untreated allergic bronchitis sometimes progresses to *asthma,* which causes attacks of severe breathing difficulty. Cats affected with asthma may breathe rapidly with their mouths open, wheeze, and/or make forced attempts to exhale. Their distress may cause them to paw at their mouths, and you may see their gums and tongue become bluish in color (a sign of oxygen deprivation). An asthmatic attack is an emergency calling for immediate veterinary care.

Although there is no permanent cure for feline chronic bronchitis of allergic origin and although signs of bronchitis from any cause are not emergency situations requiring immediate care, it is important to take your cat to your veterinarian if you suspect this condition. Only your veterinarian can distinguish between chronic allergic bronchitis and other conditions that may cause similar signs (e.g., lungworms); drugs designed to relieve the airway inflammation and thereby prevent an asthma attack can only be prescribed by a veterinarian who has determined that it is safe to use them.

LARYNGITIS

Laryngitis is an inflammation of the larynx ("voice box," vocal cords) that causes a change of or loss of voice in cats. There can be many causes. Some cases are caused by infection (viral, bacterial); others are simply the result of excessive meowing (e.g., in Siamese cats). Laryngitis unaccompanied by fever or other signs of illness usually needs no treatment and clears within about five to seven days. Laryngitis that does not heal rapidly, is accompanied by signs of illness, or seems to cause excessive discomfort to your cat requires the help of a veterinarian for diagnosis and treatment. In rare cases cancer of the larynx or paralysis of the vocal cords may cause laryngitis, and early diagnosis can be important for successful treatment.

Most respiratory diseases, if neglected, can progress to pneumonia or other serious conditions involving the respiratory system. Be sure to have your cat examined by a veterinarian in the presence of any of the following signs: persistent nose or eye discharge, difficulty breathing, fever, or any signs you do not feel confident about.

For other causes of respiratory diseases, see *toxoplasmosis* (page 93) and *Lungworms* (page 104).

MUSCLE AND BONE
(MUSCULOSKELETAL SYSTEM)

Musculoskeletal problems not related to injury are rare in cats. Diseases seen frequently in dogs such as hip dysplasia and patellar luxation (kneecap dislocation), which have a hereditary predisposition, are almost never seen in cats except for individuals from certain purebred bloodlines. Therefore you as a cat owner have little in the way of bony or muscular problems to consider when choosing a cat. Your problems with musculoskeletal disease will most likely arise following trauma to your animal.

Many musculoskeletal injuries can be difficult to diagnose, even by an experienced veterinarian. Proper diagnosis often requires the use of X rays as well as a thorough physical examination. It may be impossible to distinguish among fractures, dislocations, and sprains without the aid of X rays. In general, however, it should not be too difficult to distinguish the presence of a fracture or dislocation from the presence of a sprain, strain, or bruise. Keep in mind that, although musculoskeletal injuries often cause marked signs, they themselves are not usually emergencies (see page 200). Review the musculoskeletal section, page 6, then read this section thoroughly and become familiar with your cat's normal posture and movement in order to prepare yourself to recognize any injury to your cat's muscles and/or bones.

When actual injury occurs, keep calm and proceed with an examination in a thorough and deliberate manner. First try to localize the site of the injury. To accomplish this stand back and look at your cat as a whole. Try to determine the area (or areas) causing the change in posture or gait. If legs are involved, which are they? Which seem to hurt, look distorted, or are being "protected" by the cat? Swelling is often fairly well confined to the injured area but is sometimes extensive. The posture of an affected leg *may* be fairly normal above but not below the affected area. Once you have a general idea of the location of the problem examine each part of the limb, including each joint, gently and carefully. All legs should be examined thoroughly, but you will probably want to go over the most obviously damaged one first. Review how to perform a leg examination in the Anatomy section of this book if you feel unsure about it, and remember that comparing an injured leg to its (probably) uninjured mate can be very helpful.

SPRAINS, STRAINS, AND BRUISES

Sprains, strains, and bruises (contusions) consist of damage to the soft tissues surrounding and supporting the bones, usually without loss of weight-bearing ability. In these injuries swelling and signs of pain are often quite diffuse, so you may not be able to determine the exact site of injury, only the general area involved.

A *contusion* occurs when a blow causes the capillaries (small blood vessels) in the affected soft tissues to bleed. You may see skin discoloration, abrasion, or other skin injury at the site of a bruise. However, cats' fur often obscures the outer signs of injury. Expect a contusion to be free of significant pain in seven to ten days following injury.

Strains result from unaccustomed or excessive activity that overstresses the involved muscle, tendon, and/or site of the attachment of the tendon to the bone. Signs of a strain are often most obvious two or three days after the actual injury occurs. Strains often take one to three weeks of enforced rest to heal.

Sprains are ligament injuries that occur when these soft tissues, which directly surround and stabilize the joints, are stretched (mild or first-degree sprain), partially torn (moderate or second-degree sprain), or completely torn apart (severe or third-degree sprain). *All sprains* heal slowly even if the signs of pain disappear quickly. Radiographs (X-ray pictures) are often necessary to diagnose a sprain, as the more severe forms can easily cause signs of pain, swelling, deformity, and inability to bear weight that are indistinguishable from signs of a bone fracture. Splinting, casting, or surgery is sometimes needed to return the affected joint to normal stability.

If your cat has a mild to moderate lameness due to soft tissue injury, enforced rest is the best treatment, and it should result in rapid improvement in two to seven days. Confine your cat indoors and, if necessary, to one room or to a cage to reduce activity. You may be tempted to give pain relievers such as aspirin to your cat for such injuries. *Avoid doing so.* Most such preparations for humans are contraindicated for cats, and such drugs mask the pain that would encourage your cat to rest the injured area and that is an important clue for you to use in gauging the degree of recovery. Consult your veterinarian in more severe cases.

FRACTURES

Complete fracture (break) of any of the major limb bones usually results in the *inability to bear weight* on the affected limb, as well as some *deformity* of the limb. The deformity may consist simply of swelling or may include *angulation* (formation of an abnormal angle) usually at the fracture site, rotation or shortening of the affected limb, or other deviations from the normal position. The sound and/or feel of bone grating against bone (*crepitus*), if present, is almost always indicative of a fracture. Unless sensory nerves have been damaged or the cat is in deep shock (see page 202), evidence of pain can be elicited by manipulating the fracture. Signs of pain, however, are unreliable, since pain can be present in other conditions as well; also many sensitive cats overreact to relatively mild pain, and "stoic" cats may be less likely to react strongly to painful stimuli.

A fracture is classified as *simple* if there is no communicating wound between the outside of the skin and the broken bone. A *compound* fracture communicates to the outside. If your cat has a compound fracture with bone protruding from a wound, you should have no difficulty diagnosing the condition. Compound fractures become infected easily and should be given immediate attention by a veterinarian, if at all possible.

COMPOUND FRACTURES ARE EMERGENCIES

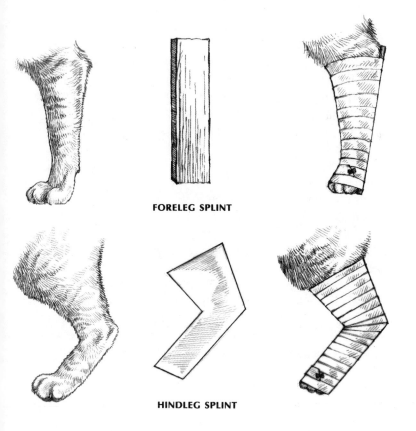

FORELEG SPLINT

HINDLEG SPLINT

If your cat is in fairly normal general condition, a simple fracture is not necessarily a veterinary emergency. The best thing to do is to localize the fracture site, then call your veterinarian for further advice. Fractures of the foot bones are rarely emergencies and can usually be left unsplinted until X-ray pictures can be taken. Whether or not you splint other limb fractures depends on the site of the fracture and the mobility of the bone ends. In many cases, splinting causes more trouble for you and pain for the cat than it's worth. In obviously mobile fractures, where you see the leg below the break dangling freely and twisting, heavy cardboard cut to the appropriate shape, roll cotton, and elastic bandage can be used to prevent bone movement, interruption of blood supply, and nerve damage. Wrap padding (even a diaper can be used) gently and *thickly* around the injured part. Then apply the splint and top it with the bandage. Compound fractures should have a clean bandage applied over the exposed bone ends if splinting is unnecessary or not possible.

SPINAL FRACTURES ARE EMERGENCIES A special case of fracture (or dislocation) is fracture of the spine. This requires professional veterinary care *at the earliest possible time* as well as careful first aid. Spinal fractures usually result in partial or complete paralysis of the rear legs and sometimes the front legs as well, often with remarkably little evidence of pain. If your cat shows such signs following trauma, *immediate* and *absolute* (if possible) restriction of movement is necessary. If you can get the cat to lie quietly, transport in a shallow open box is best. Do not, however, attempt to hold a frightened and struggling cat down—you may make the damage worse. Cooperative cats may be carried in your arms if you are careful to prevent back movement.

FRACTURE REPAIR The method a veterinarian chooses to repair a fractured bone depends on the type of fracture present, the fracture site, and the age of your cat. External devices alone, such as casts and splints, can be used in some cases. In many others surgery to place a metal pin, plate, or other internal fixation device into the fractured bone is necessary. A good veterinarian will x-ray the fracture, evaluate all the possibilities for repair, and tell you what he or she thinks is necessary to achieve the best healing. If you cannot afford the best repair, a veterinarian should offer alternative methods that may not be as ideal for healing but more within your means. (Keep in mind that the alternatives may mean slower healing or complete failure to heal.)

DISLOCATIONS

Dislocations (*luxations*) are seen much less frequently than fractures in most veterinary practices. Dislocations occur whenever a bone is displaced from its normal position in relation to another bone at a joint. *The signs of dislocation are similar to those of fracture, but are usually milder.*

Dislocations are not emergencies in the sense that they endanger a cat's life or limb. However, they should be examined by a veterinarian within twenty-four hours of occurrence because they are most easily corrected without surgery during this period. All suspected dislocations should have X-ray pictures taken to determine the true extent of bony damage. General anesthesia is given to relax the muscles and provide relief from pain while the bones are manipulated back into their proper positions. Some dislocations require surgery for permanent correction especially those causing complete disruption of the supporting and surrounding soft tissues.

NUTRITIONAL SECONDARY HYPERPARATHYROIDISM (PAPER BONE DISEASE)

Signs of this bone condition are seen most often in young, growing kittens, but the basic changes in metabolism and bone which occur are induced in *any* cat fed a diet unbalanced in calcium and phosphorus. The cause of this nutritional bone disease is usually a diet that consists solely or primarily of meat (muscle or organs such as heart, kidney, or liver). This results in an abnormally low calcium intake and abnormally high phosphorus intake (see page 68), and in turn stimulates the parathyroid glands to make metabolic adjustments in an attempt to return blood calcium and phosphorus to levels more nearly normal. Since insufficient dietary calcium is available to make the necessary adjustments, the skeleton is called upon to furnish it and demineralization of bone occurs.

Since the demand for calcium is particularly high in the first six to eight months of a cat's life, signs of paper bone disease are usually most marked in animals of this age. Bowing of the legs, abnormal spinal curvature, and reluctance to move (a sign of pain) occur and have been misdiagnosed by some owners and veterinarians as rickets. Spontaneous fractures may even occur, and if the condition is left untreated death may be the final result. Nutritional secondary hyperparathyroidism can be very deceptive. Because meat is high in protein and fat, kittens fed improper high-meat or all-meat diets can maintain a healthy appearance in terms of body weight and normal hair coat while the bony changes are occurring.

Unless you have seen the disease before, you may have difficulty recognizing paper bone disease. Your veterinarian, however, should be able to diagnose it, and you will need veterinary expertise to treat it successfully. The best thing you can do as an owner is to prevent paper bone disease by feeding your cat (young or adult) a balanced diet (see page 60).

SKELETAL ABNORMALITIES
(POLYDACTYLY, PATELLAR LUXATION, HIP DYSPLASIA)

The incidence of abnormalities of the appendicular skeleton in cats historically has been rare. The most commonly recognized abnormality has been the formation of extra complete or partially formed digits on each affected foot, particularly the front feet. This condition is called *polydactyly* and is caused by the action of a single dominant gene. Polydactyly is usually of no serious physical consequence to an affected cat. However, some cats have as many as four nearly normal extra digits on the affected feet and in these there is a tendency for the toenails on the extra toes to grow into the digital pads causing discomfort and infection if the claws are not kept trimmed.

As the popularity of purebred cats has risen so has the incidence of more serious skeletal diseases. *Patellar luxation* (dislocation of the kneecap) was first recognized in the Devon Rex breed, but is now seen in others as well. *Hip dysplasia,* a deformity of the hip joint in which the joint socket is abnormally shallow and the head of the femur is malformed, has also been diagnosed in lines of purebred cats.

Both patellar luxation and hip dysplasia are diseases that are strongly genetically influenced in dogs and appear to be similarly influenced in cats. Most cats affected with such skeletal abnormalities are not significantly impaired in their day-to-day function. However, all affected individuals are predisposed to develop osteoarthritis (degenerative joint disease, see page 232), and markedly affected animals may have problems with lameness throughout their lives.

Dog breeders who minimize the importance of skeletal abnormalities that seem to cause no obvious problems for their animals are responsible for the persistence of these problems in dog breeds. The time to stop the establishment of similar crippling, genetically influenced diseases in cats is *before* the problem becomes as prevalent as it is in purebred dogs. Be sure that any kitten you acquire (purebred or random bred) is found normal on repeated physical examination through his or her skeletal growth period and be sure that any cat selected for breeding has a normal musculoskeletal system.

DIGESTIVE SYSTEM
(GASTROINTESTINAL TRACT)

VOMITING

Vomiting is the *forcible* expulsion of stomach and/or intestinal contents through the mouth. It is important to try to distinguish between true vomiting and *regurgitation,* which is the *passive* act of returning the contents of the esophagus or pharynx through the mouth. This distinction will help your veterinarian make a diagnosis if home treatment is unsuccessful. Vomiting is a *sign* of various illnesses, not a disease in itself. For example, vomiting may accompany thyroid disease (see page 235), liver disease, kidney disease, cancer of the bowel, intestinal parasite infection, or chronic inflammation of the intestine (see page 170).

Vomiting occurs commonly in cats, and it is often accompanied by diarrhea. It seems to be caused most often by irritation of the stomach, which veterinarians call *acute* or *simple gastritis.* Gastritis is usually caused by the ingestion of an irritant substance—for example, decomposed food, grass, paper, or bones. The cat often first vomits frothy clear or yellow fluid. Cats with gastric irritation may seek grass to eat in an attempt to disgorge any irritant or foreign material which remains, but grass eating is often an enjoyable pastime for cats and not a sign of illness.

AFTER-MEAL VOMITING

Some cats vomit occasionally following meals. This type of vomiting is usually not serious in nature and may have several causes. Among the most common seem to be food gobbling, overeating, or a particular sensitivity to certain kinds of food. If your cat is an after-meal vomiter, trying one or more of the following things may help you:

1. If your cat eats with other animals, separate him or her at feeding time. Not only offer an individual food bowl but place the food bowls at a distance from one another. Competition encourages food gobbling.

2. Feed smaller meals more frequently.

3. Try a food that has to be chewed well before swallowing (e.g., large-sized dry kibbles instead of canned food).

4. See if you can associate the vomiting with the kind of food being fed. Some cats have food intolerances to certain ingredients in commercial foods, e.g., food colorings or flavorings. In such instances, you may find that only one brand or flavor of food seems to cause the vomiting. If you do find a specific food which seems to be the cause be sure to eliminate it entirely from your cat's diet.

Cats with food allergies may also develop vomiting when fed certain foods, but the mechanism causing the vomiting is more complex than that of simple food intolerance. The immune system must react to the presence of the food allergen before any signs appear. The association with a specific food may be more difficult for you to make in these instances since the particular ingredient to which these cats are allergic must usually be withheld for several weeks to resolve the vomiting problem. Be sure to consult a veterinarian for diagnostic help if a simple diet change does not stop your cat's signs.

HAIRBALLS
Hairballs can also cause vomiting of a nonserious nature, but sometimes they cause serious obstructions and must be removed surgically. When hairballs are vomited they usually are tubular, brown masses and are emited by themselves or accompanied by a small amount of clear, foamy fluid. If you look closely at such masses or tease them apart you will find that they are composed primarily of hair. If you find vomited hairballs and your cat is acting normally you may assume that the current hairball problem is solved. This should alert you, however, to do something about hairball prevention to avoid future problems, as should stools that have a large amount of hair in them. A hairball problem can also cause lack of appetite or constipation.

Prevent hairballs by brushing your cat regularly, providing some insoluble fiber in his or her diet, and by the routine administration of commercial hairball prevention preparations available through your veterinarian or at pet stores. A fiber source cats enjoy is fresh grass. Grow wheat, rye, or oats in a pot and allow your cat to nibble them a few times a week. A home remedy for hairball prevention is mineral oil or white petrolatum. Other oils are not efficient hairball preventives because they are digested and absorbed by the cat. Add mineral oil at a rate of one teaspoonful per 10 pounds of body weight to the food once or twice a week for hairball prevention. (White petrolatum can be given directly by mouth. See page 247.)

HOME
TREATMENT
FOR VOMITING
Vomiting cats may or may not be interested in their normal food. If your cat vomits once or twice, has no fever or obvious abdominal pain, and is no more than slightly depressed you can probably treat the vomiting at home. Do not feed your cat for twelve to twenty-four hours following vomiting. At the end of twelve hours (if you can't stand to wait longer), you can offer a very small (about a tablespoonful) of soft, easily digested food such as a soft-boiled egg, meat baby food, or cottage cheese. If your cat keeps this small meal down for about four hours, another small meal can be offered, then another

about four hours later. If no further vomiting occurs, the next day's meals can be normal-sized portions of bland food, and the following day you can return your cat to a regular diet. Water or other liquids should be offered frequently only in small amounts at a time to combat the tendency to dehydration that accompanies vomiting. Large amounts of food or water distend the already irritated stomach and usually cause vomiting to recur. An easy way to have water available in small portions is to place ice cubes in the water bowl. This allows the cat to drink the liquid that accumulates as the cubes melt.

Antacid liquids containing aluminum and/or magnesium hydroxide designed for humans may help soothe the irritated stomach lining. Dose aluminum or magnesium hydroxide antacids to provide 10 milligrams per pound (22 mg/kg) body weight every six hours until the signs have passed. If vomiting is present with diarrhea (*gastroenteritis*) intestinal adsorbents are best. Do not give any preparations containing aspirin.

If your cat vomits more than a few times; if the vomitus is ejected extremely forcefully (*projectile* vomiting); if there is blood in the vomitus or obvious abdominal pain; if your cat seems particularly depressed, weak, or has a fever, or retches unproductively, *do not* attempt to treat the condition at home. Even simple gastritis cannot always be treated successfully without the help of a veterinarian, and there are many other serious causes of vomiting—among them foreign objects in the digestive tract, stomach ulcers, inflammation of the pancreas, panleukopenia (see page 90), and kidney failure (see page 234). Expect your veterinarian to perform diagnostic tests such as complete blood counts, biochemical analysis of the blood, and radiographs (X-ray pictures) of the abdomen when the cause of vomiting is not immediately evident. Even more sophisticated tests are necessary in some cases, including endoscopic examination of the gastrointestinal tract and biopsy (removal of tissue for a pathologist's examination.)

TIMES TO SEEK VETERINARY HELP

DIARRHEA

Diarrhea is the passage of abnormally soft and/or frequent stools. This sign is often associated with vomiting, but may also occur by itself. When present, diarrhea often causes cats to fail to use their litter pans.

Diarrhea has many causes; the most common are related to diet. Diets containing cows' milk (see page 293) often cause diarrhea. Spicy table scraps and decomposed food are other common offenders, but any food, including commonly fed commercial diets, can cause diarrhea in certain cats. Viruses, bacteria, and intestinal parasites (e.g., worms, coccidia) may infect the bowel and cause diarrhea. This occurs most often in kittens. Diarrhea can also be caused by diseases of the liver and/or pancreas, bowel obstruction, cancer, and metabolic problems (see page 236). Even psychological stress gives some cats diarrhea. Trips to the veterinary hospital or the addition of a new cat to the household may result in stress-induced diarrhea, but this type usually subsides quickly without any treatment being required.

Inflammatory bowel disease (IBD) is also frequently accompanied by diarrhea. In this disorder, various types of blood cells that become active during bowel inflammation infiltrate the small intestine and/or colon and/or the stomach causing chronic dysfunction of the gastrointestinal tract. Unlike other causes of diarrhea, in IBD the veterinarian is not usually able to identify any specific agent that triggers the inflammatory process. However, food allergies are not uncommonly involved. Vomiting is one of the frequent signs of inflammatory bowel disease in cats, but diarrhea is also a common sign that may occur by itself or accompany the vomiting. When the large intestine (colon) is involved the affected cat may pass soft bowel movements containing excessive mucous and fresh blood. Left untreated diarrhea associated with inflammatory bowel disease can result in permanent damage to the bowel and an increased incidence of bowel cancer.

CONSTIPATION

Constipation is the difficult or infrequent passage of feces. This sign does not occur often in healthy young cats, but is relatively frequent in sick and/or old ones. Although constipation may be caused by simple things such as improper diet or excessive hair ingestion during self-grooming, when a well-fed and well-cared-for young cat has recurrent bouts of constipation it is a reason to be concerned and may require diagnosis and treatment by a veterinarian. Serious causes of constipation include rectal tumors, spinal cord dysfunction, and reduced colonic muscle function. Most normal adult cats have one or two bowel movements each day, but since each cat is an individual and diet has a great influence on stool frequency, you must learn your own cat's daily routine. One day without passing a bowel movement is not normally a crisis situation, but any change in an individual cat's normal bowel movement frequency, especially if accompanied by other signs such as straining to pass a stool, dehydration, sitting in a crouched or hunched-up position, loss of appetite, or vomiting warrants your investigation and possible veterinary evaluation.

If constipation is mild, a change in diet may relieve the problem. Canned foods containing large amounts of ground bone should be avoided; they can sometimes produce rock-hard stools only a veterinarian can remove. Feeding dry cat food will help some cats who tend to have trouble with mild constipation since dry products contain more bulk-forming fiber than canned foods. A meal of fresh liver is very laxative, and older cats who frequently do not drink enough to keep up with their obligatory water losses often benefit when extra water is added to their foods. **DIET CHANGE MAY HELP MILD CONSTIPATION**

Commercial preparations containing psyllium fiber have been designed for humans to add bulk to the diet and hold water in the stool. These products are sold in health food and drugstores. They may be used to help treat recurrent mild constipation in cats. Give 1 to 3 teaspoonfuls (5 to 15 ml) mixed in the food once or twice a day. Bran is also an effective fiber laxative when mixed with a cat's canned food. Use up to 4 tablespoons (120 ml) a day. Some cats accept canned pumpkin added to their diets (up to 4 tablespoons [120 ml per day]) more readily than psyllium fiber or bran, and it can also be an effective laxative. If you find that you must add bulk-forming preparations to your cat's diet frequently, discuss the constipation problem with your veterinarian. **BULK-FORMING AGENTS MAY ALSO BE NEEDED**

Mineral oil (1 teaspoonful per 10 pounds [1 ml/kg] body weight), white petrolatum (1 teaspoonful, [5 ml]) given orally, or docusate sodium or calcium capsules (DSS, dioctyl sodium sulfosuccinate, 50 to 100 mg orally) are all laxatives sold over the counter in drugstores that may be used to relieve more severe constipation. Infant glycerine or DSS suppositories for insertion into the rectum are also sold without prescription. These products work by softening and lubricating the stool. Like all laxatives they should not be used on a continuous or frequently repeated basis without professional advice. Once or twice a day for two days should be sufficient to relieve simple constipation. Mineral oil interferes with the absorption of oil-soluble vitamins and prolonged continuous use can cause vitamin deficiency. Mineral oil should be administered in food. *Do not* attempt to give it orally; if inhaled, it can cause severe pneumonia. Stimulant laxatives such as those containing castor oil or bisacodyl are not **LAXATIVE DRUGS SHOULD BE USED WITH CARE** recommended for home use without specific instructions from your veterinarian. Chronic use of such drugs can damage the bowel and actually aggravate the constipation problem.

An enema may be necessary to relieve *impaction* of the colon (hardened stool lodged in the lower bowel). This is best performed by a veterinarian who should give your cat a thorough physical examination before treatment. DSS-containing pediatric enemas can be purchased in drugstores if the services of a veterinarian are unavailable. To administer an enema, insert the lubricated nozzle into the rectum and administer the liquid slowly at a rate of 1 ounce per 10 pounds (about 1.5 ml/kg) body weight. Avoid enemas containing sodium phosphate. They are dangerous for cats and their use can cause death.

In long-haired cats, straining to defecate is occasionally associated with hair matted over the anus, not constipation. The cat sometimes cries, especially when making attempts to defecate. If you have a long-haired cat who makes repeated attempts to pass a bowel movement without success, be sure to examine his or her anus before concluding that the problem is internal constipation. Clip away any matted hair with scissors or clippers and wash the anus gently with an antiseptic shampoo. If the anus is very inflamed, a soothing antibiotic-steroid cream or ointment may help relieve discomfort. Prevent recurrent problems by keeping the hair around the anus clipped short.

Straining to eliminate associated with bladder problems (see page 177) and with severe diarrhea and intestinal inflammation is often confused with constipation. Be sure you know what the problem is before attempting to treat it. Veterinarians must often perform rectal examinations by inserting a gloved and lubricated finger into the lower bowel to be certain a cat is constipated. In other cases X rays must be used for diagnosis.

FLATULENCE (INTESTINAL GAS)

Having a flatulent cat around is more of an inconvenience than a real medical problem. Excessive gas formation unaccompanied by other problems can usually be controlled by changing the diet. With a little observation you can often find that flatulence occurs only when a specific flavor or brand of food is fed or only with certain types of table scraps. Some cats cannot digest oligosaccharides such as raffinose and stachyose, which are carbohydrates contained in soybeans. Since soybeans are a common ingredient in dry cat foods, oligosaccharide-intolerant cats may develop excessive intestinal gas when they are fed them. Oligosaccharide intolerance is similar to lactose intolerance, which occurs when a cat is unable to digest milk sugar (lactose) and bacteria in the gut ferment the excess carbohydrates causing gas production and sometimes diarrhea. Cats eating relatively poor-quality diets that are high in fiber may also develop flatulence, because diets high in fiber decrease the digestion of nutrients in the small intestine allowing them to pass on to the large intestine where they undergo bacterial fermentation and accompanying gas formation. Flatulence that is not reduced by a diet change and is accompanied by diarrhea necessitates thorough physical examination and treatment directed toward resolving the diarrhea. When the stool becomes normal, flatulence often disappears.

ANAL SACCULITIS

Impaction of the anal sacs sometimes accompanied by infection is an infrequent problem in cats. The most common signs of anal sacculitis are scooting the anal area along the ground and excessive grooming around the anal area and tail base. Scooting is only occasionally a sign of worms. An unusual twitching of the skin over the back or surprise "attacks" at the tail base can sometimes be explained by overly full anal sacs. Signs of simple anal sac impaction can usually be relieved by expressing the contents of the sacs. You can do this yourself. Use one hand to hold up the cat's tail. Hold a disposable cloth or tissue in the other hand. Place your thumb externally over one anal sac and your finger over the other. Press in and apply firm pressure over the sacs. This causes the contents to be expressed through the anal sac openings into the tissue so they can be discarded.

If impacted anal sacs are not emptied, one or both may become infected. Infected sacs may be painful and result in constipation due to the cat's reluctance to experience a painful bowel movement.

You may be able to express blood-tinged material or pus from

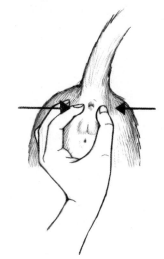

EXPRESSING THE ANAL SACS

173

the sac. If you don't notice the problem at this stage, you may later see an abscess or swelling externally at one side or the other of the anus. Infected anal sacs are best treated by a veterinarian. If they have not yet abscessed, it may be possible to treat them by expression of the infected contents and with antibiotics alone. If they are abscessed, surgical drainage is usually necessary.

OBESITY

Obesity (fatness) is almost always an owner-induced disease in pets caused by overfeeding and inadequate exercise. Excessive fat puts excessive stresses on your cat's joints, heart, and lungs and often results in an inactive cat who is a poor companion. An obese cat, as you may have discovered, is more difficult to examine thoroughly than a normally fleshed one, since excess fat interferes with listening to or feeling the heartbeat, and with feeling the pulse and abdominal organs. An obese cat is a poorer surgical risk and is more likely to develop diabetes mellitus, liver malfunction, and decreased resistance to infectious diseases. If your cat is overweight, have a veterinary examination if you want to be sure that his or her general health is good and that the obese condition is not caused by a medical problem, then start a diet. This important single step can prolong your cat's life, as calorie restriction (providing the diet itself is nutritionally adequate) is the *only* dietary manipulation scientifically shown to improve longevity.

DESIRED WEIGHT		DAILY MAINTENANCE CALORIE
POUNDS	KILOGRAMS	REQUIREMENT*
4	1.8	120
5	2.3	150
6	2.7	180
7	3.2	210
8	3.6	240
9	4.1	270
10	4.5	300
11	5.0	330
12	5.4	360
13	5.9	390
14	6.3	420
15	6.8	450

*Tomcats require 10 calories more per pound body weight.

An obese cat is 15% or more above optimum body weight. Normal cats have only a thin layer of fat between the skin and muscles covering the ribs, and each rib can be felt but not seen. They also have a defined abdomen that does not protrude far below the rib cage. Most adult cats weigh between 8 and 10 pounds; any cat weighing more than 12 pounds is likely to be obese.

SIGN OF OBESITY

Choose the weight you want your cat to reduce to. Then feed 60 to 70% of the daily caloric requirement to maintain that weight until the desired weight is reached. This could take several weeks. Never fast obese cats for weight reduction since fasting in overweight cats may trigger the onset of fatty liver disease (hepatic lipidosis), a potentially fatal condition. You can use the following table as a guide to how much commercial food will provide the proper amount of calories:

FEEDING FOR WEIGHT LOSS

TYPE OF FOOD	APPROXIMATE CALORIES PER ONE-FOURTH POUND (114 G) FOOD
Dry	400
Semi-moist	250
Canned	120

If you make your cat's food yourself, you will have to determine its calorie content. You can feed the calculated amount of food in as many meals as you desire each day, and experimental studies indicate that several small meals may result in greater weight loss than one or two larger ones, but remember *more total food is not allowed.* If your cat is accustomed to begging, dole out a portion of the daily food ration a single bite at a time. Try to distract your cat from food and increase his or her muscle tone by encouraging play with new toys.

Special low-fat, relatively high-fiber, complete and balanced diets are now commercially available for cats. Such products are reduced in calories compared to maintenance foods while still providing the proper ratio of protein to fat and all the other nutrients a cat needs. These products allow an obese cat to consume a relatively larger meal than that provided by portions of a usual maintenance diet. Although most cats can easily maintain a normal body weight when given appropriate quantities of regular commercial cat food without snacks or table scraps, weight control products are useful to cat owners who have difficulty resisting their pet's demands for food. Also, since many cats do not exercise regularly they will maintain their weight much more easily when fed diets lower in fat (therefore lower in calories) than the usual maintenance diets, which are designed for normally active cats. Weigh your cat weekly. If you are following the rules set out above and your cat is not losing weight, consult your veterinarian for further help. Once your cat has reached the desired weight you can relax the rules a little to increase your cat's calorie intake to the maintenance level for that weight.

An example: Your cat weighs 12 pounds (5.5 kg), but should weigh 9 (4.1 kg). The daily maintenance calorie requirement for this cat is about 270 calories $\times$ 60% = 162 calories to be fed while reducing. This is about 1.6 ounces (48 g) of dry food, or 2.6 ounces (78 g) of semimoist food, or about 5.4 ounces (162 g) of canned food. After the desired weight is achieved, feeding could be increased to about 2.7 ounces (81 g) of dry, or 4.3 ounces (130 g) semimoist food, or 9 ounces (270 g) of canned food.*

Keep in mind that all calculations are approximate, as individual differences in metabolism affect the actual maintenance requirements significantly. Almost one cat in seven requires 20% more or less than the average maintenance calorie level to maintain a proper body weight.

*For your own ease, it is best to weigh out the appropriate cat food portion on a food scale, then measure the portion's volume. Then on a day-to-day basis the portion can be measured out by volume.

REPRODUCTIVE AND URINARY ORGANS (GENITOURINARY SYSTEM)

If your cat has any of the following signs, genitourinary (reproductive or urinary) system disease may be present and thorough examination by a veterinarian is indicated:

Drinking increased amounts of water
Urinating very frequently
Urinating abnormally large or small amounts
Difficulty or inability to urinate
Bloody urine
Inability to hold his or her urine (urinary incontinence)
Blood and/or puslike material dripping in quantity from the penis or vulva
Abdominal pain or walking with an abnormally arched back

FELINE UROLOGIC SYNDROME
(FUS, FELINE LOWER URINARY TRACT DISEASE)

Feline urologic syndrome (FUS) is a term used by veterinarians to describe the signs caused by a number of disorders that affect the bladder and/or urethra of cats. Some veterinarians prefer to use the term *feline lower urinary tract disease* (LUTD) in place of FUS. Signs of lower urinary tract disease can be caused by inflammation of the bladder (*cystitis*) and/or urethra (*urethritis*), stone formation in the bladder (*urolithiasis*), and/or urethral obstruction. Signs of cystitis most often include bloody urine and frequent urination of small amounts, sometimes accompanied by excessive licking at the genitals. Some affected cats display signs of discomfort when the abdomen is palpated (felt) in the bladder area. Cats with cystitis may also begin urine spraying (see page 183). Inflammation of the urethra may accompany cystitis, or urethritis may occur by itself resulting in signs very similar to those of cystitis but unaccompanied by blood in the urine. Since some urine that contains blood does not look discolored to the naked eye complete urinalysis is necessary.

Urolithiasis occurs when hard stones form from mineral crystals found in the urine. The stones (urinary calculi, cystoliths) may range from very small sandlike grains to ones as big as large pebbles. Single or multiple stones may be present. These stones are irritating to the bladder itself thereby causing cystitis and the signs that typically accompany it. Bladder stones may be accompanied by stone formation in the kidneys. Veterinarians diagnose bladder stones by evaluating urinalyses, urine cultures, and X-ray and/or ultrasound studies of the urinary tract.

Small urinary stones, amorphous crystalline material (magnesium ammonium phosphate) mixed with mucoid secretions (*struvite*), or mucous alone may completely or partially block the urethra of cats, causing extreme difficulty or complete inability to urinate. This is an emergency and calls for immediate veterinary examination, since an unrelieved urinary obstruction can cause bladder rupture. Affected cats make repeated trips to the litter pan without producing any significant amounts of urine. Cases of complete urinary obstruction that go unnoticed or untreated progress until the cat becomes depressed, weakened, and dehydrated. Eventually, vomiting, total collapse, convulsions, coma and death will occur. Even if treated, cats with urinary obstruction in the later stages may not recover. Systemic body changes caused by *uremia* (toxemia caused by excessive retention of wastes normally excreted by the kidneys) and kidney damage are sometimes irreversible.

CAUSES OF FUS   Bacteria, diet, water intake, patterns of urination and activity, stress, and heredity all can play a role in producing and controlling signs of lower urinary tract disease. Viruses have been isolated from some cats with cystitis and/or urinary obstruction, and they may be the primary culprits in some cases of feline urologic syndrome. Cats with lower urinary tract disease may even have cancer of the bladder or urethra or an anatomical deformity in the area. Often more than one problem is present in a single cat with signs of feline urologic syndrome. In order to avoid recurrent signs of illness, it is important to determine exactly which factors are active in producing any individual cat's signs. A cat who is exhibiting signs of FUS should always be evaluated by a veterinarian who can perform and interpret the diagnostic tests necessary to sort out the problems.

The majority of FUS cases with stone or plug formation are diet related, and some diets promote urinary crystal formation much more readily than others. The composition of a cat's diet closely determines the urine pH (acidity or alkalinity). Some diets, notably those based on plant materials, tend to promote a more alkaline urine (urine pH higher than 7) than others, and alkaline urine is most favorable for the formation of crystals and uroliths. Mineral content of the diet, especially the quantity of magnesium present, also affects crystal formation. Vegetable materials used in the production of commercial cat foods have high magnesium content. However, diets high in magnesium will not cause stone or plug formation if the urine pH is kept on the acid side (less than 6.5). Water intake and excretion associated with diet also can affect crystal formation since a reduced urine volume raises the relative mineral content of the urine, thereby providing a more favorable environment for crystal formation. Reduced urine volume also discourages urination so urine is retained in the bladder, allowing more time for mineral crystalization. High-fat, energy-dense foods cause cats to excrete a greater proportion of water in their urine than in their bowel movements. Diets least likely to promote urolithiasis and urinary obstruction are high in fat and energy, easy to digest, low in magnesium, and produce an acid urine. Good quality canned foods readily meet these criteria. Dry cat foods, on the other hand, have ingredients that contain relatively high magnesium levels and are less energy dense, causing more minerals to be consumed to meet the same caloric level. They are less digestible, which increases the amount of stool formed and the amount of fecal water excreted, thereby lessening urine volume. Dry foods also tend to promote alkaline urine unless they have been specially modified by the addition of acidifying agents. Only specially formulated dry foods are suitable for cats with the tendency to stone formation and/or urinary obstruction.

If you think your cat has signs of cystitis try to get a look at the urine and examine the cat thoroughly. Straining to urinate associated with cystitis can easily be confused with the straining accompanying constipation or severe diarrhea and vice versa, so you need to do something to try to determine exactly what the problem is. If your cat has been urinating in abnormal places such as a sink or the bathtub, it may be easy to see whether the urine looks blood tinged. Otherwise a small urine sample can be obtained for home examination by placing an open plastic bag over the litter in the litter pan or by lining the litter pan with a fresh plastic bag and replacing the litter with nonabsorbent polystyrene foam bits. Blood-tinged urine almost always confirms the presence of severe bladder irritation and indicates that your cat should be examined by a veterinarian, who can perform a complete urinalysis and culture the urine to determine whether bacteria are present, and who can prescribe medication as needed. Bacteria that are isolated from cases of bladder inflammation and/or urinary obstruction in cats can be responsible for retrograde infection of the kidneys and permanent damage to the urinary system if they are not eliminated. Cystitis may also be present when the urine looks normal to you. In this instance only a urinalysis will confirm the condition's presence. You can present a fresh (less than thirty minutes old or kept refrigerated up to three hours) urine sample in a clean container to your veterinarian for analysis. Most veterinarians, how-

URINALYSIS IS IMPORTANT TO A DIAGNOSIS

ever, prefer to obtain their own urine samples to avoid laboratory errors associated with old and/or contaminated specimens. Many veterinarians obtain the screening urinalysis sample in the office by a safe, relatively painless, and quick procedure called *cystocentesis.* A fine needle attached to a syringe is passed through the abdominal wall and into the bladder, where a small sample of urine is withdrawn. This procedure avoids inconvenience for you as well as contamination of the urine sample that can confuse the interpretation of lab results.

SIGNS OF URINARY OBSTRUCTION

If your cat shows signs of cystitis but you cannot be *sure* urine is being passed, immediate physical examination by you or your veterinarian is necessary to determine whether or not urinary obstruction is present. Urinary obstruction is *rare* in females; their broad urethras are not easily plugged by sandy material. It almost always occurs in males (both castrated and uncastrated), whose narrow urethras become blocked quite easily. Knowing this may help you with diagnosis. Feel for the bladder (see page 30). In obstructed cats, it can be felt as a lemon-sized or larger hard object, and the cat (unless very depressed) will usually react as if in pain. (Unobstructed cats with cystitis who have urine in their bladders often urinate when you feel for their bladders.) Look at the penis. It is often extended beyond the prepuce; if it isn't visible, expose it (see page 28). In obstructed males its tip is often bloody and/or bruised looking, and sometimes a bit of white, sandy material can be seen protruding from the urethra.

A VETERINARIAN'S HELP IS IMPORTANT IN CASES OF OBSTRUCTION

If you conclude that your cat is obstructed or cannot be sure that he isn't, veterinary help is imperative to avoid bladder rupture. Only in instances of veterinary unavailability should you waste time attempting to relieve the obstruction yourself. If a veterinarian is absolutely not available, you can try the following.

1. Use firm but gentle manipulation of the penis to try to squeeze the obstructing material from the urethra. Try rolling the penis between your fingers, working from nearest the body to the tip, and try milking the penis from its base to its tip. If your motions are being effective, gritty-feeling, white or blood-tinged material will be expressed like toothpaste from the end of the penis. If you relieve the obstruction completely, urine will usually begin to flow freely from the penis.

2. If you remove some sandy material but urine doesn't flow, then try squeezing the bladder *gently* (you can easily rupture it if you aren't careful). This will sometimes result in a free-flowing stream of urine.

An obstruction relieved at home still requires veterinary care if at all possible. Acutely obstructed cats tend to become plugged again, and most cats docile enough to allow you to manipulate the penis and distended bladder are extremely ill and need the specialized supportive care only a veterinarian can give.

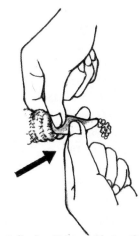

Relieving Urinary Obstruction

Veterinarians have many techniques for relieving obstruction. Unless the cat is extremely depressed, most veterinarians administer general anesthesia, and once the obstruction is relieved, a *catheter* (tube) may be sutured in place and left for a few hours or days to assure that the cat remains unblocked. Fluid therapy is administered to correct dehydration, stimulate a free urine flow, and to remove toxic wastes from the body. Blood tests (to measure uremia) are often necessary. As in cats with uncomplicated cystitis, urinalysis will be performed and appropriate medications administered and dispensed for home use.

The most common drugs used in treatment of bladder inflammation and blockage are urinary acidifiers, antispasmodics, and antibiotics. Antibiotics are useful only if bacteria are present in the urine and against the bacteria that invade the cat's body secondary to the stress of the bladder problem. Antispasmodic drugs are used to relax the smooth muscle of the bladder and urethra in an attempt to prevent reobstruction and to provide relief from discomfort. Urinary acidifiers are drugs which, as their name suggests, help promote the production of urine with an acid pH instead of an alkaline one.

Although antispasmodics and antibiotics are usually discontinued as signs requiring them resolve, urinary acidifiers often are used on a long-term basis. A commonly used one is ammonium chloride that your veterinarian will supply or that you can purchase in pet supply stores. Urinary acidification should be undertaken *only under the instruction and monitoring of your veterinarian.* Many commercial cat foods sold in pet store and supermarkets are already acidified and addition of ammonium chloride to these may cause problems. Excessive acidification can cause a potentially fatal metabolic acidosis, demineralization of bone, and low blood potassium levels (*hypokalemia*). Hypokalemia can result in profound muscle weakness, kidney damage, and death.

HOME
TREATMENT TO
PREVENT
URINARY
OBSTRUCTION
AND
RECURRENT
CYSTITIS
Measures other than urinary acidifiers designed to help prevent re-
current urinary problems all involve the management of your cat at
home.

1. Be sure to encourage adequate water intake by providing fresh
water freely available at all times. Water intake can be increased 50
to 100% by adding ordinary table salt to the cat's food. A pinch is
all that is necessary, but avoid using it if your cat is elderly or has a
disease that may be associated with high blood pressure (e.g., heart
or kidney problems), since increased salt intake may aggravate high
blood pressure.

2. Feed a diet low in magnesium. Recommended diets contain no
more than 20 milligrams magnesium per calorie (kcal) of diet consumed. This is about equivalent to 0.1% magnesium on a dry-matter
basis.

3. Avoid dry foods unless they are specifically recommended for
feeding to cats with urinary disease. Do not feed these special diets
to cats without tendencies to urolithiasis since they may promote
problems such as low blood potassium levels in cats who are especially sensitive to the effects of urinary acidification.

4. Provide a litter pan that is clean and dry at all times. Many cats
are so fastidious that they will hold their urine rather than use a litter
box they consider too soiled. This causes urinary stagnation that can
contribute to crystal formation and urinary tract infection. Some cats
will remain indoors for long periods of time to avoid going outside
to urinate in inclement weather but will use a clean litter pan if one
is provided.

5. Encourage activity in sedentary cats. Inactive cats tend to
empty their bladders less often, resulting in urinary stagnation.

Even with the best home treatment, cats with cystitis and/or urolithiasis problems often have recurrent bouts of bladder inflammation
or obstruction. It is impossible for your veterinarian to predict
whether your cat's condition will be a one-time problem or a recurrent nuisance. Veterinarians can only confirm the condition and
make sure no other complicating problems are present. Simple feline
cystitis (unaccompanied by bladder infection, bladder stones, or
tumors) in female cats is more of an inconvenience for you and your
cat than a life-threatening medical problem, since recurrences usually cause only signs of bladder irritation. Recurrent urinary obstruction in male cats, however, is a serious and life-threatening situation.
A good alternative to constant worry over the threat of obstruction
is a surgical procedure called a *perineal urethrostomy.* In this sur-

gery the small urethra of the male is enlarged so it no longer easily becomes blocked.

Although this surgery cannot cure the underlying problem, performed by a good veterinary surgeon its success rate is high, and it solves the problem of worry and the repeated expense of treatment for urinary obstruction. Cats who have undergone perineal urethrostomy need periodic urinalysis since they are more susceptible to bacterial urinary tract infections than other cats.

SURGERY CAN HELP A CAT WITH REPEATED URINARY OBSTRUCTION

URINE SPRAYING

Urine spraying is the act of squirting or spraying urine on vertical (rarely horizontal) surfaces in response to territorial stimuli, particularly the smell of other cats. This is a normal behavior for unneutered adult male cats (see page 273), but a behavior almost all cat owners find undesirable. It can usually be prevented or arrested by castration. Female cats and castrated males who have never sprayed before sometimes start spraying (or habitually urinating in abnormal places) at an advanced age. Usually this occurs as the re-

URINE SPRAYING

sult of some environmental change, such as the presence of a new cat in the house or even a change in the owner's routine. It may, however, be associated with a urinary tract disease such as cystitis. In females it is occasionally associated with incomplete neutering since urine spraying is a normal behavior for some females in heat (estrus, see page 267). Sometimes spraying is associated with defecation outside the litter box because cats occasionally use uncovered feces to mark their territorial boundaries.

The best course of action to follow when a cat suddenly starts abnormal urination behavior, such as spraying, is to have the cat examined by a veterinarian who can perform a complete urinalysis. If physical examination and urinalysis reveal no abnormalities, then you and the veterinarian can work together in an attempt to find and solve the behavioral problem.

The most successful solutions to spraying problems in cats who have already been neutered usually involve reducing the number of cats in a household and/or eliminating the spraying cat's exposure to other cats he or she can see outdoors, since the sight of another cat through a window or screened porch will trigger spraying in some individuals. Simply keeping the window blinds closed may discourage spraying behavior in some cats. However, the scents and sounds of unseen cats may continue to cause problems. Male cats even if neutered are more likely to spray (and fight) if housed with females (spayed or not) than if housed with other males.

It is also important to provide a clean, easily accessible litter pan containing attractive litter material that will encourage the cat to empty his or her bladder (and bowels) completely in an appropriate place (see page 47). At the same time, the urine-sprayed area needs to be made less desirable. Clean up all urine odor from the marked spot. Use vinegar and detergent in water, commercial pet odor removers, club soda, or a baking soda and water rinse following detergent cleaning to remove urine odor. Do not use ammonia-based cleaners, which seem to smell like urine to cats. Make the site itself unattractive by using booby traps. Hanging strips of aluminum foil frighten some cats away because they make a sound when urine is sprayed against them. Two-sided sticky tape or sheets of plastic wrap or aluminum foil placed on the cat's approach to the spraying site discourage others. Some cats will avoid areas that smell of citrus so a few peels can be left in previously sprayed areas. Heavily scented perfumes or rubbing alcohol have a similar effect, especially after a dab has been rubbed on the offending cat's nose. To use punishment to discourage spraying, stand ready with a plant mister or water pistol to administer a squirt to the face when the cat approaches the favored spraying area. Motion-sensing burglar alarms set up in the areas can also administer effective punishment in your absence by making a frightening noise when the cat approaches. Keep in mind that while effective for some cats, punishment and booby traps may cause additional stress for others and may just result in a more disturbed and insecure pet who chooses a new site for urine spraying.

Occasionally tranquilizers (e.g., diazepam) and/or progesterone-like hormone drugs are administered by veterinarians to help break the behavior pattern of spraying. If such treatments are effective for your cat, and you know that he or she is one who begins urine (or stool) marking whenever a new stress arises, these drugs can be given prophylactically anytime the cat must be moved to a new house, experience a change in routine, or endure the introduction of a new cat, dog, or human to his or her territory. Intractable cases of urine spraying have caused veterinarians to resort to surgical procedures in an attempt to stop the problem. In one, *olfactory tractotomy,* the cat's sense of smell is eliminated by destroying a portion of the brain. Such mutilating surgeries should be considered only as an extreme last resort, since a cat's sense of smell is one of the major ones he or she uses to relate to the surrounding world. A more natural solution is to give the cat free access to the outdoors via a fully enclosed run that gives a permissible place to mark territory.

FALSE PREGNANCY

For signs of false pregnancy, see page 279.

UTERINE INFECTION

PYOMETRA

Pyometra is a type of uterine infection that occurs commonly in older unspayed (or partially spayed, see page 272) females. It occurs most often in females who have never had a litter and is probably due to a hormonal imbalance that develops when cats undergo repeated reproductive cycles without breeding. In cases of pyometra where the cervix is open there is usually a sticky reddish to yellow, puslike, abnormal-smelling discharge from the vulva. *Other cases have no discharge.* A female with pyometra is often listless, lacks appetite, and has a fever. Her abdomen may look distended, and she may show signs of discomfort when it is touched. She may show increased water intake and increased urination. If not treated, this condition can cause death. Although some drugs can be used for treatment, *ovariohysterectomy* (spaying) is the treatment of choice for pyometra. Cats treated without surgery often do not recover, and if they do recover, recurrences are frequent. Females with pyometra are much poorer surgical risks than healthy young cats, so consider having an ovariohysterectomy (see page 269) performed when your cat is young, and rush your cat to a veterinarian if you think pyometra may be present.

ACUTE METRITIS

A retained placenta or fetus, or a lack of cleanliness during delivery, can result later in an infection of the uterus, *acute metritis.* It may also follow or accompany spontaneous abortion. A female with acute metritis is usually depressed, febrile (feverish), lacks appetite, and may seem uninterested in her kittens. She may seem excessively thirsty, vomit, and/or have diarrhea. The discharge from the vulva is often odorous, reddish, and watery, or later dark brown and puslike. This condition calls for immediate treatment by a veterinarian.

Kittens may have to be raised by hand (see page 289) since females with acute metritis often do not have enough milk or the milk produced may be toxic.

HEART AND BLOOD
(CARDIOVASCULAR SYSTEM)

ANEMIA

Anemia is a common sign of illness in cats. Anemia occurs whenever a fewer than normal number of red blood cells is circulating in a cat's bloodstream. It has many causes. A borderline degree of anemia may only be recognized by your veterinarian with the help of a complete blood cell count (CBC) or other laboratory tests.

SIGNS OF ANEMIA More pronounced anemia causes other signs that you may be able to recognize at home. Pale-colored mucous membranes (look at your cat's gums, tongue, roof of the mouth, and conjunctiva), decreased activity, and decreased appetite usually indicate anemia in cats. The skin that covers the nose and lines the ears may also become paler. An unusual accompanying sign seen in many anemic cats is an appetite for abnormal foodstuffs; many are seen to lick sidewalks or earthenware pots; others consume kitty litter. When anemia becomes very pronounced, pale mucous membranes become white, an abnormal *shh* sound may be heard in the heartbeat (a heart murmur), complete loss of appetite usually occurs, and any physical activity may lead to complete collapse and rapid, strained breathing. Also loss of bladder and bowel control is often seen. Anemia left untreated in these stages almost invariably becomes fatal within a few days or hours. If you recognize signs of anemia in your cat, seek the help of a good veterinarian. Discovery of the anemia is only the first step; good treatment directed at the cause of the low red blood count requires thorough investigation. Rational therapy can only be applied when the specific disease producing the anemia is identified. Repeated blood counts and other more refined diagnostic tests, including measures of organ function (e.g., liver and kidney function tests) and bone marrow biopsy (removal of a sample of bone marrow for examination) are frequently necessary when treating an anemic cat. Patience and cooperation on your part are important assets if this serious problem arises.

The causes of anemia fall into three basic categories: anemia due to blood loss, anemia due to increased destruction of red blood cells, and anemia due to decreased production of new red blood cells. Blood loss most often follows trauma, such as that which occurs when a cat is hit by a car (see page 204) or falls from a height. In cases of blood loss due to trauma, other evidence of injury is often present.

KINDS OF ANEMIA

Increased destruction of red blood cells usually accompanies *Haemobartonella felis* infection also known as *feline infectious anemia* (haemobartonellosis). This microscopic rickettsial organism attaches to the surface of the red blood cells causing them to be identified as abnormal and removed from the circulatory system. The organism responsible for this disease may be transmitted from cat to cat during fights, or through the uterus before birth. Blood-sucking external parasites such as fleas, lice, and ticks may also be responsible for its spread. Carrier cats may be infected without showing signs of disease, and the exact combination of factors necessary for *Haemobartonella* to produce significant anemia is not yet fully understood. There are no preventive vaccines or drugs available for control of infectious anemia. The best prevention is to limit your cat's exposure to other cats. The task of diagnosis and treatment requires the help of a veterinarian. The infectious anemia organism is often present accompanying other causes of anemia such as feline leukemia virus infection (see page 191). In many of these instances treatment fails since antibiotic therapy directed at *Haemobartonella* may not help correct other more significant causes.

FELINE INFECTIOUS ANEMIA

The failure to produce enough red blood cells is the more common cause of anemia in cats. This type of anemia is called *bone marrow depression,* but identifying an anemia as such is only a small part of the total picture. Cats have a very sensitive bone marrow, and almost any chronic disease can cause bone marrow depression and resulting anemia. Anemia due to bone marrow depression accompanies disease processes as diverse as bacterial infection following fighting wounds, kidney failure, panleukopenia (see page 90), nutritional deficiencies, leukemia, lymphosarcoma, and feline immunosuppressive virus infection (see page 195). Some causes are simple to diagnose and easy to treat; others are difficult to diagnose and sometimes impossible to treat successfully. In many instances the true problem emerges only after time passes and initial treatments do not succeed.

Treatment of anemia varies, of course, depending on its cause. Drugs commonly employed are antibiotics and vitamin-mineral supplements. Bone marrow stimulants and blood transfusions are sometimes necessary as well. Home nursing care is very important. In addition to administering drugs as directed, you will need to provide a balanced diet and a warm, unstressful environment.

HEART DISEASE AND HEART FAILURE

Heart disease may occur in cats of any age. Just as in people, there are many causes of heart disease in cats. They include structural defects (e.g., leaky valves, abnormal holes between heart chambers), primary diseases of the heart muscle, bacterial infections of the heart and/or heart valves, heartworms, cancer, and diseases of the heart muscle secondary to other problems such as nutritional deficiency, thyroid disease, or high blood pressure. Disease of the blood vessels that supply the heart itself, arteriosclerosis, is an uncommon problem in cats. Therefore, heart attacks that result in sudden death are rare in cats. Instead, disease in cats generally progresses gradually through several stages where it can be treated and its signs ameliorated before heart failure that requires emergency treatment or that results in death occurs. Many cats, however, go undiagnosed in the early stages of heart failure because the signs of heart disease may be very subtle and a cat may compensate for a failing heart by making changes in his or her activity level that go unnoticed by the average person.

HEART MURMURS A *murmur,* an abnormal sound in the heartbeat associated with turbulent blood flow through the heart, may be the first sign of heart disease. Kittens who have been born with heart disease (see page 295) are often diagnosed when a murmur is heard during their first physical examination given at the time of their kitten vaccinations. In older cats, a murmur may be a new finding that your veterinarian mentions at the yearly office visit for a physical exam and booster injection. Or you may hear a murmur as a *shh* sound interposed between the normal lub-dup sounds of the heartbeat when you are examining your cat at home. If the murmur is intense enough, you even may be able to feel it through the chest wall by placing your fingers in the area where the heartbeat is normally felt. The presence of a heart murmur in any age cat is not necessarily something to be alarmed about especially if there are no other associated symptoms. However, it is something that *requires* a full veterinary evaluation since there are many causes of heart murmurs. Some murmurs result from serious diseases of the heart itself, including congenital defects and heart muscle diseases. Others are associated with systemic diseases that cause anemia, fever, or high blood pressure. Still others are completely innocent and have no disease association at all. Your veterinarian will need to perform blood tests, a chest radiograph, an echocardiogram (ultrasound examination of the heart), and/or an electrocardiogram (electrical evaluation of the heart function) to differentiate among the various causes of heart murmur and to rule in or out heart disease in any age cat.

In cases of heart disease where you or your veterinarian do not detect a heart murmur or a murmur is not present, you may not notice any changes until the heart begins to fail. Sometimes the only external change is a reduction in a cat's normal activity level, which may be misinterpreted as a normal decrease caused by maturity, boredom, or simple laziness. Cats with this sign will often become abnormally short of breath if chased or enticed into play. When the heart failure becomes full blown it will usually be associated with rapid respirations and difficulty breathing (due to fluid accumulation in the lungs themselves and/or the chest cavity). The cat's body temperature may become subnormal, the mucous membranes may become pale and develop a bluish color; your cat may be reluctant to move, eat, or drink and may even vomit. The heartbeat of a cat with heart failure will often be extremely rapid and the pulses will be weak. (Heart rates persistently above 240 beats per minute are consistently associated with heart failure.) Some cats with heart failure have no femoral pulses at all, due to a blood clot that has lodged in the aorta. These cats may act as if their hindlegs are paralyzed. Death soon follows heart failure if treatment is not instituted when signs become evident.

SIGNS OF HEART FAILURE

The initial treatment of severe heart failure is directed toward lifesaving measures. Since many cats with obvious signs of heart failure are effectively in a state of shock (see page 202), the most important thing you can do is seek a veterinarian's aid. Veterinarians will administer oxygen if needed and diuretic drugs that reduce fluids interfering with effective respiration. Veterinarians may even physically drain the chest cavity with a needle to remove fluid that is dangerously compressing the lungs. Various blood-pressure and heart-contraction-modifying drugs are also employed depending on the type of disease that is causing the heart to fail. During diagnosis and initial treatment absolute confinement in a hospital cage is essential to prevent even normal activity that may place too many demands on the cat's weakened heart. This confinement is quite similar to the bedrest prescribed for people who have serious heart disease.

INITIAL TREATMENT OF HEART FAILURE

DIAGNOSIS OF HEART DISEASE Once a cat in heart failure is stabilized or if a cat with heart disease does not require emergency care, your veterinarian will need to diagnose the underlying cause of the heart problem in order to provide the most appropriate treatment. This will involve a full biochemical evaluation of your cat, including evaluation of the blood and urine, chest radiographs, and echocardiogram, and/or special X-ray studies of the heart, and/or an electrocardiogram.

DIETARY DEFICIENCY CAN CAUSE HEART FAILURE IN CATS One important form of heart disease in cats, *dilated cardiomyopathy,* in which the heart muscle loses its normal contractile ability, is often caused by a diet deficient in the amino acid taurine. Taurine deficiency may be further aggravated by potassium deficiency. The condition can be reversed when taurine supplements and a nutritionally complete diet are instituted before the heart is permanently damaged. Cases of dilated cardiomyopathy caused by nutritional deficiency can be entirely cured.

Prevent heart failure by investigating the cause of a heart murmur as soon as one is diagnosed in your cat; by feeding a nutritionally complete diet; by taking measures to diagnose and treat problems known to aggravate heart disease such as kidney failure, thyroid disease, and obesity before decreased heart function is severe.

CHRONIC TREATMENT OF HEART DISEASE The prognosis for each cat with heart problems depends on the kind of heart disease present. The prognosis will have to be discussed with your cat's veterinarian once his or her evaluation is complete. In general, heart failure secondary to other problems can often be completely controlled if diagnosed and treated soon enough. Other forms of heart disease in cats cannot be entirely cured; therefore, treatment in these instances is generally directed at improving circulatory function. Medical treatment consists of various drugs and a controlled diet. Diuretic drugs help control sodium and water retention that accompany and aggravate heart failure. Blood vessel dilating drugs are used to lower high blood pressure and lessen the work that the heart must do to circulate the blood. Aspirin in controlled doses can be safely used in cats to help prevent excessive blood clot formation that may occur when blood circulation is poor. And some cases benefit from digitalislike drugs that increase the strength of the heart muscle contraction. In addition to administration of drugs as needed, home care for cats with heart failure includes a sodium-restricted diet and confinement indoors. Cats who receive good home care may live longer, more comfortable, and more active lives than would seem likely when a diagnosis of heart disease is made.

MULTISYSTEM DISEASES

FELINE LEUKEMIA VIRUS INFECTION

Feline leukemia virus (FeLV) causes a complex group of diseases, many of which are fatal. About 50% of cats infected with the leukemia virus develop cancer. The most common type of cancer affects lymphoid tissues (e.g., lymph nodes) causing solid tumors called *lymphosarcomas.* FeLV can also cause cancer of the blood cells and their precursors in the bone marrow. Veterinarians refer to this group of disorders as *myeloproliferative diseases.* All myeloproliferative diseases caused by feline leukemia virus are serious. Depending on which blood element is affected, profound anemias, low white blood cell counts (which increase susceptibility to infection), or low platelet levels (which can cause uncontrollable bleeding) may occur. Some myeloproliferative disorders are true *leukemias* that cause cancerous cells to circulate in the bloodstream. Cats affected with myeloproliferative disorders often show signs of illness such as progressive weight loss, poor appetite, fever, and pale mucous membranes (caused by anemia). Since such signs often accompany other serious but treatable diseases (e.g., feline infectious anemia, see page 187) and since laboratory tests such as blood counts and bone marrow examinations are imperative for diagnosis, a veterinarian's help is necessary if you suspect such a problem in your cat.

Lymphosarcoma (malignant lymphoma) is the most common tumor (abnormal growth of solid tissue) in cats. The solid growths it produces have been found in almost every organ and tissue of cats because the lymphocyte cells from which the cancer cells arise are present in most body tissues. The signs of its presence depend on the site of tumor formation. The most common site of cancerous growth is the abdomen. Here kidney involvement may produce signs of kidney failure (see page 234). Persistent diarrhea, constipation, and/or vomiting may occur with intestinal or lymph node involvement. Malignant lymphoma also is frequently found in the chest, resulting in fluid formation, compression of the windpipe, and signs that may be mistaken for other respiratory or heart diseases. These include difficulty breathing and coughing. Generalized lymph node enlargement occurs in other cases. Liver and spleen lymphosarcoma can occur, and when tumor formation occurs in unusual sites (e.g., brain, spinal cord, skin, eyes) the accompanying signs may be bizarre, ranging from behavior abnormalities and urinary incontinence to paralysis or seizures, skin growths, irregular pupil size, and/or blind-

LYMPHOSARCOMA CAN CAUSE MANY DIFFERENT ILLNESS SIGNS

191

ness. Blood abnormalities (e.g., leukemia, anemia) may or may not accompany the solid tumor formation of lymphosarcoma. Clearly, a cat with signs that may indicate lymphosarcoma will require a veterinarian's care. Although a cure is not to be expected, many treatments are available that can comfortably prolong an affected cats' life.

Feline leukemia virus infection also causes health problems unrelated to cancer. It may suppress an infected cat's immune system, thereby causing loss of resistance to other infectious diseases (e.g., feline infectious peritonitis, upper respiratory infections, haemobartonellosis, toxoplasmosis). Infected cats also have more frequent and longer lasting bacterial infections. It is not unusual for FeLV-infected cats to have abscesses that fail to heal normally (see page 131), chronic diarrhea or to have chronic gum inflammation (gingivitis). Feline leukemia may encourage the cat's immune system to recognize the self as foreign, causing antibody-mediated damage to the cat's own body tissues. Cats with this problem may develop kidney inflammation, nerve damage, arthritis, or self-destruction of the red blood cells or platelets. Female cats infected with FeLV have many reproductive system disorders, including infertility, uterine inflammation, loss of kittens due to resorption before birth, spontaneous abortion in later pregnancy, or death of the kittens shortly after their birth.

HOW FELINE LEUKEMIA VIRUS INFECTION IS ACQUIRED

Feline leukemia virus is classified as a *retrovirus*. Retroviruses possess the ability to enter a cat's body cells and use the cat's own genetic machinery (DNA) to multiply. Feline leukemia virus is a particular kind of retrovirus called *oncornavirus* (tumor-producing ribonucleic acid virus) thought to have evolved millions of years ago from a leukemia virus of mice. Infected cats excrete (shed) newly formed virus mainly in their saliva, although it is also found in the blood, tears, respiratory secretions, urine, and stool. The virus is passed from cat to cat by contact with infectious materials. Female cats can transmit the virus to their kittens through colostrum, milk, and across the placenta. Sharing a litter pan with an infected cat, receiving infected blood by transfusion, or, in theory, even getting a bite from a flea from an infected cat could result in leukemia virus infection. Most often, though, transmission occurs by contact with saliva during mutual grooming, biting, or sharing of food and/or water bowls. One drop of ingested saliva can contain up to 400,000 infective viral particles! Despite this fact, prolonged (days to weeks) close contact between cats (especially adults) is usually required for transmission of FeLV and transmission via bite wounds is thought to be uncommon.

Not all cats exposed to the leukemia virus become infected, and of those who become infected *most* do not become permanently sick. Although newborn kittens usually cannot resist a terminal infection, approximately two thirds of healthy cats older than three months of age suppress or throw off the infection. The remaining one third remain infected and actively shed the virus for the rest of their lives. (In the USA only about 2% of randomly tested cats on average are infected.) These cats pose a danger to other cats even if they never show any signs of illness caused by the virus. These cats are called FeLV *carriers,* and they can be detected by blood tests performed by your veterinarian. Tests performed on saliva or tears are also available, but they miss a significant number of infected cats and may give a false positive result so they are best used only as screening tests. Carrier cats should never be allowed to contact uninfected cats. This means they should be kept indoors, isolated from uninfected cats, and provided with their own litter pans and food and water bowls. Some veterinarians advocate euthanasia of all infected cats.

Although most cats who become chronically FeLV infected will have trouble with illnesses and die within three years, many live nearly normal lifespans with few apparent illnesses. Some remain visibly healthy. Owners who are able to isolate their infected cats do not need to prematurely euthanize an apparently healthy but FeLV-infected cat. Neither should owners be overly concerned about any danger to themselves, since FeLV virus has never been shown to infect human beings naturally.

The best way to prevent leukemia virus infection in your cat is to avoid virus exposure. The safest cats are those who are kept indoors away from other potentially infected cats. Avoid introducing any new cat to your household until he or she had been blood tested negative for FeLV *at least* twice over a three- to five-month period. This is most desirable since recently exposed cats could conceivably test negative at first, only to turn positive later. The best strategy is to test the cat before bringing him or her home, then confine him or her to separate quarters until after the repeat testing is completed.

Do not allow your cat to share food or water bowls with other untested cats. It is particularly dangerous to allow your cat to share food and/or water bowls or an elimination area with other untested neighborhood cats. Providing an outdoor water source only attracts cats who may be FeLV (or other disease) carriers; and although FeLV survives for only three or four hours when it dries at room temperature, it may remain infectious for *several days* when suspended in water at room temperature. Neighborhood cats will also compete for territory with your own and the resulting bite wounds may spread FeLV.

Be sure any boarding kennel or grooming parlor you patronize is cautious about infectious diseases (see page 84). Your veterinarian may request feline leukemia virus testing of your cat before dental procedures in order to provide extra protection against dispersal of contagious saliva in the veterinary hospital.

FELINE LEUKEMIA VIRUS VACCINATION IS NOT NEEDED FOR ALL CATS Vaccines against FeLV have been available since 1985. Some were found to be ineffective and/or unsafe and were removed from the market; new ones have replaced the old. Safe feline leukemia virus vaccines pose no danger to a healthy cat; however, they are unnecessary for cats who will never be exposed to FeLV (cats living indoors alone or with other test-negative cats) and for cats already infected with FeLV. Also since most adult cats exposed to FeLV—unlike other diseases prevented by vaccination including panleukopenia, rabies, and respiratory infection—will not become sick, the risk of infection will need to be weighed against the cost of vaccination and the potential protective effect of the vaccine. This warrants a thorough discussion with your veterinarian before accepting routine feline leukemia virus vaccination of your cat. Determination of your cat's infection status prior to vaccination will require blood tests.

CLEANSE PREMISES WHERE FELV-INFECTED CATS HAVE LIVED Should you have the misfortune to have a cat die of FeLV, wait at least two weeks before introducing a new uninfected cat to a previously contaminated environment. During the waiting period be sure to clean the premises thoroughly with detergent and commercial disinfectant (all common ones including alcohol will kill FeLV). Wash all food and water bowls and litter pans, then disinfect them by soaking them in 0.16% hypochlorite solution (household bleach diluted 4 ounces/gallon water, 32ml/l). To eliminate any concerns about cleanup, you may want to discard these items. If you have any other cats who have lived with the infected one, follow the procedures for control of feline leukemia virus in catteries on page 195.

CONTROL OF FELINE LEUKEMIA (FELV) IN CATTERIES AND MULTIPLE CAT HOUSEHOLDS

1. Blood test all cats for feline leukemia virus by immunofluorescent antibody (IFA) test. This blood test is most effective for detecting cats who will excrete the virus persistently.

2. Remove all FeLV-infected cats. (This is usually done by euthanasia. If infected cats are not to be removed, *no* new uninfected cats should be introduced and infected cats should not be allowed to reproduce).

3. Isolate all cats found negative for FeLV to cleaned and disinfected quarters and provide them with cleaned and disinfected food and water bowls, litter pans, and new toys.

4. Retest all quarantined cats for FeLV three months after the initial test to detect any cats who may have been incubating the disease.

5. Repeat the removal of positive (infected) cats and continue the isolation of negative cats.

6. Continue the retesting, removal of positive cats, and isolation of negative cats until all remaining cats have blood tested negative at least twice at three-month intervals.

7. Isolate all new cats. Introduce them to other cats in the household only after two negative FeLV tests performed three months apart.

FELINE IMMUNODEFICIENCY VIRUS (FIV)

Feline immunodeficiency virus (FIV) is a member of the *retrovirus* family. This virus is found all over the world and has been present in the United States since 1968. Like feline leukemia virus and other related family members such as human immunodeficiency virus (HIV, AIDS virus), it enters the victim's body cells and utilizes their genetic machinery, their DNA, to reproduce itself. In this process the virus is able to enter the host cell's chromosomes where it may remain hidden for some time before causing obvious signs of disease, or it may immediately interfere with the normal function of infected cells causing signs of illness shortly after infection. Because FIV prefers T-lymphocytes, a specific type of white blood cell important to the immune system (see page 34), for replication many of the problems it causes are due to immune system dysfunction.

HOW FIV IS TRANSMITTED FIV is a fragile virus that cannot survive outside the infected cat. It dies quickly at room temperature, and it is easily killed by common disinfectants (e.g., household bleach). Therefore, FIV is transmitted only by close contact between cats. The virus is found in the blood, cerebrospinal fluid, and in the greatest quantities in saliva. Since infection is found most often in free-roaming male cats, it is thought that the most common way it is spread is via bite wounds. Mother cats may also transmit the virus to their kittens before they are born, but this is apparently an uncommon event.

SIGNS OF FIV Following infection with FIV, there may be no noticeable symptoms of disease, but some cats develop fever, low white blood counts, and/or enlarged lymph nodes about four to six weeks following a bite wound. The lymph node enlargement may last for weeks or even months unaccompanied by any other signs. Infected cats that show no symptoms or that appear to recover from their initial illness can seem healthy for months or even years (the *latent* phase) during which they can be particularly dangerous to other cats since unaware owners will often let these infective cats go outdoors or mingle indoors with other apparently healthy cats. Eventually, though, most FIV-infected cats develop the chronic stage of illness that is characterized by suppression of the immune system (immunodeficiency), cancer, and/or signs of illness related to almost any organ or organ system. Cats who are concurrently infected with other viruses such as feline leukemia virus are particularly likely to show early signs of illness and to die soon after infection. FIV infection also makes cats more likely to die from other infections that thrive in an immunodeficient animal (e.g., toxoplasmosis, *Haemobartonella* infection, yeast infection, calicivirus). The most common problems seen in infected cats are inflammation and infection of the gums and mouth (gingivitis, stomatitis) and nonspecific signs of illness such as weight loss, fever, lack of appetite. Other problems that may signal infection with FIV are enlarged lymph nodes, anemia and other blood count abnormalities, persistent or recurrent signs of upper respiratory disease (sinus infection), conjunctivitis, bronchial inflammation, diarrhea (indicating inflammation of the bowel), skin and ear infections (abscesses, mite infection), urinary bladder dysfunction (cystitis), eye inflammation, neurologic abnormalities, and nervous system damage that can result in seizures and/or bizarre forms of mental deterioration. Infected female cats may abort or have other reproductive difficulties. This pattern of illness so closely resembles that found in people infected with human immunodeficiency virus (acquired immune deficiency syndrome, AIDS) that the disease caused by FIV is often called feline AIDS. Up to one third of all sick cats may be carrying the feline immunodeficiency virus. Your veterinarian may request a blood test for FIV whenever your cat shows signs that are suspicious of infection and especially in cases of chronic mouth disease. Unfortunately, FIV cannot be confirmed in all cats by a blood test and sometimes false positive tests are found. This is especially true for kittens testing positive under twelve weeks of age. To assure correct results test positive young kittens should be retested after twelve weeks of age.

If your cat does test FIV positive, he or she should be kept indoors and away from other test-negative cats to limit further spread of the disease. Should you consider euthanasia a positive screening test should be confirmed by other blood tests before taking this final step.

TREATMENT OF FIV

Treatment for FIV is directed primarily against secondary infection and toward the organs that are malfunctioning. Antibiotics, fluids, vitamins, and nursing are important aspects of supportive care to insure the longest, most comfortable survival of an affected cat. Antiviral drugs are also sometimes beneficial. Protect your cat against FIV by not allowing him or her to roam unsupervised outdoors where an infected cat may be encountered. It is also important not to admit new cats (especially strays) to your household until they have been quarantined for at least one month and blood tested for FIV.

FELINE INFECTIOUS PERITONITIS

Feline infectious peritonitis (FIP) is a viral disease of cats that is almost invariably fatal. FIP is caused by a *coronavirus,* which can invade certain white blood cells called macrophages and other body tissues. This virus is similar to other members of the same virus family that infect pigs, dogs, and humans, but the FIP virus itself can cause disease only in cats. It does so only under certain specific circumstances. Problems with FIP are found primarily in cats who live in or grew up in multicat environments. Many catteries raising purebreds produce kittens who later develop FIP, and it is a more frequent problem among cats who live in crowded, stressful surroundings where there are concurrent problems with other infections (e.g., respiratory infections, see page 152; feline leukemia infection, see page 191) than in more well-managed environments. Some genetic strains of cats may even be more susceptible than others to disease caused by FIP virus.

FIP infection is transmitted from cat to cat by close contact. Virus is shed (excreted) in oral and respiratory secretions, stool (feces), and urine so it may contaminate food and water bowls, litter pans, clothing, and bedding. Spread via the feces is most common. Virus does not, however, survive longer than a few weeks in the environment and it is easily killed by common household detergents, disinfectants, and bleach. Therefore, problems with FIP infections only persist in households with actively infected cats. In some cases, queens (female cats) transmit the virus to their kittens while they are still in the uterus. This can result in disease that occurs within a few days of birth.

SIGNS OF FIP

A cat may develop symptoms within a few weeks after or many years after infection with FIP virus. Why there is so much variation in the onset of symptoms is not understood. One theory is that related but harmless coronaviruses that infect the bowel (*feline enteric coronaviruses*) must mutate to the illness-causing FIP form in an infected cat. It is known, however, that most often affected cats are between six months to two years of age. The most characteristic sign of infection is a persistent fever that does not respond to antibiotic treatment. Some cats lose weight, have poor appetites, and become lethargic and depressed. They may also be anemic. Some cats remain alert and eat well until more specific signs of illness appear and become severe, but *all* cats sick with FIP have a fever that may fluctuate from just slightly above normal to very high. Other signs of FIP are classically grouped and used to categorize the illness into "wet" *(effusive)* or "dry" *(noneffusive)* forms. In effusive FIP fluid accumulates in the abdomen and/or chest cavities resulting in abdominal distention and/or respiratory distress. In noneffusive FIP signs of almost any organ involvement may be seen. Common symptoms include those caused by kidney failure (increased water drinking and urination), liver disease (jaundice, loss of appetite, vomiting), or pancreatic disease (diarrhea, vomiting, signs of diabetes mellitus). Eye inflammations that may lead to blindness and involvement of the nervous system causing a wide variety of signs ranging from hindleg weakness, loss of balance, to seizures and behavior changes may all be seen. Some cats may have signs found in both wet and dry FIP at once. All these signs are caused by antibody-mediated damage to the small blood vessels (vasculitis) as the body's own immune system tries to eliminate the virus.

DIAGNOSIS OF
FIP

Since signs of FIP can be so wide ranging and thereby mimic other diseases, a veterinarian's aid is necessary for diagnosis. Analysis of fluids from the chest and/or abdomen, biopsy of affected organs, and blood and other laboratory tests are all used to aid diagnosis. Because FIP antibodies in the blood cross-react with other common but harmless coronaviruses found in healthy cats, and because cats not made ill by FIP virus may still harbor antibodies formed during previous exposure, it is *not* possible to diagnose FIP on the basis of blood tests *alone*. Many cats have been euthanized unnecessarily on the basis of inaccurately interpreted blood tests. Lab tests that can detect the damage caused by the virus or the FIP virus itself will make diagnosis easier. Currently veterinarians are able to avoid problems in diagnosis only by thoroughly understanding the disease and by carefully evaluating all available information before making any treatment decisions for their patients.

There is no specific treatment for FIP. Cats who have not become too debilitated or who have signs limited to one organ system (e.g., the eyes) may live comfortably for weeks or months when various kinds of supportive care, such as fluids, vitamins, antibiotics to treat secondary infection, antiviral drugs, and drainage of excessive fluid, are given. A very rare cat may even recover. It is up to you and your veterinarian to decide together what treatment plan is best to follow if your cat is diagnosed as having FIP. **TREATMENT OF FIP**

A vaccine against FIP was introduced in 1991. It was designed to help solve the problem of recurrent FIP in multicat environments but has been found to be less effective and more dangerous than originally anticipated. Cats at low risk of infection should not receive FIP vaccination. Most household pets fall into this category. Ask your veterinarian for information about FIP vaccination if you have a household where FIP is an ongoing problem.

EMERGENCY MEDICINE AND FIRST AID

An *emergency* is any situation that requires immediate action in order to prevent irreversible damage to or the death of your cat. Each of the following signs indicates an emergency:

> Uncontrollable bleeding
> Extreme difficulty breathing (including choking)
> Continuous or recurrent convulsions
> Unconsciousness
> Shock
> Sudden paralysis
> Inability to urinate
> Repeated or continuous attempts to vomit, repeated unproductive vomiting, and/or diarrhea

Conditions such as injury to the eyeball or snakebite are usually emergencies; others, such as certain leg injuries, are not so clear-cut. Therefore, in many cases you will have to use your intuition to judge the best action to take.

It is to both your own and your veterinarian's benefit that you are able to recognize an actual emergency. No veterinarian I know enjoys being taken away from dinner, pulled from the bathtub, or awakened in the middle of the night by a hysterical pet owner who obviously does not have an emergency. Most veterinarians value their leisure time more than any emergency fee they may collect. Rational pet owners are often unhappy to find out upon reaching the veterinary hospital that the "emergency" could have safely waited until morning and that the emergency fee could have been saved. Usually, getting emotionally upset leads to restricted judgment. Try to remain calm and use this section as a reference for making that emergency decision.

Most emergencies are the result of trauma (hit by a car, bitten by a dog) or poisoning. Most could have been easily prevented if the owner had confined his or her pet when unable to provide supervision. Medical emergencies due to failure of a vital organ could often have been prevented by consulting a veterinarian soon after the earlier signs appeared. Look ahead. If a weekend or holiday is coming up, it may be a good idea to take your cat in for an examination even if the signs seem minor. An emergency could follow directly. It is also a good idea to make up a first-aid kit to have on hand and to take with you on trips during which your pet will be far from veterinary care. It should include the following:

A SIMPLE FIRST-AID KIT FOR PETS

Instruments:
  Rectal thermometer
  Penlight flashlight
  Scissors
  Fine-toothed tweezers
  Nontoothed tweezers
  Magnifying glass
  Needlenose pliers
  Small wire snips
  Sewing needle
Antiinfectives:
  Povidone-iodine solution and scrub (shampoo) and/or
  Chlorhexidine solution and scrub
  Neomycin/polymixin B/bacitracin topical cream (or ointment)
  Rubbing alcohol (70% ethyl or isopropyl alcohol)
  3% hydrogen peroxide (poor disinfectant but good for removal of blood)
Poisoning antidotes:
  Syrup of ipecac
  Activated charcoal liquid
Bandaging materials:
  Nonstick wound pads (2" × 2", 3" × 3", 4" × 4")
  Gauze squares (2" × 2", 3" × 3", 4" × 4")
  Roller gauze (1", 2" wide)
  Roll cotton (disposable diaper or sanitary pad pieces can often be substituted in an emergency)
  Adhesive tape (½", 1", 2" wide)
  Elastic bandage (2", 3" wide)
Miscellaneous:
  Cat muzzle (see page 255)
  Cotton-tipped swabs
  Styptic powder (or pencil)
  Toenail trimmer
  Medical-grade cyanoacrylate glue (rarely needed)

All of the materials above should be easy to obtain in any well-stocked drugstore except for the cat muzzle and the needlenose pliers and metal snips, which can be purchased in hardware stores. Commercial first-aid kits intended for people can be easily expanded to make them appropriate for use with pets.

SHOCK

The term *shock* is one that is frequently misused. It is extremely important to know whether or not shock is truly present, because its presence or absence often determines whether or not a condition is an emergency. Shock can be simply defined as *the failure of the cardiovascular system to provide the body tissues with oxygen.* There are several causes of shock; the most common in veterinary medicine is blood loss. The following are signs that may indicate the presence of shock:

SIGNS OF SHOCK IN ORDER OF INCREASING SEVERITY

1. Depression (quietness and inactivity) and lack of normal response to external environmental stimuli. This may progress to unconsciousness.

2. Rapid heart and respiratory rate.

3. Rapid pulse that becomes weak and may become absent as shock progresses.

4. Poor capillary refilling time. To test for capillary refilling time, press firmly against the gums, causing them to blanch (whiten) beneath your finger. Lift your finger away and see how long it takes for the color to return to the blanched area. The normal refilling time is no more than one or two seconds. Poor capillary filling is an early and constant sign of shock. It precedes the pale, cool mucous membranes present in advanced shock.

5. Lowered body temperature. The extremities (legs and paws) and skin become cool to the touch, and the rectal temperature often drops below 100°F (37.8°C).

If your cat shows signs of shock following injury or prolonged illness, contact a veterinarian immediately. But first wrap your cat in a towel or blanket (if possible) to preserve body heat during the delay before treatment.

EXTERNAL BLEEDING AND HOW TO STOP IT
(HEMOSTASIS)

Most cuts through the skin will stop bleeding within five or six minutes of their occurrence. Those that do not or that are bleeding profusely need some kind of immediate care, especially if it's going to be a while before you can enlist professional veterinary aid.

HOW TO USE A PRESSURE BANDAGE

A *pressure bandage* is the best method of hemostasis or stopping bleeding. If a gauze pad is available, place this directly over the wound, then apply the bandage over it. Any clean strip of material can be used for a bandage. Gauze roller bandage, a strip of clean sheet, or an elastic bandage are best since persistent bleeding causes seepage that you can see through such bandages. If the wound is on the trunk or you plan to bandage a limb only temporarily, apply several wraps of bandage firmly (not tightly) and directly over the wound. If the bandage is to be left on a limb for several hours or more, it should be applied over the wound and down the leg to cover the foot as well. This will prevent swelling and *ischemia* (lack of blood and oxygen) of the part of the limb below the bandage. This rule applies to bandaging the tail as well. If you cannot apply a pressure bandage, firm, *direct* pressure (with your bare hand, if necessary) over the wound for several minutes will often stop bleeding.

APPLYING A PRESSURE BANDAGE TO THE TAIL

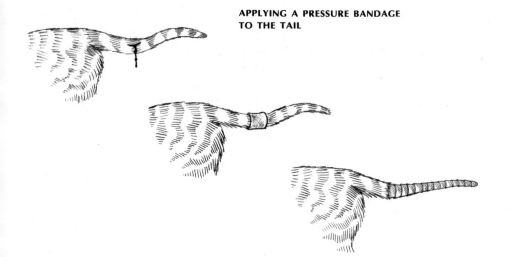

If a pressure bandage successfully stops the bleeding and no other problems are apparent, you can usually wait several hours or overnight, if necessary, to have the wound examined and treated. An exception is a chest wound in which there are air bubbles in the blood or that is accompanied by the sound of air moving in and out of it. Wounds like this may be associated with air leakage into the chest cavity from outside, which can cause difficulty breathing and fatal lung compression. Once covered, such wounds should remain so, and immediate veterinary aid should be sought. Do not disturb any foreign body protruding from such a wound before seeking a veterinarian's advice.

Most wounds severe enough to require a pressure bandage will need *suturing* (sewing closed) for proper and most rapid healing. (Any wound that gapes open is likely to benefit from suturing.)

TOURNIQUET

HOW TO APPLY A TOURNIQUET

A *tourniquet* is a second and *much less desirable* method of achieving hemostasis. Tourniquets are useful only for bleeding involving a limb or the tail. They should be loosened *at least* every fifteen minutes to allow reoxygenation of tissues. Use any strong cord, rope, bandage strip, or even a piece of panty hose to make a tourniquet. Form a loop and apply it to the extremity between the body and the wound. (It is easiest to apply it at a joint to prevent slippage.) Watch the change in blood flow to determine how tightly to tie the tourniquet. Proper application will usually cause an immediate and definite slowing of blood seepage. When you achieve sufficient slowing, stop tightening the tourniquet. (Don't expect a completely blood-free area.) Then consider replacing the tourniquet with a pressure bandage if at all possible.

HIT BY A CAR

The first thing to do if you find your cat hit by a car is to try to remain calm. This isn't easy, since your animal is so important to you, but hysterics will not help you or your cat. Try to assess the damage that has been done. You must gather information to help your veterinarian decide on the seriousness of the injuries before you get to the hospital. So concentrate your attention on this plan of action while administering first aid.

Many seriously injured animals try to run from the scene of the accident in fright, thereby increasing their injuries or becoming lost and unavailable for veterinary care. *Do not* leave your cat unattended for one second. If necessary ask a bystander to telephone your veterinarian, or carry your animal with you to the telephone. (But before moving any injured cat check for possible fractures or spinal cord damage. See below.)

First, evaluate your cat's vital signs. Look for signs of shock, consciousness, airway obstruction, breathing, and heartbeat. If the airway is obstructed, the cat is not breathing or seems unconscious, and you cannot detect a heartbeat, cardiopulmonary resuscitation (CPR) may be needed (see page 206). A fracture or large cut can be spectacular and frightening, but this matter takes secondary consideration. If signs of shock are present, be sure your cat gets professional veterinary care *at once.* If this is not possible and shock is present, indicating the possibility of internal bleeding, an elastic bandage wrapped firmly around the abdomen can be effective in raising blood pressure and limiting blood loss until veterinary aid can be obtained. Be sure any wrap you apply is firm but does not further compromise the breathing. **EVALUATE VITAL SIGNS**

Even a small amount of blood can make a wound appear to be more serious than it is. Try to determine the source of the blood loss. When you find the site, you will often find that the bleeding has stopped. **EXTERNAL AND INTERNAL BLEEDING**

If there is a great deal of bleeding from the wound, apply a makeshift pressure bandage (see page 203) or direct pressure to it. Persistent bleeding from the nose and/or mouth requires immediate veterinary care, as does blood in the urine or signs that indicate internal bleeding and/or injury (shock, abdominal pain, difficulty breathing).

A veterinarian should be consulted if you think your cat has a fractured limb, but the fracture itself may not be an emergency if the cat is doing well otherwise (see page 162). **BROKEN BONES**

Paralysis or partial paralysis may indicate spinal cord damage and requires that you keep the vertebral column as immobile as possible from the time of the accident until you arrive at the veterinary hospital (see page 164). A small box or cat carrier is the best means to carry a severely injured cat. If you can't determine the extent of the injury or do not have a makeshift carrier available, try carrying the cat as illustrated.

CARRYING AN INJURED CAT

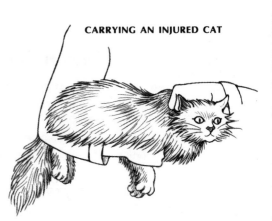

If you find that your cat seems essentially normal following an accident, you may not need to see a veterinarian. You should be aware, however, that certain major internal injuries may not be apparent for several hours (sometimes days) following such trauma, for example, diaphragmatic hernia.

A *diaphragmatic hernia* results when a tear in the diaphragm allows the abdominal organs to move through it into the chest. If the tear occurs at the time of an accident but the actual hernia does not (or is mild), you may not see any signs. When the abdominal organs herniate (or a small hernia gets worse), strained respiration ensues. Lack of appetite, difficulty swallowing, or vomiting may be seen. If you try to hear the heart sounds, they may be absent or muffled. If a large portion of the abdominal organs have moved into the chest, you may notice a "tucked up" abdomen. Watch for signs indicating possible diaphragmatic hernia for several weeks following any severe accident.

Be sure to watch for signs of normal urination following incidents involving abdominal trauma, such as that suffered when a cat is hit by a car. Cats with ruptured bladders may act normal at first, then later develop abdominal pain or their abdomens may be very tender when first examined. If urination is completely absent, or urine is blood-stained, or if normal-looking urine is passed with some difficulty, suspect a ruptured bladder, which is a surgical emergency.

If your cat is not examined by a veterinarian following an accident be sure to perform a thorough physical examination yourself, and watch your cat closely for signs of shock for twenty-four hours (keep the animal indoors). Don't forget to examine the abdomen thoroughly by palpation. If your cat shows signs of pain such as tensing (contracting) the abdominal muscles more than usual or crying out, or if the abdomen feels unusual to you (too few, too many, or unusually shaped masses present), be sure to arrange for an examination by a veterinarian.

CARDIOPULMONARY RESUSCITATION (CPR)

Cardiopulmonary resuscitation (CPR) is an important emergency life-saving technique to know, although it is rarely needed by pet owners. CPR is used whenever there is an event or illness that causes breathing or the heartbeat to stop, such as drowning, electric shock, or choking. It can also be used to assist severely impaired breathing or heart function. Signs that indicate the need for CPR include unconsciousness accompanied by absence of a heartbeat, absence of a pulse, mucous membranes that are gray, blue, or white (pale pink or normal pink color may be present if aid is administered immediately), dilated pupils, and failure to breathe. CPR must be administered within three to five minutes of respiratory and/or cardiac arrest to be effective. Its two components, artificial respiration and external heart massage, are described below.

ARTIFICIAL RESPIRATION

Any occasion in which you have to resort to artificial respiration is an emergency (except perhaps in a newborn kitten that is slow to start breathing). Don't spend all your time trying to revive the cat on the spot. As soon as your veterinarian is contacted, head for the clinic while continuing attempts at resuscitation.

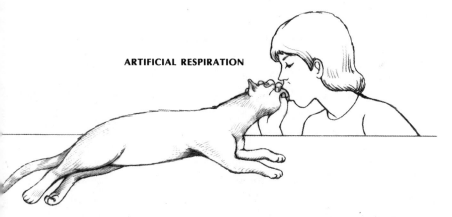

ARTIFICIAL RESPIRATION

SIGNS OF DEATH Artificial respiration serves no purpose in an already dead animal. Place your ear on the unconscious cat's chest and listen for a heartbeat; feel for a pulse (see page 32). If no pulse or heartbeat is detectable and the pupils are dilated and nonresponsive to light, it is probable that death has already occurred and that your first aid will be useless. However, you can try external heart massage (see page 208).

To administer artificial respiration, open the cat's mouth, pull out the tongue, and look as far back into the pharynx as possible to see if there are any obstructions. If you can't see anything, it is a good idea to feel for obstructions with your fingers and remove any you find. However, you must take extraordinary care when doing this as a bite from a semiconscious animal can be severe. Wipe away excessive mucous or blood in the pharynx that might interfere with the flow of air. Extend the cat's head and neck. Then close the cat's mouth. Inhale. Holding the cat's mouth closed, place your mouth over his or her nose (cover it completely) and exhale, forcing the exhaled air through the cat's nose into the chest. Since cats are small your mouth may cover the whole *anterior* (front) part of the muzzle. Watch for the chest to expand as you blow. After inflating the lungs in this manner, remove your mouth to allow the chest to return to its original (deflated) position. Repeat the inflation-deflation cycle twelve to twenty-four times per minute as long as necessary. If the heart is beating and you have been quick to relieve an airway obstruction, respiration may resume within a few minutes. These procedures put the resuscitator at significant risk of accidental injury and should be undertaken only by those willing to assume such risk.

EXTERNAL HEART MASSAGE
(EXTERNAL CARDIAC COMPRESSION)

External heart massage is used in an attempt to maintain circulation when cardiac arrest has occurred. If you cannot feel a pulse or heartbeat in an unconscious and nonbreathing cat, you may try external cardiac compression.

Heart arrest automatically follows respiratory arrest; when heart arrest occurs first, breathing soon stops. Therefore, *cardiac massage must be combined with artificial respiration if any benefit is to be gained.* Irreversible damage to the brain is believed to occur after three minutes without oxygen. This implies that heart compression must be started within three to five minutes following cardiac arrest to be of benefit. Place the cat on his or her side on a firm surface. Place your hands on the side of the chest over the heart and compress the chest firmly. Then completely release the pressure. Don't be rough, but don't worry too much about damage to the chest: getting effective circulation going is more important, and it has been shown that chest compression, not actual heart compression, is probably most important in maintaining blood circulation. The compression/release cycle should be repeated 120 times per minute.

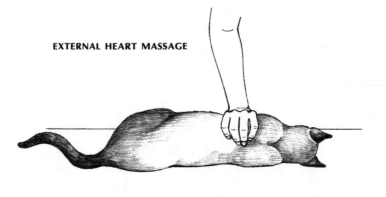

EXTERNAL HEART MASSAGE

You can also achieve effective cardiac massage by applying pressure on the heart area with one hand on each side of the chest wall or with the fingers of a single hand wrapped around the chest. If your actions are effective, you should be able to feel a pulse (see page 32) with each massage. If you are unassisted, try to intersperse an artificial respiration for every ten cardiac compressions. Otherwise have your assistant give a respiration at the same time as every other heart compression, since simultaneous chest compression and lung inflation have been shown to provide the best circulatory results.

While attempts to restart the heart are being made, try to get the animal to a veterinarian. Don't expect the animal to revive during your attempts at resuscitation before obtaining veterinary services. If consciousness resumes, however, keep the cat warm and quiet and proceed to a veterinary hospital where observation can continue.

CONVULSIONS

Convulsions (seizures) include a wide variety of signs consisting primarily of abnormal behavior and/or abnormal body movements. The most easily recognized signs are *loss* (or disturbance) *of consciousness, loss of motor control,* and *involuntary urination* and/or *defecation.* Convulsions fall into two main categories in terms of whether or not they are emergencies:

1. The single convulsion, which lasts for a minute or two and does not recur for at least twenty-four hours.
2. Repeated or continuous convulsions.

Convulsions in the second category require immediate veterinary attention. Cats with convulsions in the first category should be examined by a veterinarian, but may not require emergency care.

The most important thing for you to do if your cat is having a **RESTRAINT IS** convulsion is to provide gentle restraint so he or she will not become **IMPORTANT** injured. One of the best ways is to place a light blanket or towel over the cat. It's not a good idea to place your hand on the cat or in or near the cat's mouth unless you are willing to risk serious scratches or bites. Airway occlusion by the tongue rarely occurs. While one person restrains the cat, another can try to reach a veterinarian. Seizures in the first category are often past by the time you get in touch with a veterinarian.

POISONING

Emergency situations involving convulsions occur commonly follow-ing poisoning. Cats are extremely sensitive to the effects of many chemicals used commonly in the house and garden, but because of their habits they are seldom seen ingesting poisonous substances. Instead, an owner often becomes aware the poisoning has occurred only after signs of toxicity, such as convulsions, develop. Try to prevent poisoning from common household products by reading their labels carefully and using them appropriately. Any product labeled hazardous for humans should be assumed to be toxic to your cat as well. Outdoors, avoid the use of organophosphate and chlori-nated hydrocarbon insecticides (see chart), snail bait, herbicides, fungicides, and rodent poisons if there is even the slightest chance your cat may come into contact with them.

GENERAL TREATMENT OF POISONING

1. If you see your cat ingest a toxic substance, read the label to see if specific instructions for treatment are given. If not, induce vomiting unless the material is corrosive (a strong acid or alkali or a petroleum distillate, e.g., kerosene). The most reliable way to cause vomiting is to administer *syrup of ipecac, USP* (2% alcohol, 7% glycerine, sold over the counter in drugstores), about 1 teaspoonful per 5 pounds of body weight (2 ml/kg). Vomiting should occur in 10 to 30 minutes. Another home remedy to induce vomiting is 3% *hydrogen peroxide* by mouth; give about 1 teaspoonful per 5 pounds of body weight, (2 ml/kg). If vomiting does not occur within 5 to 10 minutes, you can repeat the dose up to two more times. A much less effective way to cause vomiting is to place a teaspoon of salt on the back of the cat's tongue. As this method itself is potentially toxic, avoid it unless induction of vomiting is critical and there is no other product available. Then give milk mixed with a raw egg at ¼ cup per 10 pounds of body weight (13 ml/kg). If milk is not available, plain water can be used. (See the poison chart for treatments and times to use activated charcoal as the universal antidote.) *Do not induce vomiting if your cat is already losing consciousness or is beginning to convulse.* If veterinary care is immediately available, *do not waste time with home treatment.*

2. If your cat gets a toxic substance on his or her skin or in the eye, flush with large volumes of water while (or before) someone calls a veterinarian. Be sure to protect yourself from toxic exposure when rinsing or washing toxins from the fur.

3. If convulsions occur, try to restrain the cat.

4. Try to bring a sample of the suspected poison *in its original container* to the hospital. If this is not possible, bring a sample of any vomitus you find.

There are thousands of potentially toxic substances in the environ- ment, and new toxins are developed every day, making it impossible for any single book to provide current information on every toxic substance. Regional animal poison control centers in the United States and Canada help with this problem. The pioneer animal poison control center, the National Animal Poison Information Center, provides a twenty-four-hour toll-free number, (800) 548-2423, to assist with poisoning problems in animals. Information is available to both pet owners and veterinarians for a fee that must be paid at the time the call is made (credit cards are accepted). Local human poison control centers can also provide information on toxic ingredients in pesticides, insecticides, medicines.

COMMON HOUSEHOLD POISONS AND THEIR IMMEDIATE TREATMENT

POISON	TYPICAL PRODUCTS CONTAINING IT	SIGNS THAT MAY OCCUR AFTER EXPOSURE	IMMEDIATE TREATMENT
Acids	Car batteries, some metal cleaners, antirust agents, swimming pool cleaners	Local white, gray, or black burns; pain, shock, vomiting, respiratory distress, other	*Externally*: Flush copiously with water. *Internally*: Do not induce vomiting, give milk or water to dilute.
Alkali	Cleaning products, lye, drain openers	Local white, gray, or black burns; pain, shock, vomiting, respiratory distress, other	*Externally:* Flush copiously with water. *Internally:* Do not induce vomiting; give milk or water to dilute

POISON	TYPICAL PRODUCTS CONTAINING IT	SIGNS THAT MAY OCCUR AFTER EXPOSURE	IMMEDIATE TREATMENT
Amphetamines, caffeine	Diet and stimulant pills	Dilated pupils, restlessness, rapid heartbeat, muscle tremors, vomiting, seizures, coma	Induce vomiting; follow with activated charcoal*
Arsenic	Ant poisons, herbicides, insecticides	Vomiting, restlessness, abdominal pain, diarrhea, (may be bloody)	Induce vomiting; follow with milk or tea.
Brodifacoum, bromadiolone, diphacinone, fumarin, pindone, valone, warfarin, chloro-phacinone	Rodent poisons	Hemorrhage, mainly internal; pale mucous membranes, weakness, vomiting or diarrhea (may be bloody), pain, difficulty breathing	Induce vomiting; consult veterinarian immediately. No effective home remedy. Signs may not appear for hours or days.
Bromethelin	Rodent poisons	Weakness, paralysis, tremors, seizures	Induce vomiting; consult veterinarian immediately. No effective home remedy. Signs may not appear for hours or days; repeated doses of activated charcoal* necessary.

POISON	TYPICAL PRODUCTS CONTAINING IT	SIGNS THAT MAY OCCUR AFTER EXPOSURE	IMMEDIATE TREATMENT
Carbamates	Antiflea sprays, powders, foggers; slug and snail bait; ant, roach, and water bug baits	Drooling, small pupils, abdominal pain, vomiting, diarrhea, difficulty breathing, muscle tremors, weakness, paralysis, restlessness, seizures, coma	*Externally:* Flush copiously with water followed by mild detergent baths. *Internally:* No good home remedy; rush to veterinarian. If veterinary care not available, induce vomiting before convulsion stage. Follow with activated charcoal.*
Cholecalciferol	Rodent poisons	Vomiting, depression, not eating, excessive thirst and urination, kidney pain	Induce vomiting; consult veterinarian immediately. No effective home remedy. Signs may not appear for hours or days.
Ethylene glycol	Antifreeze (2 tsp. will kill a 5-lb. animal)	Immediate treatment necessary to prevent death; *do not* wait for signs to appear	Induce vomiting and rush to veterinarian.

POISON	TYPICAL PRODUCTS CONTAINING IT	SIGNS THAT MAY OCCUR AFTER EXPOSURE	IMMEDIATE TREATMENT
Fertilizer (NPK)	Houseplant and garden plant food	Vomiting, diarrhea, dehydration	Give water or milk to dilute. Take to veterinarian if signs develop.
Lead	Paints, solder, fishing weights, used motor oil, food or water fed from improperly glazed pottery	Lack of appetite, vomiting, diarrhea, constipation, abdominal pain, behavioral changes from subtle to seizures and blindness	*Externally:* Bathe thoroughly using nonalcohol-based detergent. *Internally:* Induce vomiting followed by Epsom salts (250–500 mg/kg diluted in 5–10 volumes water). All exposure suspects need a veterinarian's evaluation as signs may not develop until long after exposure.
Metaldehyde	Snail bait	Restlessness, incoordination, muscle tremors, vomiting, convulsions	Induce vomiting if signs not yet present.

POISON	TYPICAL PRODUCTS CONTAINING IT	SIGNS THAT MAY OCCUR AFTER EXPOSURE	IMMEDIATE TREATMENT
Methanol, other alcohols	Windshield washer fluid; automotive, medicinal, and cleaning products; fuels, wood finishes	Excitability, incoordination, depression, coma, respiratory and cardiac arrest	*Externally:* Flush copiously with water followed by soap baths. *Internally:* Activated charcoal.* Rush to veterinarian.
Nonsteroidal anti-inflammatory drugs (NSAIDs)	Pain, cold, cough, or allergy remedies containing, e.g., acetaminophen, aspirin, ibuprofen	Vomiting, diarrhea, gastrointestinal bleeding, lack of appetite, abdominal pain, death	Induce vomiting followed by activated charcoal.* Consult veterinarian.
Organochlorines	Antiflea dips, insecticidal shampoos, ant and roach baits, garden insecticides	Drooling, small pupils, abdominal pain, vomiting, diarrhea, difficulty breathing, muscle tremors, weakness, paralysis, restlessness, seizures, coma	*Externally:* Flush copiously with water followed by mild detergent baths. *Internally:* No good home remedy; rush to veterinarian. If veterinary care not available, induce vomiting before convulsion stage. Follow with activated charcoal.*

POISON	TYPICAL PRODUCTS CONTAINING IT	SIGNS THAT MAY OCCUR AFTER EXPOSURE	IMMEDIATE TREATMENT
Organophosphates	Antiflea sprays, powders, foggers, dips, collars; ant and roach killers; dewormers, pest strips	Drooling, small pupils, abdominal pain, vomiting, diarrhea, difficulty breathing, muscle tremors, weakness, paralysis, restlessness, seizures, coma	*Externally:* Flush copiously with water followed by mild detergent baths. *Internally:* No good home remedy; rush to veterinarian. If veterinary care not available, induce vomiting before convulsion stage. Follow with activated charcoal.*
Petroleum distillates, turpentine	Kerosene, gasoline, solvent carriers for pesticides, wood finishes, furniture polishes, lighter fluids, lamp oils	Difficulty breathing, vomiting, diarrhea, skin irritation	*Externally:* Bathe thoroughly with nonalcohol-based detergent. *Internally:* Do not induce vomiting. Consult vet. Minimal exposure may not be serious.

POISON	TYPICAL PRODUCTS CONTAINING IT	SIGNS THAT MAY OCCUR AFTER EXPOSURE	IMMEDIATE TREATMENT
Phenol (carbolic acid)	Household disinfectants and antiseptics, wood preservatives, fungicides, herbicides, photographic developer	Incoordination, muscle tremors, depression, unconsciousness	Wash with soap and water. Induce vomiting.
Phosphorous	Strike-anywhere matches (safety matches are nontoxic), rat poison, fireworks	Vomiting, diarrhea, abdominal pain; apparent recovery may be followed by relapse and death	Induce vomiting followed by activated charcoal.* Consult veterinarian.
Salicylate (aspirin)	Aspirin	Weakness, lack of appetite, vomiting, fever, incoordination, convulsions	Avoid use; spontaneous consumption unlikely
Strychnine	Rodent poisons, malicious poisonings	Restlessness, incoordination, muscle tremors, convulsions	Induce vomiting if signs not yet present.

POISON	TYPICAL PRODUCTS CONTAINING IT	SIGNS THAT MAY OCCUR AFTER EXPOSURE	IMMEDIATE TREATMENT
Theobromine	Chocolate (3 oz. baking or 1.5 lb. milk chocolate can kill a 20-lb dog; equivalent quantities are unknown for cats)	Dilated pupils, restlessness, rapid heartbeat, muscle tremors, vomiting, seizures, coma	Induce vomiting; follow with activated charcoal*

*Do not waste time trying to administer activated charcoal if veterinary aid is nearby. It can be both difficult and messy to administer. Activated charcoal is available over the counter in drugstores in tablet or liquid form. The recommended initial dose is 1 to 4 grams per pound of body weight (2 to 8 gm/kg body weight). Multiple capsules are needed even for small pets. The liquid form is more effective. Familiarize yourself with the appropriate dose for your pet.

See page 113 for chemical names of typical insecticidal poisons.

POISONOUS PLANTS The list of potentially dangerous garden and houseplants is extremely long. Any plant not normally used for food is potentially toxic, so the best rule to follow to avoid problems is to not keep poisonous houseplants and to correct your cat whenever you find him or her chewing on any plant or floral arrangement. You can make houseplants somewhat more undesirable by spraying them with a dilute solution of perfume, hot pepper sauce, or citrus oil. Cats who have proper diets, plenty of attention and activity, and who are offered their own patch of catnip or fresh grass (see pages 80 and 168) rarely chew other plants. Although some plants have only certain poisonous parts, consider all parts, *including the roots, tubers, and bulbs,* dangerous until proven otherwise. Many plants considered poisonous have only local irritant properties, so a reasonable strategy to follow if there is no veterinary care available when a pet is found chewing on a plant is to rinse the mouth carefully with a stream of water. If there is evidence that some of the plant has actually been consumed, induce vomiting and follow with activated charcoal. When local veterinary care is unavailable, a call to the regional or veterinary poison control center may also yield advice.

Poinsettia (*Euphorbia pulcherrima*); *Philodendron* species; dumbcane (*Diffenbachia* species); members of the rhododendron family including azaleas; and mushrooms are the potentially poisonous plants pets consume most often. Although once thought to be highly toxic, poinsettias are now regarded as plants that are mainly gastrointestinal irritants. Most pets who chew on poinsettias develop no signs. A few begin to drool or vomit and have diarrhea. Similarly, a minimal exposure to philodendron or dumbcane may cause local irritation followed by drooling or vomiting. However, moderate exposure can result in swelling of the lips, tongue, and throat, which may produce laryngitis, tongue paralysis (rarely), and difficulty breathing (rarely). In rare cases, ingestion of philodendron or diffenbachia has resulted in later death from kidney failure.

Members of the *Rhododendron* genus and wild-growing outdoor mushrooms have great potential to cause death in any pet that eats them. As there are no specific antidotes for the toxins they can contain, a veterinarian's emergency aid is needed for animals poisoned by these plants.

TYPICAL POISONOUS PLANTS

Araceae family—dumbcane (*Diffenbachia* spp.), *Philodendron* spp., ceriman (*Monstera* spp.), elephant's ear (*Alocasia antiquorum*), calla lily, caladium, skunk cabbage, wild calla or water arum, malanga (*Xanthosoma* spp.)

Algae—blue-green algae bloom contaminates pond water in hot weather (*Microcystic aeruqinosa, Anabaena flos-aquae, Aphanizomenon flos-aquae*)

*Azalea (*Rhododendron* spp.)

Black locust (*Robinia* spp.)

Bleeding Heart (*Dicentra* spp.)

Bulbs—narcissus, daffodil, jonquil (*Narcissus* spp.); *Amaryllis* spp., naked lady amaryllis (*Brunvigia, Iris* spp.); Easter lily (*Lilium longiflorum*); glory lily (*Gloriosa* spp.); autumn crocus (*Colchicum* spp.)

Buckeye (*Aesculys* spp.)

Buttercups (*Ranunculus* spp.)

*Castor beans—castor oil plant, palma christi (*Ricinus communis*)

Chinaberry (*Melia azedarach*)

*Chokecherry (*Prunus virginiana*)
Daphne (*Daphne* spp.)
English ivy (*Hedera helix,* fruits especially)
*Foxglove (*Digitalis* spp.)
Golden chain (*Laburnum*)
Helleborus
Hydrangea
Larkspur (*Delphinium* spp.)
Lily of the valley (*Convallaria* spp.)
Marijuana (*Cannabis* spp.)
Mistletoe (*Phoradendron flavescens*)
*Monkshood (*Aconitum* spp.)
*Mushrooms—*Amanita, Gyromitra, Coprinus, Inocybe* spp.,
Clitocybe spp.
Nettles—*Urtica* spp., *Laportea* spp., *Cnidoscolus* spp.
Nightshade family—*Solanaceae* spp. all contain toxic agents at
some growth stage or in some plant part: *Datura stramonium*
(thornapple, jimsonweed); *Datura inoxia* (tolguacha, trumpet
vine, angel's-trumpet); *Datura arborea*; *Nicandra physalodes*
(apple-of-Peru); *Solanum nigrum* (black nightshade, common
nightshade); *Solanum dulcamara, Atropa belladonna, Pseudo
capsicum* (deadly nightshade, Jerusalem cherry, European bit-
tersweet, climbing nightshade); tobacco, potato; and tomato
leaves and stems
*Oleander—*Nerium oleander;* yellow oleander, yellow bestill
tree (*Thevitia peruviana*)
Poison hemlock (*Conium maculatum*)
Pokeweed (*Phytolacca*)
*Precatory beans (*Arbus precatorius*)
Spurges—snow-on-the-mountain, crown of thorns, candelabra
cactus, tinsel tree, poinsettia (*Euphorbia* spp.)
Walnut hulls (*Juglans regia, Juglans nigra*)
Water hemlock (*Cictua maculata*)
*Yew (*Taxus* spp.)

*Extremely toxic; ingestion of *very* small amounts often results in death.

SNAKEBITE

Although cases of snakebite in cats are rare, you should be aware of the first aid necessary in order to try to prevent death if your cat should be bitten by a snake. Prompt action by you and your veterinarian is necessary.

Bleeding puncture wounds or small tooth marks are common signs of envenomation. Bites of poisonous snakes may also cause severe pain if venom has been injected, so a bitten cat will often become excited and run. You should attempt to prevent this response, since exercise helps spread the venom. Immobilize the cat as soon as possible.

If the bite is on an extremity, apply a flat tourniquet between the body and the wound nearer the wound. The tourniquet should be loose enough barely to slip the end of one finger under it, and it should not be fully loosened until the bite is treated by a veterinarian or until two hours have passed. (This type of application allows some oxygen to reach the tissues beyond the tourniquet while inhibiting the flow of venom in the lymph and venous blood.) If possible, keep a bitten limb on a level horizontal with the heart. Then make a linear incision (not X-shaped) over the fang wounds and apply suction for at least thirty minutes, preferably not by mouth but with a suction cup. The value of suction in limiting the spread of venom is controversial. For coral snake bites, in particular, copious flushing of the wound with water and germicidal soap is recommended. Another excellent alternative is to apply a tight compression bandage that includes both the bite wound and a wide area on both sides of it. Elastic bandage material or strips of panty hose are good for this purpose. Do not remove the bandage before getting veterinary aid within twenty-four hours. If veterinary care is nearby, don't waste time with prolonged attempts at first aid. The successful treatment of serious snake bite requires prompt antivenin injection and prolonged intensive supportive care in a veterinary hospital. Since a cat in pain is difficult to handle, the best first aid may be only to apply a tight tourniquet and acquire veterinary aid within fifteen minutes. Besides antivenin the veterinarian will administer antibiotics and pain relievers, and can administer other medical treatment as called for. It may be necessary to remove a large portion of the wound surgically. Even if this is not done, snakebites often cause large portions of skin to die and slough off, leaving a large wound that must be treated. Plan on your cat being hospitalized for a minimum of twenty-four to forty-eight hours.

TOAD POISONING

Toads have glands in their skin that secrete substances that are bad tasting to cats and that can cause local irritation and drooling. At least two toad species, the Colorado toad (*Bufo alvarius*) and the marine toad (*Bufo marinus*) are very toxic. Should you observe your cat mouthing or playing with a toad, flush his or her mouth thoroughly with water (a carefully directed stream from a garden hose can be effective). Contact with poisonous toads requires *immediate* veterinary care as well, since heart irregularities often develop that can result in death less than thirty minutes after contact.

FISHHOOKS IN SKIN

Fishhooks become embedded easily in the skin. Once the barb has passed under the skin, a hook will not fall out on its own. The only way to remove it is to push the barb through the skin. Once through, cut the curved part of the hook just below the barb and pull the rest of the hook back out through the original hole. Often this procedure is too painful to be accomplished without anesthesia, so don't be surprised if you need the help of a veterinarian. Veterinary services are needed to administer appropriate antibiotics as well. Unless the hook was *extremely* clean, this type of wound is likely to become infected.

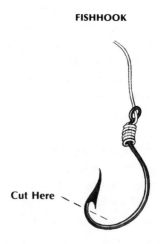

FISHHOOK

Cut Here

PORCUPINE QUILLS IN SKIN

The important thing to remember about a porcupine quill in the skin is to remove the *whole* thing. Grasp the quill with a pair of pliers near the point where it disappears into the skin, then, with a quick tug, pull it out. If the quill breaks off as you try to remove it or if some of the quills have broken off before you had a chance to try to remove them, you may need a veterinarian's help. *Do not* ignore pieces of quill you cannot pull from the skin. They can migrate long distances (sometimes into bone or internal organs), carrying sources of infection with them. And remember to check for quills inside the mouth as well as in the body surface.

INSECT BITE OR STING

Owners usually become aware of insect bites or stings long after they have happened. Usually a large swelling of the muzzle tissue or a foot is noticed with no particular evidence of pain. Other times, but rarely in cats, hives (bumps in the skin) appear. These are allergic reactions to the bite or sting. If there is no fever and if the cat acts normally (even though abnormal in appearance), no treatment is usually necessary, but pull out the stinger if you see it. Swelling should go away within forty-eight hours. With spider bites, the swelling may last for days or weeks and may sometimes be accompanied by death and sloughing off of tissue at the site of the bite. If you catch the bite early; if your cat receives multiple stings from bees, wasps, or hornets; or if the signs are progressing to those of severe allergic reaction, *anaphylaxis,* (e.g., difficulty breathing, vomiting, diarrhea, urination followed by shock and collapse), consult a veterinarian. Emergency supportive care may be needed, and various drugs including corticosteroids may be administered to prevent signs or further progression of signs that are already apparent.

BURNS

THERMAL BURNS

Burns may be thermal, chemical, or electrical (electric shock). The severity of *thermal* (heat) burns in cats may be underestimated because the appearance of burns in cats differs considerably from those in humans. The type of blister characteristic of superficial burns in humans may not form in the burned skin of a cat. In a superficial burn, the hair remains firmly attached. If you pull on the hair in the area of a burn and it comes out easily, the burn is deeper and more serious.

Immediate treatment of thermal burns consists of applying cold water or ice compresses for twenty minutes. The affected area should then be washed with povidone-iodine or chlorhexidine disinfectant. Neomycin–polymixin B–bacitracin cream can then be applied topically if the burn is minor. Deep burns or burns covering large areas need emergency veterinary care. Because of the difficulty in evaluating the severity of burns in cat's skin immediately after their occurrence, it is a good idea to have all burns examined by a veterinarian within twenty-four hours.

ELECTRICAL BURNS (ELECTRIC SHOCK)

Electrical burns occur often in kittens who chew on electric cords. These burns cause severe damage to the skin of the mouth and may result in *pulmonary edema* (fluid in the lungs). Cats sustaining such burns should be thoroughly examined by a veterinarian as soon as you become aware of the injury. If difficulty breathing or coughing occurs, pulmonary edema may be present. In severe cases the tongue and gums may look bluish. If you find your cat unconscious and not breathing after electric shock, administer artificial respiration (see page 207) once you have carefully and safely removed the cat from the electrical source. Even if general signs do not develop after electric shock, mouth tissue damaged by the burn often dies and sloughs off several days later and needs veterinary attention. Electrical burns are characteristically cold, bloodless, pale yellow, and painless.

CHEMICAL BURNS

For information on chemical burns, see *Acids and Alkali* in the chart of common household poisons, page 211.

HEAT STRESS (HEAT STROKE, HEAT PROSTRATION)

Heat stress occurs most often in cats who have been confined to a car (or other enclosure) with inadequate ventilation on a warm day. Temperatures inside a parked, poorly ventilated car can rapidly reach over 100°F (37.8°C) on a relatively mild 75 to 80°F (23.9 to 26.7°C) day even in the shade. Heat stress can also occur in cats suddenly transported to a hot climate to which they have not previously been acclimatized. Kittens, short-faced cats such as Persians, fat cats, and older cats are more subject to heat stress than others are.

SIGNS OF HEAT STRESS *Signs of heat stress are panting, increased pulse rate, congested mucous membranes* (reddened gums), *and an anxious or staring expression.* Vomiting may occur. Stupor and unconsciousness may follow if the stress is allowed to continue long enough. Rectal temperatures are elevated (106 to 109°F, 41.1 to 42.8°C). Immediate treatment by immersion (up to the cat's neck) in cool water is necessary. If you cannot immerse the cat, spray him or her with cool water. Cold packs applied to the neck and abdominal area can help. Fanning will speed cooling by evaporation. Massage the skin and flex and extend the legs to return blood from the peripheral circulation. Then get your cat to a veterinary hospital where treatment can be continued.

Cats sustaining heat stress should always be examined by a veterinarian, but if this is impossible, the cat's temperature should be taken frequently over a twenty-four-hour period because elevation of the rectal temperature often recurs after the initial drop and first signs of improvement. It has been suggested that if the rectal temperature has not reached 103° F in ten to fifteen minutes after starting treatment, a cold water enema should be given. Following this treatment, however, the rectal temperature is no longer accurate.

Prevent heat stroke by carrying water with you when you travel on hot days and by frequently offering your cat small amounts to drink. Wet towels placed directly over your cat or over the carrier will provide cooling by evaporation, as will wetting your cat's fur with water. Open the car windows when a cat is left inside, or better yet, don't leave the animal in the car. Although clipping a long-haired cat's fur may provide a little more comfort in hot weather, it is not an effective way to prevent heat prostration.

YOU CAN PREVENT HEAT STRESS

FROSTBITE AND/OR HYPOTHERMIA

Cats rarely experience frostbite (cold injury caused by freezing of tissue) or hypothermia (lowered body temperature) when left outdoors in cold weather if they have been properly acclimatized, are adequately fed, and have access to shelter that prevents their fur from becoming wet. However, even short periods can be dangerous for animals who have recently moved from a warm climate to a cold one, for very young, very small, short-haired, sick, and/or old cats, and for any animals whose fur is wet in cool and/or windy weather. Kittens under four weeks of age may become hypothermic at room temperatures between 65° and 85°F (18.3° and 29.4°C) if they are separated from their mother or littermates (see page 289). Although frostbite and hypothermia often occur together, a severely frostbitten pet may not become hypothermic and vice versa. Prevent frostbite and hypothermia in cold weather that you would consider unsafe for a child by never leaving your pet outdoors without access to warm, dry, draft-free shelter.

Frostbite usually affects the tips of the ears, tail, and the foot pads. When first frostbitten, the skin looks pale and feels cool to the touch, and it is insensitive to painful stimuli. Later the skin may die and fall (slough) off. In less serious cases of frostbite, the skin may never slough off, but hair may fall out and grow back white although it was previously dark colored.

Signs indicating hypothermia may not be accompanied by frostbite. They include decreased mental alertness, shivering, weak or absent pulse, slowed heart rate, and slowed, shallow respirations. Shivering stops when the body temperature drops below 90°F (32.2°C). Animals whose temperatures drop to 75°F (23.8°C) usually die.

Rewarming is the treatment for both frostbite and hypothermia. If veterinary care is immediately available, do not attempt home treatment. Wrap your pet (and a hot-water bottle, if available) in a blanket, warm jacket, or other insulator to retain any remaining body warmth, and rush to the veterinary clinic for treatment. Should veterinary care be unavailable, home care will be necessary.

If frostbite is unaccompanied by signs of hypothermia, treatment is directed only at the injured areas. Do not rub the areas, but apply moist heat by immersing the part in warm water (102 to 104°F, 38.9 to 40°C) or by applying warm, moist towels. Rapid return of sensation, pink color, and warmth to the skin indicate successful treatment.

If the cat's temperature is above 86°F (30°C), simple home treatment for hypothermia is often successful. Bring the pet into a warm room and cover him or her. Warm water bottles (102 to 104°F, 38.9 to 40°C) placed inside a blanket wrapped around the cat help speed rewarming. Be sure to rewarm the water as soon as the temperature drops below 100°F (37.8°C). This can be done in a microwave oven to avoid repeated refilling of bottles. Electric heating pads may also be used if they are well insulated with toweling and the animal is turned frequently to prevent burns. Water-circulating heating pads or chemical gel warming bags are safe and ideal for providing heat. Immersion of the body in warm water (102 to 104°F, 38.9 to 40°C) can also be done if a hair drier or heater is available to prevent rechilling on removal of the pet from the water. The body temperature should be maintained just above 100°F (37.8°C) until thermoregulation resumes and the animal's temperature returns to normal.

CHOKING

Cats have a highly developed gag reflex, and they rarely try to swallow large pieces of food or objects that could cause choking. However, should your cat look as if he or she is choking, a thorough examination of the mouth and pharynx must be performed immediately, since suffocation will occur if the airway is blocked. *If your cat has been choking and is unconscious and not breathing, follow the procedures for artificial respiration on page 207.*

If resuscitation is not needed, remove any obstructing debris from the mouth that you can reach with your fingers or a pair of tweezers, keeping in mind that any cat, and especially a distressed one, can inflict severe bite wounds to fingers and hands placed in or near the mouth. So do not attempt to remove obstructing debris by hand if you are unwilling to risk a bite.

If you can't reach an obstruction, grasp the cat around the abdomen just behind the ribs, tip his or her nose toward the ground, and give a quick squeeze to cause a forced exhalation that may dislodge the object. (This is a Heimlich maneuver for cats.) Avoid swinging a cat by his or her hindlegs to achieve the nose-down position, as you may dislocate the hips. **HEIMLICH MANEUVER**

An alternative maneuver is to lay the cat on his or her side and use the heel of your hand to exert a thrust toward the head just behind the last rib. Three or four quick, firm but controlled pushes will cause forced exhalation that may dislodge the object. If you are unsuccessful with these actions, seek immediate veterinary assistance.

(Rabid cats have been reported to act as if they were choking. Do not attempt to examine the mouth of any cat whose rabies vaccination and exposure status is unknown if you are not willing to assume the risk of rabies exposure).

FALLS (HIGH-RISE SYNDROME)

Cats are renowned for their agility and their jumping and climbing abilities. The saying that "Cats always land on their feet" has some truth to it, since cats' air-righting reflexes are highly developed and they will normally turn in the air to land with their feet facing the ground if dropped from any significant height. Nevertheless, cats are not immune to injury from falls.

Falling is a particularly serious danger in the city where apartments may be located several stories above the ground. Cats fall so often and are injured so characteristically that veterinarians have begun to call the problem the "high-rise syndrome." Cats who fall two stories or more usually suffer severe injuries that include a split hard palate, nose bleed, free air in the chest due to rupture of the lung (pneumothorax), and fracture of the lower jaw. Broken teeth, broken legs, and limb dislocations are also common. Some cats suffer ruptured diaphragms and/or bladders and injury to other abdominal organs such as the liver and kidneys. **THE HIGH-RISE SYNDROME**

Cats receiving proper emergency care often survive even after falling more than eighteen stories. In fact, the number of fractures that are sustained actually decreases in cats falling more than seven stories. Prevention, though, is far better and far less expensive than any treatment. **PREVENTION IS THE BEST TREATMENT FOR FALLS**

Prevent serious injuries to your cat by keeping windows closed if you live on upper floors or by confining your cat to a safe, interior room or travel crate when windows must be opened. Closely supervise any outdoor activity on patios, decks, or balconies above ground level. A cat sleeping peacefully in the sun one minute can easily be leaping over the balcony edge after a bird in the next, and kittens are even more likely to leap before they look.

ECLAMPSIA (PUERPERAL TETANY, MILK FEVER)

Eclampsia (*puerperal tetany*) usually occurs in mother cats within two or three weeks after delivery, although it can occur before delivery. Though the exact mechanism is unknown, it is due to a defect in calcium metabolism that results in an abnormally low blood calcium level when calcium stores cannot be mobilized to keep up with calcium losses in the milk. Although it occurs infrequently in cats, heavily lactating females with large litters seem predisposed to the disease.

The first signs are often restlessness, distressed meowing, and rapid breathing. Spontaneous recovery may result, or the signs may progress to stiffness and muscle spasms, incoordination, inability to stand, convulsions, and fever. *Progressive tetany is an emergency that must be treated by a veterinarian.* Calcium preparations are given intravenously. Kittens are removed from nursing for at least twelve to twenty-four hours. Sometimes they may be returned for restricted nursing later, but this must be supplemented by hand-feeding. Kittens old enough to eat solid food are weaned. Calcium-phosphorus-vitamin D supplements are often prescribed for queens who must continue restricted nursing.

Certain females seem predisposed to milk fever, and it may be advisable not to rebreed these females. A ration adequate in calcium, phosphorus, and vitamin D should be fed throughout pregnancy. Veterinarians feel that oversupplementation with calcium may help induce milk fever. Therefore, supplementation during pregnancy should be with balanced vitamin-mineral preparations used cautiously. Discuss this problem in detail with your veterinarian if your female will be bred.

URINARY OBSTRUCTION

Obstruction of the urethra is a common cause of inability to urinate in cats. If the obstruction is not relieved it may cause rupture of the urinary bladder. For more information, see page 177.

GERIATRIC MEDICINE
(CARE AS YOUR CAT AGES)

The life expectancy of cats varies considerably between individuals and with the kind of health care received throughout their lives. Most well-cared-for cats can be expected to live between ten and fifteen years, and many reach the age of twenty. A few cats have even been reported to have lived more than thirty years. The record is claimed to be 36.

In general the older cat is less adaptable to stress. Sudden changes in diet, routine, or environment are probably best avoided if they have not been part of the cat's routine in the past. Many old cats do not adapt well to hospitalization and therefore need special care when ill. Good veterinarians are aware of this and provide special attention or make special arrangements for the care of such older animals.

OLD CATS MAY NOT ADJUST WELL TO CHANGES

If you have been feeding your cat a well-balanced diet throughout his or her life, few if any changes will be needed in old age unless special health conditions develop. Special diets need to be provided for older cats with degenerative changes of major organs such as the kidneys. Many other times the addition of a balanced vitamin-mineral supplement to the normal diet is sufficient to meet any special needs imposed by aging. Sometimes strong-smelling foods, such as those containing fish or fish oil, stimulate a lagging appetite that is the result of decreased ability to smell or taste. Since each cat is an individual and ages as an individual, the need for a special diet should be discussed with a veterinarian familiar with your aging cat before any major dietary changes are made.

GERIATRIC DIET

Most cats continue to exercise and play to the degree they have most of their lives well into old age. Only rarely is there a reason to restrict an older cat's activity, and the best rule to follow is to allow your cat to exercise as he or she chooses. Watch carefully for sudden changes in activity and exercise intolerance; they can indicate illness.

GERIATRIC EXERCISE

Some conditions that are likely to develop in cats with age are covered in this section. Not all are disabling or progressive, and most, if recognized early, can be treated at least palliatively. To use this section for diagnosing signs, refer to the Index of Signs on page 305 as well as to the General Index.

DEAFNESS

Gradual loss of hearing occurs as cats age, but not as frequently as in older dogs. The anatomical changes responsible for hearing loss in old cats are not well established, and treatment is not possible. Inattentiveness or unresponsiveness to calling is often one of the first signs of hearing loss. A crude test for hearing ability is to stand behind the cat and make a sudden sound, such as a whistle, hand clap, or sharp call. Most cats will cock their ears toward the sound or turn their heads. Hands clapped near the ear (but not near or in front of the eyes) may cause both eyes to blink in response to the sound. Most cats also come running when they hear the sounds of food preparation in the kitchen. If your elderly cat is hungry at mealtime but no longer responds to these auditory cues, suspect hearing impairment. Since hearing-impaired cats are at greater risk of injury they are safest when kept indoors and allowed outdoors only under close supervision.

DIABETES MELLITUS

Diabetes mellitus (diabetes) is a disease that occurs most often in cats older than seven. It develops when an absolute or relative deficiency of the pancreatic hormone *insulin* occurs, interfering with the normal transport and utilization of glucose (blood sugar). Diabetes mellitus in cats is identical to the disease that occurs in people and in dogs, sometimes called "sugar diabetes."

Signs of diabetes mellitus include increased drinking and urination and increased appetite. As the disease progresses weight loss occurs despite the increased appetite. Eventually, lethargy, vomiting, diarrhea, rapid respiration, weakness, and complete collapse will occur in untreated cats. A veterinarian can confirm the diagnosis of diabetes mellitus by a combination of blood and urine glucose tests.

TREATMENT OF DIABETES MELLITUS Treatment includes controlled feeding of special reduced calorie/high fiber diets and the administration of insulin. Oral drugs used to lower blood sugar in humans are occasionally used in treatment of cats. Traditionally insulin has been given by injection, but other methods of administration such as implantable insulin pumps or permeable insulin administration units may be available when the cost is not prohibitive. Veterinarians train owners of cats who require ongoing insulin administration to control blood sugar levels to give the injections at home.

Diabetes has been shown to be more prevalent in obese cats and in neutered male cats (who are often allowed to become obese). It is also more prevalent in cats who have been given certain drugs such as adrenocorticosteroids (see page 262) or progesterone-like drugs that are sometimes used to treat certain behavioral problems or skin diseases. Cats weighing more than 15 pounds (6.8 kg) are twice as likely to become diabetic than those weighing less, and many diabetic cats' blood sugar levels return to normal when they are treated with diet restriction and weight reduction alone. Help prevent diabetes in your older cat by avoiding unnecessary drug administration and by maintaining a normal weight. (For information on weight reduction, see page 174.)

HEART DISEASE

Heart disease may occur in cats of any age. When it develops in an older cat it may be overlooked until the heart is in severe failure and the animal is in a crisis situation. The first outwardly visible compensation a cat may make for decreased heart function is reduced activity that many owners attribute incorrectly to the aging process, thereby overlooking the signs of heart disease. If you suspect heart disease in your elderly cat, count his or her heart and pulse rates. Heart rates slower than 100 beats per minute, above 160 beats per minute in a relaxed, resting cat (above 200 in a *slightly* agitated cat), or heart rates that are irregular and/or are unaccompanied by an equal pulse rate should prompt you to have a veterinarian examine your cat. Do not attribute any unexplained decrease in activity to the aging process alone until a thorough medical workup rules out other causes. For more information on heart disease in cats, see page 188.

IRIS ATROPHY

Iris atrophy is a degenerative condition of the iris that is not uncommon in old cats. The normally solid-looking iris tissue takes on a "moth-eaten" or "Swiss cheese" like appearance due to the breakdown of the iris fibers that is followed by the development of actual holes. Iris atrophy causes no problems for affected cats and needs no treatment.

LENS SCLEROSIS

The formation of new fibers in the lens of the cat's eye continues throughout life. As new fibers are formed the older ones are compressed and pushed toward the center of the lens. This results in a continually increasing density of the lens. The lens also loses water as it ages, another factor contributing to increased density. This process is called *nuclear sclerosis* and should be recognized as a normal part of the aging of the cat's eyes. It results in a bluish or grayish-white haze in the part of the lens that can be seen through the pupil. It does not normally interfere with vision and does not need treatment. This condition is often erroneously referred to as *cataracts* (lens opacities that interfere with light transmission to the retina). In truth, senile cataracts, which usually appear very white and dense and which interfere with vision, occur much less commonly.

If your cat does develop cataracts as an aged (or sometimes young) animal and loss of vision occurs, there are surgical procedures that can be used to remove the opacity and restore vision. Surgery is best performed by a veterinary specialist because cataracts are relatively uncommon, and the best results are obtained only by those individuals who perform the operations most frequently. Most cats seem to adjust completely to a gradual loss of vision should surgery be unavailable or contraindicated.

OSTEOARTHRITIS (ARTHRITIS)

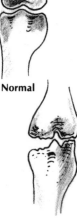

Normal

Arthritic

Osteoarthritis is a joint disease in which the *cartilages* (fibrous caps) covering the articular surfaces of the bones degenerate and bony proliferation (excess bone growth) occurs. This condition usually results in pain and lameness of the joints involved. It may occur in single joints of young animals with congenital joint defects or following any kind of joint trauma. When it occurs as an aging change it usually affects several joints, although lameness may not be apparent in all of them. The lameness present with arthritis is often most severe on arising and improves with exercise. Sometimes all you will notice in your cat is a generally decreased ability to move freely or jump effectively. If you gently move the affected joints you may hear or feel *crepitus* (cartilage or bone grating against cartilage and/or bone). X-ray pictures will show the affected joints and the severity of bone changes. Although you may not become aware of the disease until signs occur, the changes characteristic of arthritis have usually been occurring over a long prior period.

There is no effective means of arresting the progression of osteoarthritis in older cats, so treatment is usually symptomatic, directed at relieving any significant pain and assisting the cat in getting to his or her favorite resting spot. Unfortunately most drugs useful for the symptomatic relief of arthritis in people, dogs, and other animals are toxic to cats. One of the safest drugs for people or dogs, aspirin, can cause severe signs of illness in cats and should only be used with care under the direction of a veterinarian. Fortunately, few cats with osteoarthritis show discomfort and intermittent lameness or lameness that is only present on arising usually needs no treatment. Weight reduction often significantly improves lameness in obese cats with arthritis. Soft bedding, warm, dry quarters, and access to a towel-covered heating pad set at a safe, low temperature also help relieve discomfort. Acupuncture may help cats who don't respond to more conventional treatments, as do some nutritional supplements with antiinflammatory effects. Ask your veterinarian what is appropriate for your cat.

TUMORS (NEOPLASMS, CANCERS)

A *tumor* is an abnormal growth of tissue (*neoplasm* means new growth). *Benign tumors* are those that are likely to remain at the site of their original growth. *Malignant tumors* (cancers) are neoplastic growths that invade surrounding tissue and travel via blood vessels or lymph channels to other body sites where they start to grow anew. Although cats have a comparatively high incidence of cancer (see page 191), the likelihood of any tumor occurring increases with age.

Many tumors occur internally where you would not likely be aware of them until they have grown quite large. You should, however, watch carefully for growths in the mouth and on the outside of your cat's body. On both males and females it is wise to check each mammary gland periodically (e.g., once a month) for new growths. Breast cancer is the third most common tumor in cats, and about 85% of the tumors that occur are malignant. It is seven times more common in unspayed females than in those who have been neutered. Although unspayed females at least ten years old are the most likely to develop breast cancer, all cats are at risk including males and young, spayed females. (Siamese cats have a particularly high incidence of aggressive, malignant breast tumors.)

Since about two thirds of all cats with breast cancer have more than one tumor at the time of diagnosis and the likelihood of surviving the disease decreases as the number and size of the tumors increase, early diagnosis and prompt surgical treatment by removing the affected and surrounding breast tissue is very important. Consult your veterinarian without delay if you feel a growth in your cat's mammary area.

EARLY DIAGNOSIS AND TREATMENT IS IMPORTANT IN CANCER

If you find any kind of tumor in any age cat, it is always best to discuss its removal with a veterinarian. If you don't feel that you can see a veterinarian, watch the tumor carefully for growth. Some malignant tumors *metastasize* (spread) while the original tumor is still very small; and for some tumors, such as melanomas, microscopic examination by a pathologist is the only reliable way to differentiate benign from malignant growths.

COMMON SIGNS OF CANCER IN ANIMALS

1. Abnormal swellings that persist or continue to grow
2. Sores that do not heal
3. Weight loss
4. Loss of appetite
5. Bleeding or discharge from any body opening
6. Offensive odor
7. Difficulty eating or swallowing
8. Hesitation to exercise or loss of stamina
9. Persistent lameness or stiffness
10. Difficulty breathing, urinating, or defecating

Source: The Veterinary Cancer Society

CONSTIPATION

Difficult or infrequent passage of stools (constipation) is one of the more common but usually not serious problems of older cats. Aging changes often result in loss of muscle tone that, when combined with a suboptimal diet or changes in digestive process, result in recurrent constipation. Many older cats, especially those with kidney disease, develop subnormal blood potassium levels that affect muscular function and may aggravate constipation. Home remedies for constipation discussed on page 171 can be used to treat constipation in older cats. Don't rely on any methods repeatedly except the dietary changes mentioned unless your veterinarian directs you to do so after giving your cat a clean bill of health.

KIDNEY DISEASE

Many older cats have decreased kidney function due to aging changes and/or urinary tract diseases that have gone undetected earlier in life. Because the kidneys have a large amount of tissue reserve, signs attributable to progressive kidney disease are often not apparent without laboratory tests until damage is severe and often irreversible. Special testing is also necessary to detect high blood pressure that may cause and/or result from kidney disease.

Increased water drinking accompanied by increased volume of urination are often the only external signs of kidney disease. As the kidneys degenerate, less functioning tissue is available to excrete the same amount of wastes produced by the body as when the kidneys were healthy. In an effort to maintain a normal physiological state, a larger volume of urine in which the wastes are less concentrated must be excreted and the cat must drink more water daily. The need to excrete large volumes of urine will sometimes cause an old cat without a litter box and without convenient access to the outside to urinate in the house. This cat has not "forgotten his or her housetraining" or "grown senile"; the volume of urine is just too great to be held for many hours. The only way to remedy this situation is to provide a litter pan indoors or to provide more easy access to the outdoors. Restricting water availability will not help, but can actually make the cat sick, since it interferes with waste excretion.

When a cat cannot compensate for failing kidneys, other signs that may develop are vomiting, lack of appetite, and weight loss. The cat's teeth may be unsightly and his or her breath abnormally odorous (ammonialike). If you feel the kidneys they may feel abnormally small (most common in older cats) or abnormally large. If your cat has any signs of failing kidneys consult your veterinarian immediately. Other diseases (e.g., *diabetes mellitus,* see page 230) may have similar signs, and diagnosis requires laboratory tests including urinalysis and blood tests. Your veterinarian will try to find out if the disease process can be arrested and advise you on care that can prolong your cat's life comfortably in spite of diseased kidneys. The cornerstone of treatment for chronic kidney disease is a diet that provides only restricted quantities of high-quality protein, phosphorus, and sodium. Drugs that adjust blood pressure may be used when kidney disease is associated with high blood pressure. Cats also often need vitamin and potassium supplements to make up for continuing losses in the urine. Your veterinarian will advise additional treatment as required by monitoring your cat's blood and urine tests.

HYPERTHYROIDISM

Hyperthyroidism occurs when there is overproduction and excessive secretion of thyroid hormone by the thyroid gland. It is the most common disorder of the endocrine glands of cats. In most instances, hyperthyroidism results from a benign increase in the number of active cells in the affected gland (adenomatous hyperplasia, thyroid adenoma), but rarely it is caused by thyroid cancer (thyroid adenocarcinoma). Hyperthyroidism has developed in cats as young as three years of age, but most cases occur in cats older than nine years.

Cats affected by hyperthyroidism may have many different clinical signs at once, since thyroid hormone affects the function of so many different organ systems in the body. Sometimes, though, only one or just a few symptoms predominate.

Weight loss despite a normal or increased appetite and hyperexcitability are seen most often. Many cats seem more restless and irritable than usual. About one out of five cats will have periods of decreased as well as periods of increased appetite. A few may even refuse to eat, but this is usually only in the advanced stages of the disease when the cat has become depressed and weak. Many hyperthyroid cats vomit and/or have diarrhea, drink a lot, and urinate excessively.

High levels of thyroid hormone increase the blood pressure, thereby indirectly increasing the heart's work load. They also have a more direct effect on the heart muscle itself, increasing its demand for oxygen, and they cause an increase in the body's metabolic demands on the heart. Extremely rapid heart rates (greater than 240 beats per minute) and/or irregular heartbeats may result, further compromising heart function. Affected cats may develop heart disease, or those with preexisting heart disease may develop heart failure if the hyperthyroidism remains untreated. High blood pressure associated with thyroid disease may aggravate existing kidney malfunction or initiate it. Some cats with thyroid overproduction develop excessive shedding that may be accompanied by fur matting or by visible thinning of the hair. Others seem to have abnormally rapid toenail growth.

BLOOD TESTS
ARE
NECESSARY TO
DIAGNOSE
THYROID
DISEASE The cause of feline hyperthyroidism is unknown, so no measures can be taken to prevent it. It is most important to be aware of the disease and to make an early diagnosis to prevent severe body changes that can be caused by excess levels of thyroid hormone.

If you think your cat is exhibiting signs of hyperthyroidism you can feel along both sides of his or her neck near the windpipe (trachea) to see if you can find an enlarged thyroid gland. It could be located anywhere from the level of the larynx down to the chest level (or even inside the chest). Although many cats with hyperthyroidism do not have anything you can feel, any unusual lump under the skin in this area should prompt you to arrange for a veterinarian's evaluation.

In addition to physical changes you and your veterinarian may detect on physical examination, blood tests that measure thyroid hormone levels are needed to diagnose hyperthyroidism. Urinalysis, complete blood counts, biochemical evaluation of the blood, and chest radiographs (X-ray pictures) are also usually needed to determine any adverse effects the abnormal hormone levels have had on other organ systems and to evaluate whether your cat (especially if aged) can undergo treatment. In some cases, special studies such as echocardiograms, electrocardiograms, and radionuclide thyroid scans that can locate the exact site and size of an enlarged thyroid gland are needed.

Treatment for feline hyperthyroidism consists of antithyroid drugs, surgical removal of the affected tissue, or the administration of radioactive iodine-131 which specifically destroys the abnormal tissue. Many veterinarians use antithyroid medications only as temporary measures to stabilize a patient until a more permanent treatment is given, since these drugs can be associated with many serious side effects. Although it is very safe for the patient, radioactive iodine-131 can only be administered at special centers that are licensed to properly dispose of radioactive wastes. Therefore, access to this treatment is limited in some geographic areas. Your veterinarian can give you the name of a veterinary specialist who can administer radioisotope treatment should you need it for your cat. Thyroid surgery can usually be performed in any well-equipped veterinary clinic, but it may be contraindicated in certain patients such as those with advanced heart and/or kidney disease. The best choice of treatment for your cat will need to be discussed with your veterinarian and based on several factors including treatment availability and cost, as well as the presence of physical problems in addition to thyroid malfunction. Cats treated adequately and early enough can regain perfectly normal thyroid function and normal general health even if they are elderly.

SEVERAL TREATMENTS ARE AVAILABLE FOR HYPER-THYROIDISM

EUTHANASIA

It would be nice if all old pets who died did so peacefully in their sleep with no previous signs of illness. This doesn't always happen, though, and sometimes you must decide whether to end your cat's life or allow a progressive disease to continue. This is never an easy decision. A mutually close and trusting relationship with a veterinarian established when your cat is still young may help if you ever have to face this problem. A veterinarian familiar with your cat's medical history can tell you when a condition is irreversible and progressive and give you an opinion as to when that condition is truly a burden for your cat.

It is unfair to you, your cat, and the veterinarian to take an animal to a new veterinarian and request euthanasia. A veterinarian who does not know your cat may perform euthanasia because you requested it when the condition was actually treatable. A veterinarian unfamiliar with you may refuse to carry out this heartrending act because your cat seems healthy, not knowing that continuing to live with the cat is an extreme burden on you. Most veterinarians enter the profession to make animals well, not kill them. Many people react emotionally without knowing the facts and insist that their pet be "put to sleep" for a condition that can be treated and with which their cat can live happily. In other cases euthanasia is requested because buying a new pet is less expensive than treatment. For most people the joy of life outweighs minor discomforts, and this is probably true for most pets. The monetary value of a pet's life, of course, depends on each individual's point of view. If you decide you just don't want an unhealthy animal anymore, give the cat to a friend who does want it or take the cat to a shelter or pound where humane euthanasia is performed only after all other avenues for adoption are explored.

When you and your veterinarian are in agreement about ending the life of a pet, you need not worry about discomfort. Euthanasia in veterinary hospitals is performed by the intravenous injection of an overdose of an anesthetic drug. Death is both rapid and painless.

It's a good idea to approach the subject of euthanasia with your veterinarian soon after the possible need for it enters your mind. Your veterinarian should be willing to discuss the procedures used and to explain all the options available for disposal of the remains. Local laws prescribe whether dead pets may be buried. Veterinary hospitals and humane organizations often offer cremation services with or without return of the cat's ashes.

Many veterinarians allow an owner to remain with the pet at the time of euthanasia. A request for this service should not be considered unusual at any small animal hospital. Again, a discussion regarding its pros and cons is important to you and your cat's well-being at such an emotional time.

A useful book that explores the subject of euthanasia and grief more extensively is *When Your Pet Dies: How to Cope with Your Feelings,* by Jamie Quackenbush and Denise Gravine, Pocket Books, New York, 1985. Also, many veterinary associations and veterinary schools sponsor pet loss support for grieving owners. Feel free to ask your veterinarian for a referral to an appropriate group.

4

HOME MEDICAL CARE

∽

NURSING AT HOME

DRUG INFORMATION

YOUR CAT'S MEDICAL RECORD

Date	Tem-perature	Appetite/ Water Intake	Stool	Urine	Miscellaneous—include here medication, times given, times wounds cleaned, unusual signs, changes, etc.

Photocopy this page to use for record keeping while nursing your pet at home.

NURSING AT HOME

Although the average cat has few illnesses requiring prolonged hospitalization during his or her lifetime, many minor illnesses can become severe if proper home care is not provided. Most veterinarians are anxious to have your cat recuperate at home if you can provide adequate nursing. It also saves money and will draw you closer to your animal. This section is designed to give you the information you need for basic home nursing. If you become familiar with its contents you should be able to treat at home most minor illnesses diagnosed by your veterinarian. In cases where there are no alternatives to hospitalization, familiarity with basic nursing techniques should allow the hospital stay to be shortened and more of the convalescence to occur at home.

RECORD KEEPING

If your cat has a serious illness, regular and accurate record keeping is invaluable for the veterinarian helping you treat your cat at home. Take your cat's temperature at least once daily (preferably around the same time) and record the values. Record how much your cat eats and drinks, the frequency of urination and the type of bowel movements passed. This, of course, requires that your cat be kept indoors and a litter box be provided. In some instances it is best to confine the recovering cat to one room or a small area; other times the cat can be allowed to wander freely around the house. Your veterinarian can help you decide on the best kind of confinement. In no instance, however, should a sick cat be allowed to roam unsupervised outdoors. Sick cats frequently disappear, only to be found later in much worse condition than when they left, or else never return at all. Additional helpful information to keep in your records includes an indication of the times and amounts of medication given and a record of any unusual signs (e.g., vomiting) that develop or any other change in condition. Take these records with you whenever you visit the veterinarian.

TEMPERATURE

Use a rectal thermometer to take your cat's temperature. An oral thermometer can be used in a pinch, but the bulb is more likely to break off. Before inserting the thermometer into the rectum, shake the mercury column down below 99° F (37.2°C) and lubricate the tip of the thermometer with any nontoxic, greasy substance (petroleum jelly, lubricant jelly, vegetable oil). Place your cat on a table or other level platform, hold your cat's tail up with one hand, and insert the thermometer into the rectum with a firm, gentle push. You may feel some resistance to the thermometer just after you pass it through the anus; this is due to

RESTRAINT WHILE TAKING A CAT'S TEMPERATURE

the cat's strong internal anal sphincter muscle. When you encounter this resistance just continue to push gently but firmly until the muscle relaxes and allows the thermometer to pass, or rotate the thermometer gently. This is most easily done with the cat standing, but can be done while he or she sits or lies down. How far you need to insert the thermometer to get an accurate rectal temperature depends on the size of the cat—an inch to an inch and one-half (2.5 to 3.75 cm) is usually sufficient. If you feel the thermometer go into a fecal mass when you insert it, try again. The thermometer should be left two or

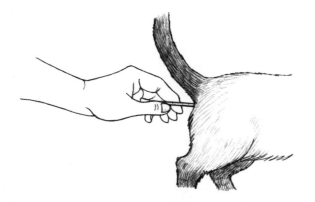

three minutes although many thermometers will register an accurate temperature in about one minute. (Helpful information if you have an uncooperative cat!)

To read the thermometer, roll it back and forth between your fingers until you can see the thin mercury column inside. The point where the column stops is the temperature. Each large mark indicates one degree, each small mark two-tenths of a degree. Normal is usually 101.0 to 102.5°F (38.3 to 39.2°C).

PULSE, HEART RATE

For how to take your cat's pulse and measure the heart rate, see page 32.

HOW TO GIVE YOUR CAT A PILL

The only way to be sure your cat has really swallowed medication in pill, capsule, or tablet form is to administer it in the following way: Place your cat on a table or other similar platform and get your pet to sit or stand relatively quietly. Grasp the pill between the thumb and forefinger of one hand so you have it ready to administer. Then place the opposite hand over the top of your cat's head, thumb and index finger near the corners of the mouth as illustrated on page 244 and tilt the head backward until the nose points toward the ceiling. Press against the cat's lips with your index finger and thumb to open the mouth and use the third finger of your pill-containing hand to hold the lower jaw open. Then quickly drop or place the pill over the back of the cat's tongue. (With practice, you can give the pill a quick and gentle shove with your index finger to send it on its way down the throat.) Then immediately allow the cat's mouth to close and hold it lightly closed until the pill is swallowed. If your cat licks his or her nose as soon as you release your grip, you can be fairly

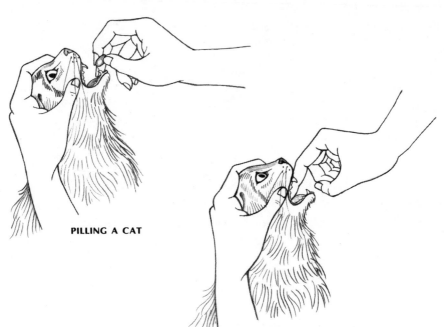

PILLING A CAT

PUSHING THE PILL DOWN

PILL GUN

certain the medication has been swallowed. (To be successful be sure to keep the cat's nose pointed upward during the whole procedure.) If pilling is to be successful it is extremely important to perform these maneuvers quickly and smoothly. If you spend too long in preparation, an uncooperative cat has mustered his or her full counterforces by the time you actually attempt to give the drug, and you are destined for failure. Although it may seem difficult at first, with a little practice giving medication in solid form to all but the fiercest cats becomes very easy. For these cats, tubular plastic pill "guns" are available in pet supply stores or through your veterinarian to hold the tablets, pills, or capsules and shoot them into the back of the cat's throat. In preparation for the day when you may have to nurse your cat at home, it is a good idea to go through the motions of administering medication to develop your skill while your cat is still young, cooperative, and healthy. You can use a small piece of dry kibble as a practice pill. If you have trouble with the above-described traditional restraint method and/or your cat is an uncooperative type, you can try the alternative method illustrated at right. This method (sometimes called the Hilton technique in honor of the veterinarian who first published it) induces many cats to reflexively remain still while their ears are grasped and their neck is turned sharply.

Problems most often occur when the pill is not placed or dropped properly over the base of the tongue. If you drop the pill off center or not far enough back, the cat will spit it out or bite into it. If this happens and the cat is still co-operative, try again. Many times when this occurs the cat tastes the medication and begins to drool profusely. This is no cause for concern, but usually requires that you wait a few minutes before trying to administer the medication again. Buttering uncoated tablets helps with this problem and is also useful if the pills don't seem slippery enough or seem a little on the large side. If you find it absolutely

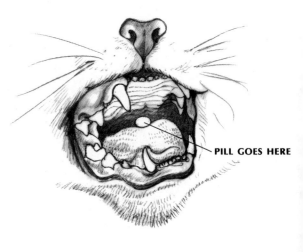

PILL GOES HERE

impossible to give solid medication in the manner described you can try crushing a tablet or pill (pill cutters and crushers are available at drugstores) or emptying the contents of a capsule and mixing the drug thoroughly with a small portion of meat or some other

HILTON RESTRAINT TECHNIQUE

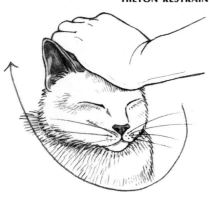

Rotate Head as Shown
While Hand Pulls Back on Ears

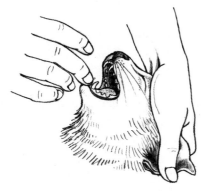

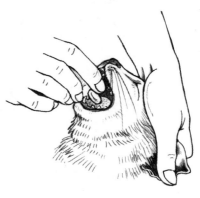

favorite food. Sometimes the medicine can be mixed with water and administered as a liquid. Most medicines taste so bad, however, that a sick cat will not take them voluntarily in food or liquid. So if it can be avoided, do not use these methods of administration. You can never be sure that your cat has taken all the medication when it is administered in food, and some drugs are inactivated in the presence of food. If you grind an *enteric-coated* (coated to be absorbed in the intestine) tablet or empty the contents of a capsule into food you may be preventing normal absorption of the drug from the gut. Coverings are often designed to remain intact until the drug reaches the part of the gut where it is best and most safely absorbed.

LIQUID MEDICATION

The simplest way to give your cat liquid medication is to squirt it into the back of the mouth using an eyedropper or syringe (hypodermic or infant ear type). For most liquid medicines your veterinarian will provide you with the tool necessary to administer the medication; if not, request the necessary item and also request a demonstration of its use. To administer a liquid, grasp your cat's head as if you were going to give a pill (see page 243), then slip the dropper between the rear teeth and squirt in the liquid; or if the mouth is open far enough, just squirt the liquid onto the back of the tongue. Keep the cat's nose pointed upward while the liquid is swallowed. Otherwise, the cat will tend to shake his or her head and spit out the medicine. Give only small amounts at a time ($1/4$ teaspoonful, 1 cc) and allow swallowing to occur between each portion to avoid causing the cat to choke or inhale the liquid.

ADMINISTERING LIQUID BY EYEDROPPER

FORCE-FEEDING

Since lack of appetite (*anorexia*) accompanies many feline illnesses, coaxing or force-feeding is often necessary to insure that sufficient calories and nutrients are consumed and to maintain the nutritional health necessary to the vital functions and repair of injured or diseased tissues. The effects of one day without food, of course, are not irreversible, but prolonged refusal to eat forces the cat's body to draw upon its own vital tissues to obtain the calories necessary for survival. If this process is allowed to continue for too long it can itself result in death although the original disease would not have. Water is also very important to your cat's health and recovery, since dehydration begins as soon as water intake does not meet daily water need. (For more about dehydration, see page 128). Water can be administered by the techiques used for force-feeding liquids, and since most foods used for force-feeding contain a high proportion of water, hand administration of food helps meet the cat's daily water need. Use the following information about hand-feeding whenever your veterinarian suggests that it is necessary and to help stabilize a sick cat's condition until veterinary help can be obtained. Do not, though, use hand-feeding in lieu of a diagnosis; unless proper treatment is given, hand-feeding alone cannot usually bring a cat back to health.

Liquid diets can be force-fed to a sick cat in the same way liquid medication is given (see page 246). It is easier to feed solid or semisolid diets by using your finger or a tongue depressor (available in drugstores) to wipe the food onto the roof of your cat's mouth. (Grasp the cat's head as if giving a pill. Insert your finger or the tongue depressor full of food and wipe it against the roof of the mouth.) Solid food can also be given rolled into small pellets like pills.

You can use any nutritionally complete commercial food for hand-feeding a sick cat; just remember to take the time to feed enough to

FEEDING WITH A SYRINGE

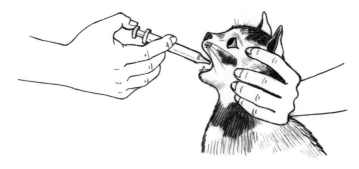

supply your cat's daily caloric needs (about 30 to 40 calories per pound, 65 to 85/kg daily for an adult). Multiple small feedings will be necessary in most cases. Strained baby foods are often easier to administer than the usual commercial foods. Strained egg yolk is best because of its high calorie content and high digestibility, but if your cat finds meat flavors more palatable, you can use strained chicken, turkey, lamb, or beef baby foods, adding two egg yolks per 3-ounce jar (for a high-protein, high-calorie diet) or 1 tablespoon corn oil and 1 tablespoon corn syrup per 3-ounce jar (for a high-fat, high-calorie diet) or a combination of egg yolks, oil, and/or corn syrup. Corn syrup and corn oil may also be added to egg baby foods to liquify them while increasing the calorie and carbohydrate or fat content. Feed an adult cat *at least* four jars of plain strained egg yolk or two jars of baby food or egg yolk mixture daily. If necessary your veterinarian can supply you with special dietary products designed specifically for hand-feeding sick cats. In addition to foods, you should provide a balanced vitamin-mineral supplement as recommended by your veterinarian while your cat is sick to meet his or her daily vitamin-mineral needs and any increased requirements caused by the illness.

Feed no more than 1 to 2 tablespoonfuls ($\frac{1}{2}$ to 1 ounce, 15 to 30 ml) food or liquid per pound body weight at each feeding, or vomiting is likely to occur. Maintain your cat's proper hydration by measuring his or her water intake and supplementing it by hand as necessary to provide about 2 to $2\frac{1}{2}$ tablespoonfuls per pound body weight (65 to 80 ml/kg) daily. (You can use milk if it doesn't cause diarrhea.) Don't forget that water or other liquids mixed with foods to liquify them for force-feeding contribute to meeting the cat's daily water need. If you find that your cat has signs of dehydration (see page 128) and is not improving as expected with hand-feeding and your other treatments, be sure to consult your veterinarian. Sometimes only the specialized techniques available in veterinary hospitals can fill the needs of a sick cat.

FOOD	APPROXIMATE CALORIE CONTENT
Strained egg yolk baby food	34 per ounce (30 per ml)
Strained beef baby food	13 per ounce (30 per ml)
Strained lamb baby food	16 per ounce (30 per ml)
Strained turkey or chicken baby food	20 per ounce (30 per ml)
Egg yolk (medium)	55
Whole egg (medium)	70
Whole milk	20 per ounce (30 per ml)
Honey	60 per tablespoonful (20 per g)
Corn syrup	55 per tablespoonful (20 per g)
Corn oil	70 per tablespoonful (8 per g)

For calorie content of commercial cat foods, see page 175.

Any of the above foods are suitable for making hand-feeding mixtures for sick cats unless the illness requires a special diet. If a mixture must be fed longer than two or three days strict attention must be paid to nutritional balance. Therefore commercial products are probably best for long-term feeding. Whole eggs should be cooked (e.g., soft boiled) before feeding or mixing with other foods. Add no more than 1 tablespoonful of corn syrup or honey and 1 tablespoonful of corn oil per 3-ounce jar of baby food unless otherwise directed by your veterinarian. Add milk, meat or chicken broth, or water as necessary to liquify the foods for hand administration and to help meet the sick cat's daily fluid requirement.

EYE MEDICATION

Ophthalmic ointments are most easily applied into the conjunctival sac (see page 18). Use your thumb or forefinger to roll the lower eyelid gently downward and squeeze the ointment into the space exposed. Approaching the eye from the outside corner helps

USING EYE DROPS

prevent the cat from seeing the tip of the tube and can facilitate instillation of the medication. Eyedrops should be instilled with the cat's nose tilted silghtly upward. Use one hand to grasp the cat's muzzle and hold the lower lid open. Rest the base of the hand holding the dropper bottle above the eye to hold the upper lid open, then drop in the medication. Avoid touching the end of the ointment tube or dropper bottle to the eye to prevent contamination of the solution and injury to the eye.

EAR TREATMENT

When your cat's ears become inflamed (see page 149) a more thorough cleaning than you give them routinely is often necessary. In most cases inflamed ears should be examined by a veterinarian, and if cleaning is necessary it should be done by a veterinarian who will have the necessary tools for observing the ear canal and eardrum during and after cleaning. Also, if the ears seem painful when touched, anesthesia is usually necessary to make most cats hold still for a thorough and safe ear cleaning. Fortunately, instances when ear cleaning in cats is necessary are infrequent.

CLEANING EARS Veterinarians use several methods for cleaning ears. In one method a rubber bulb syringe filled with warm water–antiseptic soap solution or a wax-dissolving solution is inserted into the ear canal and used to flush the fluid in and out of the ear. This is done several times and is followed by clear water or antiseptic rinses. The clean ear canal is dried with cotton swabs and appropriate ear medication is instilled. Another method relies on cotton-tipped swabs and the use of an instrument called an ear loop to remove debris.

If you cannot take your cat to a veterinarian, the best way to clean his or her ears at home is to use a cotton swab in the following manner. Grasp the end of the pinna (see page 18) and hold it straight up over the cat's head. Insert the swab into the ear canal parallel to the side of the head. You cannot damage the eardrum if you keep the swab vertical and parallel to the side of the head, but even if you

CLEANING EARS

CLOTH   COTTON SWAB

don't, cat's ear canals are so narrow that it would be difficult to reach the eardrum with a cotton-tipped swab unless you were very rough and forceful. Use the swab to clean out debris before you start medication and once daily to remove old medication before instilling the new. Turn the swab gently and try to lift out debris rather than compacting it. Only a rare cat will allow you to clean the ears with the bulb syringe method without anesthesia. If you try it, warm any solution you use to body temperature and flush the fluids in and out gently until all debris is removed. Do not wedge the syringe into the ear to form a tight seal as the pressure can build up in the ear canal sufficiently to rupture the eardrum. After flushing the ear dry the canal gently with cotton-tipped swabs.

After your cat's ears are cleaned you will usually have to instill medication in them at least daily for one or two weeks. Many ear preparations are sold in containers with long nozzles that are placed into the ear canal. Liquids can be dropped into the canal. After the medicine is in the canal, grasp the lower part of the auricular cartilage through the skin and massage it up and down vigorously. If you are doing it properly you will hear the medicine squishing around inside the ear. This will spread the medication down the length of the ear canal and is a very important part of caring for the ear properly. Once daily before instilling new medication it's a good idea to partially clean the ear to remove old medication and accumulated debris. Use a cotton swab as described above or wrap your finger in a soft cloth or tissue and clean out the ear as far as covered finger will reach.

MEDICATING EARS

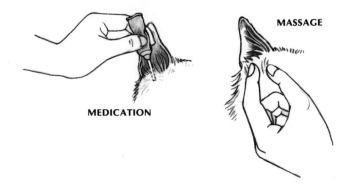

MASSAGE

MEDICATION

RESTRAINT

Unlike well-trained and frequently handled dogs, most cats cannot be commanded to sit, stand, or lie quietly while unpleasant nursing procedures are performed. So to be successful in caring for your cat's health at home you need to learn the best ways to provide restraint when necessary to avoid injury to yourself and your cat and to allow the nursing procedure to be carried out. Cats vary greatly in their personalities, and restraint must be tailored to the individual. The best general rule to follow is to use the *minimum* amount of restraint necessary to achieve your goal. Never use two people when one is adequate, and always try the gentlest method first, unless you know from experience with the cat that very firm restraint is necessary. All the basic home nursing procedures explained in this section are described as if performed by one person, since most cats begin to struggle when firm restraint is applied and since gentle control is the least stressful for the cat. If you find that these simple methods don't work for you, provide more firm control as necessary, but be sure to proceed firmly (not roughly) and deliberately or as the cat begins to object, you will lose your grip and may be scratched or bitten.

Never attempt treatment with the cat on the floor, on the bed, couch, or in your lap unless the cat is very cooperative. To achieve the best success place the cat on a smooth-surfaced table or other level platform that allows you to stand alongside. The simplest form of restraint involves the use of one hand and/or arm, leaving the other free for treatment. Light restraint includes placing one hand firmly over the cat's shoulders while he or she lies down or placing a hand in front of the chest while the cat is standing or sitting, to prevent forward movement. One arm wrapped around the cat's body, so the cat's head is held between your arm and body and so your hand can grasp his or her tail, provides good restraint for many procedures involving the rear legs and tail, as well as for taking a cat's temperature (see illustration, page 242). For more control grasp the cat's *scruff* (skin at the base of the neck) tightly and firmly or grasp

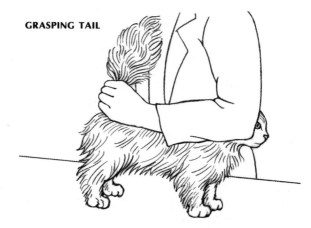

GRASPING TAIL

GRASPING SCRUFF

the cat at the base of skull and press firmly with your thumb and fingers just below the ears. When using one of these methods, you can, if necessary, rest the arm of your restraining hand down on the cat's back to give you greater control.

If these simple holding methods fail and you have no one to help you, try rolling the cat in a towel or placing the cat in a pillowcase. To give oral medication, allow the cat's head to protrude, then follow the directions given for administering solid or liquid medicines (see page 246). For other treatment just expose the area that needs care while leaving the rest of the cat covered. It is not always necessary to physically roll a cat in a towel. A towel just placed over an uncooperative cat often seems to provide a calming effect and will sometimes allow you to grasp and treat an otherwise "impossible" patient. If at any time during these or the following procedures the cat begins to pant or becomes visibly weaker, stop your restraint

WRAPPED IN TOWEL

and allow the cat to regain strength and composure before proceding. Weak cats overly stressed by fighting restraint may collapse.

Having two people working together makes nursing a very unco-

ASSISTANT HOLDING BOTH LEGS

operative cat much easier. When giving oral medication, your assistant can wrap his or her arms around the cat and grasp the front legs firmly, applying downward pressure to prevent the cat from reaching up while you handle the head and mouth. Or your assistant can wield the towel if you find that it is easier to give treatment with the cat partially covered. For other instances when firm restraint must be used your assistant can hold the cat in one of the following illustrated ways. Trimming the cat's toenails (see page 56) prior to restraint can be helpful. Do not attempt any restraint procedures for cats if you are unwilling to risk a scratch or bite since even the most experienced veterinarian is occasionally injured when handling a difficult cat.

GRASPING SCRUFF AND REAR LEGS

HOLDING FRONT AND REAR FEET

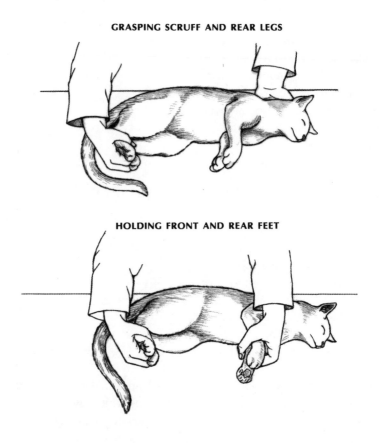

Although most veterinarians rarely muzzle a cat and the times you would have to do it are few, a muzzle can be very helpful when treating a cat whom you know bites or when moving an injured cat. A muzzle must be applied *before* attempting to move or handle the cat. It is difficult, if not impossible, to apply one properly to an already aroused and struggling cat.

The traditional muzzle is made from a long strip of cord, gauze bandage, or cloth. Form a loop and slip it over the cat's nose as far as possible. Draw the loop tightly around the nose with the ends under the chin. Then bring an end along each side of the cat's head and tie them together firmly at the nape of the neck. Now slip one end of the bandage under the nose loop as illustrated, bring it back to the nape of the neck, and tie the ends tightly. If the muzzle is applied properly the cat's biting efforts will be ineffective, and the muzzle itself may provide enough distraction for the cat for you to be able to complete the treatment. Washable nylon muzzles that slip over the face of a cat and have quick release Velcro strap closures that wrap along the sides of the face and around the back of the neck are now commercially available. They are much easier and safer to apply to a fractious cat than the traditional type. Purchase one through your veterinarian or other pet supplier if your cat is uncooperative. Place it in your first aid kit for use in emergencies.

NYLON MUZZLE

CORD MUZZLE

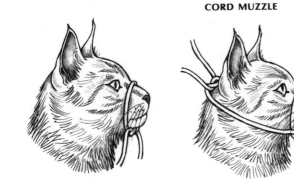

WOUNDS AND BANDAGES

Wounds that require repeated cleansing at home are infected traumatic wounds and abscesses. These wounds are left open or partially open when treated to allow pus drainage and cleaning (see page 131). Other fresh wounds usually need only a simple disinfection and/or cleansing when they are physically contaminated with foreign material such as dirt, plant parts, or hair.

CLEANING OPEN WOUNDS Solutions of povidone-iodine (0.001% to 1%) or chlorhexidine (0.05%) can be made up at home from stronger antiseptic solutions purchased in a drugstore or directly from your veterinarian. (For information on hydrogen peroxide, see page 130.) If the opening of the wound is large enough, you can pour disinfectant directly into it. A bulb syringe or turkey baster can be used to flush the solution into smaller wounds, providing you are careful not to build up excessive pressure that could force foreign material further into the surrounding soft tissue. The disinfectant can be applied to a gauze pad or cotton-tipped swab that can be inserted into very small wounds. As the solution is instilled, it may sting. Some cats find this uncomfortable. Clean the wound until the visible tissue looks free of foreign debris and/or until the solution runs clear. Repeat the cleansing once or twice a day if there is a tendency for debris to reaccumulate. Since the stronger antiseptic concentrations also damage normal tissues, stop the daily application as soon as the wound has finished draining.

Simple wounds usually heal most rapidly when left uncovered. In cases where the wound is continually becoming contaminated or when the cat licks at the area so much that it cannot heal or is made worse, it must be protected. Fortunately these occasions are rare with cats because bandages are more difficult to apply and to keep on these small animals than on larger ones such as dogs.

BANDAGING THE FOOT A light bandage for a foot can be made by placing an infant's or doll's stocking over it and taping the sock to the leg with several wraps of adhesive tape applied to the top of the sock and the leg. (Be sure the tape is loose enough to allow normal blood circulation to the foot.) This type of wrap leaves most of the sock loose and allows some air circulation. It is best for covering the nails of the rear feet to prevent damage when a cat is scratching an area or to protect the bandaged foot from licking. Ointments can be applied under such bandages, and the sock will keep the medication on the foot and off the carpet.

When cats object to a lightweight bandage such as the stocking and repeatedly tear it off, a more substantial foot bandage can be

SOCK BANDAGE   **TAPE BANDAGE**

made by covering the whole stocking with tape or by using roll or tubular gauze and adhesive tape. Before applying a substantial bandage try to pad the areas between the toes with small pieces of cotton. Depending on the site of the wound, you may want to cover it with a gauze or nonstick wound pad. Wrap the foot firmly with the roll gauze applying several layers vertically as well as around the foot. Follow the gauze with adhesive tape. First apply several tape strips vertically, then wrap more tape around the area to be covered. The long vertical strips not only form the end of the bandage, but help prevent it from wearing through. Try to apply even pressure from the toes to the top of the bandage so normal circulation to the foot is maintained. Don't be too concerned if your first bandage doesn't stay in place. A little practice is required to learn how to apply a bandage to a cat's paw properly so it won't slip off, and it is much safer to apply a bandage too loosely than too tightly.

Flexible wire or electrical tape may be wrapped over the bandage to help prevent your cat from chewing at it and removing it. Usually, however, such measures are not necessary. After a few minutes of vigorous objection, most cats begin to tolerate these artificial coverings. Bandages should be changed at least every third day unless your veterinarian directs you differently.

ABDOMEN, BACK, AND NECK BANDAGES

Many-tailed bandages can be made from any rectangular or square piece of clean cloth. These bandages are best used to try to prevent a cat from licking at a wound (e.g., incision following surgery) or to help cover open wounds such as abscesses to prevent wound drainage from damaging carpeting or furniture. If necessary, gauze or cotton padding may be placed between the wound and the bandage. This type of bandage is useful to help you cover an area on the neck, abdomen, or back, but don't be surprised if your cat wriggles out of even the best one. An infant T-shirt can serve the same purpose as a many-tailed bandage and usually remains in place better. It is especially effective if a string or ribbon is run through the hem tunnel to provide a drawstring.

MANY TAILED BANDAGE

INFANT T-SHIRT BANDAGE

ELIZABETHAN COLLAR

A rare cat will not leave wounds or other irritations alone no matter what bandaging method you try. Also, there are occasional wounds, such as those on the head, that cannot be easily protected by bandaging. In these instances you can try an Elizabethan collar.

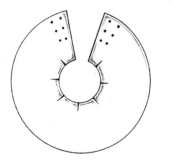

Ready-made plastic or cardboard Elizabethan collars can be purchased at some pet stores or from veterinarians. Or you can make one from heavy cardboard as illustrated. This device will prevent most cats from disturbing wounds on their bodies and will prevent the scratching of head or ear wounds. A determined cat can usually wriggle out of even the best applied collar, so be prepared to apply it several times and to administer tranquilizers if recommended by your veterinarian while your cat adjusts to the collar. Also, many cats cannot or will not eat or drink while wearing an Elizabethan collar. Be sure to allow for this by removing the collar when you are home to supervise the cat. Also be sure you know the cause of the problem. A collar will prevent your cat from scratching at his or her ears, for example, but if ear mites are present it won't eliminate them.

DRUG INFORMATION

Drugs are identified by their formal *chemical* name, their *generic* name, and their *brand* (proprietary) name. The generic name is usually simpler and easier to remember than the formal chemical name. For example, *acetylsalicylic acid* is the formal chemical name for the drug with the generic name, *aspirin.* If your veterinarian needs to write a prescription, request that he or she uses the generic drug name rather than the brand name, if possible. This allows the pharmacist to give you the same drug usually for less money than the brand-name drug would cost. However, keep in mind that some generic drugs have been shown to be badly formulated and it is not always possible to make a successful substitution.

In general, veterinary drugs are the same as human drugs, but less expensive when they are sold under a veterinary label. However, many veterinarians dispense the drugs you need instead of writing prescriptions for you to take to a pharmacy. Although veterinary hospitals make a profit from this practice, for the most part dispensing needed medication this way is a convenience for you and may be less expensive than purchasing the equivalent medicine at a drugstore. If you would like to comparison shop, ask your veterinarian for a written prescription so that you can take it to several pharmacies. In some cases there are no equivalent human drugs or appropriate dosage sizes available and you must purchase the drug in the veterinary clinic. Some companies sell drugs directly to people who are not veterinarians. In some cases the drugs are the same ones veterinarians use. In other cases, however, they are less effective or more likely to be toxic than the drugs a veterinarian would choose. I believe that many of the companies that sell these drugs to the public are interested primarily in profits, not animal health. They usually make few attempts to be sure the drugs are used properly and sometimes fail to warn of possible side effects. Try to avoid such drugs unless recommended by a veterinarian you trust.

All drugs dispensed by a pharmacist or veterinarian should be labeled with the generic or brand name, expiration date, concentration, and clear directions for use. This avoids misunderstanding in treatment and helps others who may treat the case later. Since drugs are helpers, not magic potions, your veterinarian should not be secretive about what is being dispensed. Neither should you regard drugs as universal panaceas to be dispensed and used without caution. Caution is particularly important when prescribing medication for cats because they have many idiosyncracies of metabolism that may cause them to react unfavorably to many drugs considered ordinary for use in people or in dogs. Follow your veterinarian's directions for prescription use carefully, and do not use any drug unless it has been recommended by a veterinarian or other *reputable* source for use in your cat. Also keep in mind that drugs are changing all the time. Although some generic drugs safe for use in cats are mentioned in this book, better drugs may become available after this book is published. Your veterinarian is usually the best source for the most current information.

ANTIBIOTICS

Technically, *antibiotics* are chemical substances produced by microscopic organisms that interfere with the growth of other microorganisms. In practice, antibiotics include a large number of substances, many synthetically made, that are used primarily in the treatment of bacterial infections. Antibiotics are miracle drugs when properly used. They enable us to cure infections that in the past would have certainly been fatal. They can, however, be easily misused.

All antibiotics are not effective against all bacteria. A veterinarian's decision to use a particular antibiotic is based on the probable bacterium causing the disease and/or the results of laboratory tests in which the infective organisms are grown and tested for antibiotic sensitivity. If the wrong antibiotic is chosen, there is no beneficial effect. If the proper antibiotic is chosen and given at the correct dosage, growth of the bacteria is stopped or at least controlled sufficiently that the body's own natural defense systems can overcome the infection. If the antibiotic is not given as frequently as prescribed or if the medication is discontinued too soon, forms of bacteria resistant to the antibiotic may multiply, or the infection may recur. Antibiotics are not always effective alone. Other drugs and special nursing techniques must often be combined with their use. In cases of localized infection such as abscesses, antibiotic treatment must often be used with proper surgical intervention for success.

Many people seem to believe that antibiotics are useful in combating *any* infectious or febrile disease. This is certainly untrue. A particularly common case where antibiotics may be of no help is the viral infection.

ANTIBIOTICS ARE NOT EFFECTIVE AGAINST VIRUSES

Viruses exist in body cells and depend on the cells metabolic process for reproduction. Since the methods of viral metabolism are unlike those of bacteria, which for the most part survive outside of cells and multiply independently, drugs effective against bacteria are ineffective against viruses. When antibiotics are prescribed for use during viral infection, it is to combat bacteria that invade after the virus has weakened the animal (secondary infection). There are very few drugs available for treatment of viral infections. Since viral reproduction is so intimately tied to normal cellular function, most drugs found effective against viruses also destroy body cells.

DRUGS HAVE SIDE EFFECTS

Like other drugs, most antibiotics have potential side effects. Since bacteria are single-celled organisms similar in many ways to individual body cells, antibiotics can sometimes act against body cells in ways similar to the ways they adversely affect bacteria. Among the possible side effects are allergic reactions, toxic effects, alteration of metabolism, and alteration of normal (and beneficial) bacteria inhabiting the body. A good veterinarian will tell you if there are any side effects you should watch for when antibiotics are prescribed. Side effects can be made more likely by the use of outdated drugs, combining antibiotics with certain other drugs, and by certain illnesses.

Indiscriminate use of antibiotics is to be avoided. Use with proper guidance will avoid toxic effects and stem the development of antibiotic-resistant bacteria. Be glad, not disappointed, if your veterinarian feels that the condition can be treated without antibiotics (or other drugs) and sends you away empty-handed. And don't use leftover antibiotics unless directed to by your veterinarian. Antibiotics are available over the counter as ointments for *topical* (on the body surface) use. Common effective ones contain *bacitracin, neomycin,* and/or *polymixin B.* These are suitable for applying to superficial wounds to achieve a local antibacterial effect. They should not be applied into deep wounds, as the carrier ointment for the drugs may interfere with healing.

ADRENOCORTICAL STEROIDS

Adrenocortical steroids (corticosteroids) include hormones produced by the adrenal glands and synthetic drugs similar to these natural substances. This group of drugs has a wide range of actions on the body, among them effects on fat, protein, and carbohydrate metabolism, water balance, salt balance, and cardiovascular, immune system, and kidney function. They are very important in the individual's ability to resist certain environmental changes and noxious stimuli.

Steroid drugs are commonly used in veterinary medicine for their antiinflammatory effects (for example, to give relief from itching due to allergies or other skin diseases). Because of the remarkable response sometimes possible following administration, some pet owners and some veterinarians are inclined to misuse these drugs. Keep in mind that steroid drugs are only palliative, relieving but not curing disease, unless the condition is caused by deficiency of adrenal gland function. Also, keep in mind that steroids are not without side effects. Although they are safe, even lifesaving when used properly, misused they constitute a threat to your cat's health. Avoid preparations containing steroids sold in pet stores and rely on the advice of a good veterinarian regarding the use of steroids in maintaining the health of your cat. Some names of common steroid drugs are *prednisone, prednisolone, cortisone, hydrocortisone, triamcinolone, betamethasone, flumethasone,* and *dexamethasone.* Some have less wide-ranging effects than others.

DRUGS YOU MIGHT HAVE AROUND THE HOUSE

TRANQUILIZERS   *Tranquilizers* are drugs that work on the brain in several different ways to modify behavior. They have legitimate uses in relieving anxiety and producing sedation, and have been helpful in some instances in changing undesirable behavior patterns. Veterinarians use tranquilizers most often to relieve the anxiety that makes some cats uncooperative when they enter veterinary hospitals, and as preanesthetics. Other common reasons for tranquilizing cats include prolonged confinement (as when traveling), noisy situations (as when being shipped), for appetite stimulation, and for sedation to prevent self-trauma (as in wound licking).

If you can anticipate the need for tranquilization, it is best to discuss the pros and cons with your veterinarian who can then write a prescription for tranquilizing drugs. Cats sometimes react unfavorably to tranquilizers and once tranquilized become less cooperative and more "ferocious" than before. If an unanticipated need arises, two human tranquilizers that can be used in cats are *diazepam* (Vallium) and *chlorpromazine* (Thorazine). In such situations call your veterinarian and ask about the advisability of using the drug you have, and ask what the correct dose for your cat should be. Over-the-counter pet tranquilizers contain antihistamines (such as *methapyrilene*) and other drugs (e.g., *scopolamine*) that produce sedation normally thought of as a side effect of their normal uses. In high doses such drugs may produce excitement or may be toxic to cats, and their use is not recommended. *Do not* use tranquilizers merely for your own convenience; attempt to deal with recurrent problems by training (conditioning your cat to the situation). *Do not* use tranquilizers to sedate your cat following trauma or severe injury (e.g., being hit by a car); they can have undesirable side effects on blood pressure in such situations and can contribute to shock.

Aspirin (acetylsalicylic acid) is a common household drug that is **ASPIRIN** often misused when owners attempt to treat their cats. It relieves fever, mild pain, and has some antiinflammatory effects, but is not a specific cure for any disease. Aspirin relieves fever by acting on the brain biochemistry to reset the body's "thermostat." It is believed to do this by inhibiting the production of *prostaglandins* in the preoptic region of the anterior hypothalamus. Prostaglandins, formed in the body cells by metabolism of fatty acids, are potent chemical mediators of inflammation. Aspirin also relieves local pain and blocks inflammation in tissues by interfering with the formation of prostaglandins. *It is known that aspirin can be very toxic to cats in dosages safe for other animals.* Misused aspirin can cause severe signs of illness, including vomiting, weakness, lack of appetite, hypersensitivity, blood in the stool, and convulsions. Stomach ulcerations and death have often followed the misuse of aspirin in cats. Since the indications for use of aspirin in cats are few, do not administer aspirin at home. Let your veterinarian decide whether aspirin is necessary and advise you how to administer it so over-dosage and toxicity do not occur.

Other nonsteroidal antiinflammatory drugs often used by people such as acetaminophen, ibuprofen, and naproxen are even more highly toxic to cats than aspirin. *Never* administer them to your pet.

ANTACIDS   The use of antacids is discussed on page 169.

LAXATIVES   The use of drugs with laxative action is discussed on page 171.

HYDROGEN   See page 130 for how to use hydrogen peroxide to clean wounds and
PEROXIDE   abscesses. To use it to induce vomiting, see page 210.

ISOPROPYL   You can try isopropyl alcohol (rubbing alcohol) for treatment of
ALCOHOL   inflamed ears; see page 149.

ANTIFUNGAL   To use over-the-counter antifungal medications such as miconazole
MEDICATIONS   or clotrimazole, see page 137.

5

BREEDING
AND REPRODUCTION

M ale (tom) and female (queen) cats usually reach puberty between six and twelve months of age, although some are not mature until fifteen months. The actual onset of sexual maturity and the time of first breeding vary greatly with the individual cat because these are influenced by many factors; among them are day length, nutrition, characteristics of the breed, and "psychological" maturity. (Some females have had their first estrus cycle as early as four months or as late as twenty-one months.) In general, male cats mature physically and breed later than female cats. Although a tomcat may be able to produce sperm and copulate as early as four or five months of age, the actual time he first breeds is dependent on attaining a minimum body weight (usually 7 to 8 pounds, 3.3 to 3.6 kg) and on many social factors not associated with physical maturity. A male cat not yet "psychologically mature" and secure in his social position may not breed in spite of the physical ability to do so.

Queens undergo a cyclical physiological rhythm of reproductive function called the *estrous cycle.* This cycle is divided into four stages: *anestrus, proestrus, estrus,* and *diestrus* (formerly called *metestrus*). Of the four stages, however, only two, anestrus and estrus, are easily differentiated without laboratory tests.

During anestrus the ovaries are quiescent. This period usually lasts three to four months and usually occurs during the fall and early winter (September or October until January or February in the Northern Hemisphere). It may, however, occur any time of the year. The anestrous state can be artificially induced by the *ovariohysterectomy* or "spaying" operation (see page 269). Anestrus is followed by proestrus, estrus, and diestrus, which occur sequentially and repeatedly during the spring and summer months. During this period of active sexual cycling (*seasonal polyestrus*) breeding occurs. The *estrus* or "heat" period, during which the queen is sexually receptive and breeding will occur, is usually marked by an obvious change of behavior and voice.

The meow becomes lower and very frequent *(calling),* and the cat usually becomes much more affectionate toward humans, rubbing against them (or against inanimate objects) and rolling. Occasionally the estrus female will lose her appetite or spray urine (see page 183). Sometimes you may notice increased size of the vulva, but this is extremely variable and is not a reliable sign of heat. If grasped at the nape of the neck with one hand and stroked along the back or genital area with the other, female cats in estrus usually elevate their hind-quarters, move their tails to one side, and tread (step up and down) with the hindlegs. These same postures occur when a queen accepts a tom for breeding (see page 278).

ESTRUS POSTURE

The changes associated with estrus are most easily detected in queens who are kept indoors and not allowed to breed, since the signs may persist up to twenty days (average six to ten days) in the absence of breeding. Cats with free access to the outdoors or to a tom may pass into and out of heat before you recognize it. Cats are induced ovulators (ovulating in response to breeding), and, if bred, signs of estrus soon pass and pregnancy almost always results. The estrus period in females allowed to breed at will usually has a maximum length of four days. During the breeding season female cats will return to signs of heat about every two or three weeks unless bred or artifically stimulated to ovulate (see page 269). Remember, however, that these time periods are only averages. Each queen has her own normal cycle that, once established, tends to repeat itself.

PREVENTING PREGNANCY

Because the estrous cycle shows a large amount of individual variation and since the onset of heat and breeding can be easily overlooked if your cat has free outdoor access, you must keep an unspayed female indoors and isolated from unneutered male cats to prevent pregnancy. Although several companies are working on products to prevent pregnancy in cats and dogs, there are no reliably safe and effective nonsurgical methods available now to prevent pregnancy in cats. This means that if you choose to live with an unneutered female cat, you must effectively deal with the recurrent behavioral changes that occur during the breeding season if pregnancy is to be prevented. This can be difficult to do, especially if your cat is one of the more vocal and affectionate breeds (e.g., Siamese). Your veterinarian can help you by providing tranquilizers, which may quiet the behavior to some extent, or he or she may be able to artifically induce ovulation, thereby reducing the length of the heat period.

Artifical induction of ovulation is achieved by allowing mating with a vasectomized (sterile, see page 274) male cat or by stimulation of the vagina with a smooth glass or metal rod or moistened cotton-tipped swab. A technique using acupressure over the lower spinal area may also work. Such sterile matings produce a state of false pregnancy (see page 279) and can result in a delay of a month or longer before signs of heat occur again. If you desire, your veterinarian can show you the best way to use a rod, cotton swab, or the acupressure technique for sterile mating or may be able to put you in touch with an owner of a male cat that has had the vasectomy surgery. Unless your cat is a female valuable for breeding purposes, however, these methods are usually more trouble than they are worth. The best way currently available for preventing pregnancy and eliminating heat behavior is the ovariohysterectomy or spaying operation.

ARTIFICIALLY INDUCED OVULATION

Many misconceptions surround the spaying surgery. One of the most prevalent is that the spay will cause a female to become fat and lazy. Not so. As mentioned earlier, this surgery induces a permanent condition comparable to the anestrous state. Cats become fat only if they are using fewer calories than they are eating. Inactivity (laziness) usually accompanies excess weight. Fatness can be caused by metabolic abnormalities (e.g., low thyroid activity), but this is rare. It is most often caused by *overfeeding* and is not *caused* by the ovariohysterectomy. Another common misconception is that it is important for a cat to have a litter before being altered (spayed), that having a litter is important to "personality development," or that it "calms a cat down." In fact, the heat cycle or process of having a litter has no persistent beneficial effect. Although a female cat often has marked changes of personality during estrus, while pregnant, and

OVARIOHYSTER-ECTOMY OR SPAY

when nursing, once the kittens are gone most females return to their usual anestrous personalities.

The best time to perform the ovariohysterectomy is before the first heat. Most veterinarians recommend not earlier than about four to six months of age. The surgery is easiest to perform while the cat is still young (therefore, easier on the cat) and it is usually least expensive for you at this time. It is uncommon for a cat to come into estrus before six months, but it does occur so be aware of your unneutered female's behavior in case an earlier heat cycle calls for surgery sooner. Some veterinarians and humane organizations have experimented by performing ovariohysterectomies on kittens less than ten weeks of age. Although this practice has not yet been proven harmful, it does subject incompletely vaccinated and physiologically less mature cats to the stress of a major surgical operation. Pet owners should consider these facts when selecting the age at which to spay their females. If you fail to have the surgery performed before heat or breeding occurs, however, don't worry that you will have to have an unwanted litter. Spaying can be easily performed during heat and can also be done during pregnancy, although it will probably be more expensive than if performed earlier. *Although there are individual variations,* the procedure for an ovariohysterectomy in most good veterinary hospitals is similar to the following:

Your veterinarian requests that you withhold food from your cat *at least* eight to twelve hours preceding surgery. This allows time for the stomach to empty, preventing vomiting and aspiration of the vomitus into the trachea and lungs during general anesthesia. Preanesthetic drugs are given to reduce apprehension before surgery and to prepare the body for general anesthesia. Anesthesia is usually induced with a short-acting drug given intravenously. Its effects last just long enough to allow the veterinary surgeon to place an *endotracheal tube* into the cat's windpipe (trachea). This airway is the path via which gas anesthetic agents and oxygen are administered to maintain sleep during surgery; it also provides a ready means for resuscitation if any emergency arises.

After the cat is sleeping, the abdomen is clipped free of hair, washed with surgical soap, and disinfected. The cat is then transferred to the surgery area and placed on the operating table belly up. An assistant stands by to monitor anesthesia, breathing, and heart function. The veterinarian, who has been scrubbing his or her hands and donning sterile clothing—cap, mask, and gloves—while the cat is prepared for surgery, steps in and places a sterile drape over the patient before surgery begins.

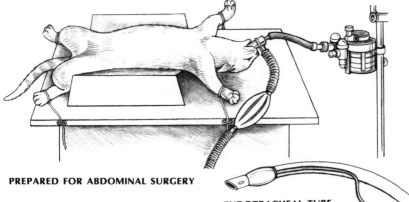

PREPARED FOR ABDOMINAL SURGERY

ENDOTRACHEAL TUBE

An incision into the abdomen is made at the midline. The length of the incision varies with the size of the cat and the difficulty of the surgery but is usually not more than an inch long. Most veterinarians use a special hooklike instrument to reach into the abdomen and pick up one horn of the uterus where it lies along the body wall. The uterine horn is brought out through the incision and followed to the ovary. Clamps are applied, and the blood supply to the ovary is interrupted by *ligatures* (ties placed around blood vessels) or metal vascular clips. The ovary is cut away from its blood supply, which is allowed to return to the abdomen. The other uterine horn and ovary are brought to the incision and treated in the same manner. Then the uterine horns are followed to their point of attachment to the body of the uterus. Its blood supply is interrupted by ties or clips and the uterine body itself is ligated. An incision is made through the uterus to free it, and the horns and ovaries are removed. (Turn to Anatomy, page 29, if you need to review the structure of the uterus and ovaries.) The inner part of the incision is closed with layers of absorbable suture material or stainless steel; then the skin is *sutured* (stitched) closed. With modern anesthesia, the cat begins to wake up shortly following the last stitches and is ready to go back to an enclosure for final recovery. Most healthy cats are acting and eating normally one or two days following surgery. In fact, most feel so good that it is often a chore to try to restrict their exercise.

When you take your female home following surgery, it's a good idea to take her temperature and examine the incision daily even if you are not given specific instructions to do so by your veterinarian. (These are good things to do following any surgery.) Fever and/or swelling, redness, or discharge at the incision site should alert you to call your veterinarian for advice. Normal feeding should resume within forty-eight hours following surgery. Many veterinarians allow you to take your cat home before this time; so if you do, provide meals and water frequently, but in small amounts to avoid stomach upset. Vomiting that occurs more than once or twice, especially if accompanied by inactivity, should again prompt you to call the hospital where the surgery was performed for advice.

TUBAL LIGATION, HYSTER-ECTOMY Rarely veterinarians and spay clinics perform *tubal ligations* (tying of the fallopian tubes so the ova cannot pass into the uterus). This involves the same type of abdominal entry as an ovariohysterectomy and, although it is effective in preventing pregnancy, it has definite disadvantages compared to an ovariohysterectomy. It does not prevent *pyometra* (see page 185), and it does not prevent signs of heat. If you are *sure* you won't mind living with repeated signs of heat, then you may choose a tubal ligation or, better in terms of health, a *hysterectomy* (removing the uterus but leaving one or both ovaries). Remember, however, that neither prevents the signs of heat or has a benefial effect against breast cancer (see page 233). People who choose a hysterectomy or tubal ligation often change their minds a year or two later and request additional surgery to remove the ovaries. Tubal ligation and hysterectomy are not considered standard practice for female neutering in veterinary medicine.

ACCIDENTAL BREEDING

If your cat was bred accidentally, there are alternatives to having an unwanted litter. If you were planning to have your female spayed, as mentioned before, your veterinarian will usually go ahead with the surgery. Usually this is the best and safest step to take. Particularly in the early stages of pregnancy, surgery is not much more difficult than for a female in heat and the fee may be the same. In the later stages of pregnancy the surgery becomes more difficult and the fee usually increases accordingly.

If you have not yet decided on the question of spaying, and if you can get your cat to a veterinarian soon after breeding (within the first twenty-four hours or so, assuming you know your cat has been bred), injections of an estrogenlike compound can be used to prevent pregnancy. The compounds used for this purpose work by preventing implantation of the fertilized ova into their "beds" in the uterine wall. These drugs should be used to prevent pregnancy only if you are unwilling to choose another alternative and are willing to accept possible side effects. Their use in cats is not usually recommended by veterinarians since they may cause uterine changes leading to infection or death of the bone marrow (followed by death of the patient), and most owners cannot be sure when breeding has actually occurred.

Some drugs will induce abortion in cats. Ask your veterinarian for information if you think your cat needs such treatment. A surgical abortion can be performed late in pregnancy if absolutely necessary. Methods similar to those used in humans are not used in cats. Surgical abortions in cats consist of *cesarean sections* in which the kittens are removed through uterine and abdominal incisions. This procedure usually results in blood loss, is stressful on the female, and is not encouraged by most veterinarians.

MALE BIRTH CONTROL

Castration (removal of the testes) is the traditional method employed for neutering (altering) male cats. Although castration renders a male cat sterile and unable to impregnate a female and is the socially responsible thing to do, the birth control aspect is of minor importance unless other neighborhood males are also neutered. (One roaming tom can impregnate all the unaltered females in a neighborhood.) The prime significance of castration for most owners of male cats is the changes of behavior that follow it.

Breeding, fighting, roaming, and urine spraying are behavioral patterns that are activated when the blood level of testosterone (a hormone secreted by the testes) rises markedly, following sexual maturity. Roaming results in encounters between cats—by nature loners—and fighting often results. The wounds and abscesses that follow are not only extremely stressful for the cat but can also become very expensive when they occur repeatedly and require veterinary treatment. Urine spraying is a kind of scent-marking behavior associated with territorial identification (see page 183). Both neutered male and female cats may spray, but this behavior is most characteristic of tomcats. The male who is scent marking backs up to the object to be marked, raises his tail to a 45- to 90-degree angle, and as the tail quivers sprays or squirts a small amount of urine onto the vertical surface of the object. Occasionally squat spraying occurs where the urine is deposited on the ground. Although perfectly normal, this behavior is not acceptable to most cat owners when it is performed around the house. Tomcat urine has a strong and objectionable odor that, together with the stains left from spraying, can be difficult to get rid of.

Castration before puberty prevents the development of behavioral patterns most often considered objectionable by owners of male **BENEFITS OF CASTRATION** cats. Castration later in life, after roaming, fighting, and/or spraying has developed, often stops objectional behavior within two weeks, although in some instances improvement takes several months. In a few instances (6 to 13%) fighting, roaming, and/or spraying persist and are independent of the age of the cat at castration or time of the onset of behavioral problems. Castration also helps prevent the development of "stud tail," (see page 13). And castrated males are generally more affectionate and docile. In other words, a castrated cat is usually a much better pet and companion than his unneutered counterpart.

Castration can be performed by your veterinarian as early as six months of age. Many animal population control advocates encourage the surgical neutering of toms by castration before six months of age. Although this effectively prevents breeding, males neutered at this age do not develop the characteristic secondary physical sex characteristics that distinguish mature male cats (e.g., larger heads and bodies and better defined muscles). Their behavior toward people is *not* adversely affected by early neutering. Should you desire normal male development and if you will be careful to prevent random impregnation of queens by your pet, castration can be delayed until adulthood or until objectionable behaviors develop.

The surgery is simple and should be inexpensive. A short-acting general anesthetic is usually administered intravenously. The hair is plucked from the scrotum (see page 27). After disinfection, two incisions are made in the scrotal sac, one over each testicle, and the testes are removed through them after the spermatic duct and the blood supply are interrupted. The incisions are allowed to heal as open wounds. Most veterinarians will send your cat home to recover the same day or within twenty-four hours following surgery. It is a good idea to examine the castration site for signs of infection and to take your cat's temperature daily until the castration wounds are healing well. No special care is necessary later except perhaps to watch your cat's diet. Although castration does not *cause* a cat to become fat, the lower daily calorie needs of an altered male may result in obesity if you allow free-choice feeding or overfeed him.

VASECTOMY   *Vasectomy,* surgical removal of a portion of the *vas deferens* (see page 27) that conducts the sperm from the testes to the urethra, is rarely performed on male cats. Although vasectomy renders a male cat sterile and unable to impregnate a female, it has no effect on his ability or desire to breed, or on other behavior undesirable in a pet, because it does not remove the source of testosterone—the testes. A vasectomy may be useful to the owner of a purebred cattery who desires to keep a sexually active but sterile male available to bring queens out of heat. But since it has no effect on fighting, roaming, urine spraying, grooming, or docility, it is not desirable for most house pets. Also, vasectomy is a more difficult, and therefore more expensive, operation than castration.

CRYPTORCHIDISM
(RETAINED TESTICLES)

A *cryptorchid* ("hidden testicle") cat has only one (unilateral cryptorchidism) or no (bilateral cryptorchidism) testicles descended into the scrotum. Males with these conditions should not be allowed to breed because the defect is usually inherited. The parents and siblings of these male cats should also be removed from the breeding pool as they can carry this genetic trait. Since both testes are normally present in the scrotum at birth or shortly thereafter, if they have not descended by six to eight months of age, you should assume that the condition is permanent. Although retained testicles do not produce sperm, they continue to secrete testosterone and must be removed unless you want your pet to continue to act like a tomcat. As some testicles have a delayed descent, castration is usually delayed until after one year of age. Retained testicles may be more subject to tumor formation, and although this is a rare problem in cats, it is another reason to be sure that retained testicles are removed. To check the testes, see Anatomy page 27.

BREEDING

Before you decide to breed your cat, ask yourself several questions. The first is are you sure you will find good homes for the kittens? Except for the most sought-after purebred cats, *permanent* good homes are difficult to find. There is an extraordinary excess of cats (and dogs) in this country. More than twenty-seven *million* cats and dogs are impounded annually and more than seventeen million are killed every year. Most animals entering animal shelters and pounds are killed. These are not just cats who have strayed from home; many are pets that have been taken to the pound by owners who know that they will almost certainly be destroyed. They include cats given as unwanted gifts, cute Christmas kittens who have grown into adults and have lost their cuddly charm, cats bought on impulse from pet shop windows, and whole litters intentionally and unintentionally produced for which homes could not be found. Statistics don't include those hundreds of animals who die following abandonment or

DECIDING TO
BREED

275

straying before reaching a shelter or pound, or those killed by humans maliciously or when homes for them could not be found. If you are not *sure* that your kittens won't end up in a pound or pet shop, and if you are not willing to provide a good home for kittens you can't place in other homes, do not allow your cat to reproduce.

Do you have a good place to keep kittens and are you willing to care for them if the mother can't? Even the smallest apartment is usually suitable for raising a litter of kittens since a mother and kittens take up little space, and the mother usually cares for them, at least until around four weeks of age when the kittens begin to consume solid food. But what if the female refuses to care for the kittens or is unable to care for them? Are you ready to assume the responsibility and devote many hours of your time? And what if the mother has difficulty at the time of delivery? You must be willing and able to pay veterinary expenses—perhaps for a cesarean delivery—if real difficulties occur.

Why do you want to breed your cat? Almost everyone is awed by birth and hardly anyone can resist the charm of a kitten, but the cat population cannot afford another litter bred solely so that your children or you can watch the birth. If this is the only reason for breeding, it might be best to make arrangements with a dairy, horse farm, or established cattery to watch a birth, or to take advantage of films and books available on animal reproduction. If you are breeding for profit, you will find that it can be a full-time business to produce *quality* purebred cats, care for them properly, and still make a profit. Many purebred breeders raise cats as a hobby because they know they are likely to break even at best or even take a financial loss. If you are breeding so the female can "have the experience of being a mother" or so she will "calm down" you are being too anthropomorphic and possibly falling prey to old wives' tales. Cats can't anticipate the experience of having kittens; a few will even neglect their litters to be with their owners. The fact that breeding has no permanent effect on personality has already been discussed. Until the pet cat population reaches a more manageable size, these fascinating and beautiful creatures will continue to experience mistreatment and neglect. Everyone, purebred breeders and pet owners alike, should think very seriously before deciding to let males or females breed and produce even a single litter.

BEFORE BREEDING If you decide that it is reasonable to breed your cat you need additional information. *Only outstanding individuals should be selected for breeding.* Both temperament and health should be given equal consideration, and if either is lacking, reproduction should not be permitted. In general terms, no animal affected with an heritable disease or whose littermate or parent is affected should be allowed to reproduce. Many physical abnormalities of cats including forms of retinal atrophy, deafness, patellar luxation (kneecap dislocation), head and facial abnormalities, and heart and kidney defects are genetically influenced diseases and can be elimated by appropriate selection of toms and queens. Genetic selection against shy, nervous cats is also possible. Genetically influenced problems cause unnecessary and extraordinary suffering for pets and expense for their owners. For more information on how to avoid them, consult: Foley, C.W., J.F. Lasley, and G.D. Osweiter, *Abnormalities of Companion Animals: Analysis of Heritability,* Iowa State University Press, Ames, Iowa, 1979; and Robinson, Roy, *Genetics for Cat Breeders,* 3rd ed., Pergamon Press, New York, 1991.

Before a female is bred, she should be vaccinated against infectious diseases (see page 85). She should also test negative for feline leukemia virus (see page 191) and feline immunodeficiency virus (see page 195). Live vaccines should not be given during pregnancy (killed type can be given to a pregnant animal), but the female should be fully protected before breeding so she can pass on a protective level of antibodies to her kittens in the colostrum (first milk). Take a fecal sample to a veterinarian for examination to be sure that a female to be bred is free from intestinal parasites that compete with her for nutrients. It is best to avoid breeding most queens on the first heat unless they are definitely full grown. Generally, this means waiting until the cat is at least one year old so she won't have to try to get enough nutrients to meet both her growth requirements and those of pregnancy. No special feeding is necessary before breeding, assuming your cat is already on a balanced diet, but avoid breeding obese females because they will have more difficulties at delivery. If your cat is over five years old at the time you first consider breeding (most unusual for a cat), definitely consider preventing pregnancy. The incidence of difficult births is much higher in animals first delivering in their later years.

The ideal way to insure that breeding will occur is to take the estrus female to the male's home and let breeding occur at will. "Emotional" factors play an important role in determining whether or not a male cat will breed. Often breeding will not occur in an environment unfamiliar to the male; therefore, it is best to take the female to the male. If the male must be brought into the female's home, keep in mind that it may take several days or even several weeks until the male will readily mate, and allow for this when planning breeding schedules. Planning ahead is also important to allow adequate time to test the male cat for parasites and other transmissible diseases

BREEDING PROCEDURES

before allowing him to meet the queen. To help insure conception, queens should be bred within the first four days of estrus and allowed to copulate at least four times to help insure ovulation. Even when the male feels comfortable and the female is in heat, breeding sometimes will not occur. Female cats in estrus do show preferences for certain males and will sometimes reject one male while readily accepting another. (Males will also occasionally reject estrus queens, but this is uncommon.)

BREEDING BEHAVIOR When placed together, a receptive female (see page 267) and an interested tom will often sniff one another's noses, and the female will rub against the male or roll on the ground. The male moves toward the female's back and grabs the skin at the nape of her neck with his teeth. At this time the female will begin treading with her hindlegs, move her tail to one side, and strongly curve her back downward and her pelvis upward. The male slips over the female's back and then moves backward until genital contact occurs. This is

MATING

followed by several strong and rapid pelvic thrusts resulting in intromission, quickly followed by ejaculation. Within five to ten seconds after actual breeding has occurred the female usually emits a loud, sharp cry, and the male rapidly dismounts and springs away to avoid being scratched by the female. The female usually licks her vulva, then rolls and rubs on the ground (the after reaction). If the cats are left together, this series of events may be repeated three to five (or sometimes more) times in an hour.

The female may lose her receptivity to the male (willingness to breed) as early as twelve hours following mating, but, on the average, ovulation occurs twenty-seven hours following breeding. A return to the nonreceptive state follows ovulation. After breeding, be sure to confine your cat until you are sure receptivity has passed. If another male is accepted and breeding occurs again before all the ova have been fertilized by the desired father, the litter could have more than a single father.

DETERMINING PREGNANCY

The first external sign of pregnancy you may see is a change in nipple color from a pale to a dark rose pink, and hair loss around the nipple area making them more prominant. These changes appear about three weeks after successful mating. About three or four weeks following conception it is often possible for a veterinarian to feel the fetuses in the uterus through the abdominal wall. At this time they are distinct round lumps in the uterus. Later, the fetuses are not so distinct, but usually a veterinarian can confirm pregnancy by palpation, since cats are small and the abdominal wall is thin. If necessary, an ultrasound examination can be used to detect kittens at two or three weeks. An X-ray film taken after five and one-half weeks of pregnancy (when the kittens' bones are ossified) can also be used for confirmation of pregnancy and to determine the number of kittens present.

Following a sterile mating, which occasionally occurs in cats, false pregnancy (*pseudopregnancy*) may occur. Although signs are not usually marked, milk production may occur, and a rare cat may even make a nest and go through a pseudolabor. False pregnancy usually terminates spontaneously about five weeks after breeding. Hormones and/or *prolactin-* (lactation-stimulating hormone) inhibiting drugs can be administered by a veterinarian to relieve severe signs of pseudopregnancy. It is best, however, to avoid hormone treatment if possible, since reproduction-modifying drugs have side effects in cats, and following hormone treatment some cats appear to remain in continual estrus or anestrus. Cats with repeated pseudopregnancies should have an ovariohysterectomy to prevent recurrent signs.

FALSE PREGNANCY

CARE DURING PREGNANCY

Pregnancy usually lasts sixty-three to sixty-six days, although some normal pregnancies have lasted as long as seventy-one days. Most queens kitten around sixty-six days. If delivery occurs before sixty-three days many kittens are stillborn or die shortly after birth. Pregnancy increases the protein and calorie requirements of the mother, but if you have been feeding a good quality, well-balanced diet, no major changes in content or calorie supply are necessary during the first two to three weeks.

FEEDING DURING PREGNANCY AND LACTATION Sources of high-quality proteins, such as milk products, eggs, and muscle meat, can be used to improve the protein content of maintenance foods and to increase their palatability without sacrificing nutritional balance if they are added at no more than 10% of the diet's dry matter. Kitten milk replacement formulas (see page 291) can also be offered as a supplement to maintenance foods.

After three weeks of pregnancy, well-balanced commercial foods adequately formulated for kitten growth are nutritionally satisfactory for the rest of the pregnancy and for lactation. Good products will provide at least 1,800 to 2,300 calories per pound dry matter (4 to 5 calories per gram fed) and contain at least 30% high-quality protein. The amount of food offered will have to be increased as pregnancy advances. By the end of pregnancy expect to be feeding about twice the volume of food your cat ate before she was bred. Although food intake increases, calorie requirements on a *per-pound* basis increase only slightly during pregnancy—from a baseline of about 40 to about 50 calories per pound (from 85 to 110 calories per kilogram) body weight per day. It is because the mother is gaining weight due to the growth of the fetuses that her food intake must increase as much as it does. Since it is often impossible for the queen to take in all the necessary food in two meals, particularly as the uterus enlarges and begins to compress the other abdominal organs, you must increase the daily number of meals throughout pregnancy and lactation or offer food on a free-choice basis.

It is not unusual for a queen to partially lose her appetite and perhaps lose a little weight over a few days during the third week of pregnancy, but after that period a steady increase should be evident until twenty-four to forty-eight hours prior to delivery. Ask your veterinarian for advice if you don't think your queen is eating adequately to maintain a healthy pregnancy. Vitamin and/or mineral supplements are not usually required if the diet you offer is nutritionally sound, but you may also wish to discuss this issue with your veterinarian.

Throughout pregnancy it is extremely important not to overfeed and/or underexercise, to prevent obesity and poor muscle tone that can cause a difficult delivery. Most cats restrict their exercise as the time for delivery approaches. If your cat seems too active during the last week of pregnancy, however, you may have to confine her to certain areas of the house where jumping and running can be prevented.

To minimize psychological stress and to prevent your cat from having her kittens in an undesirable place (like the middle of your bed!), accustom her to a warm and draft-free delivery area well before the time of delivery. If your cat has her own bed, which she prefers, this is all that is really necessary.

Otherwise, provide a maternity box (queening box). The best, most simple kind is a cardboard box with an opening cut on the side about four or five inches from the bottom. This design provides a convenient entrance and exit for the mother, but keeps the kittens from falling out. The box should have a top that can be opened or removed to provide access to the kittens when necessary but left in place at other times to provide a dark, secure environment for the queen. Introduce the cat to the box daily, beginning at least a week before delivery and encourage her to sleep in it by lining it with soft clean towels. If you find that she is not interested but attempts to make a nest in a closet or some other area, you may need to place the nest box there to get her to use it. Since newspapers are easy to remove and discard, it is simplest to line the box with several layers of them at the time of delivery. Clean sheets, towels, or diapers, however, are just as satisfactory and may be more pleasing to your cat.

GIVE YOUR CAT A MATERNITY BOX

MATERNITY BOX

If you have a very long-haired cat, you may wish to gently clip (not shave) the hair away from the vulvar area and the nipples before delivery. It makes delivery a little more tidy and allows the kittens to reach the nipples a little more easily, but is not a necessity.

DELIVERY

A week or two prior to *parturition* (delivery) some queens may become restless and search for a nesting area. Even if there are no behavioral changes, you will usually be able to detect rapid enlargement of the mammary glands in the week before delivery. Milk (colostrum, see page 87) can usually be expressed from the nipples within forty-eight hours of delivery. In some cats the rectal temperature drops for a short time around twelve to thirty-six hours before delivery from the normal 101 to 102°F (38.3 to 39.2° C) to as low as 98°F (36.7°C). However, this is not a reliable sign, and it is necessary to watch for others that more accurately signal the impending birth.

Usually a day or two before delivery the queen will lose her appetite, become anxious and more vocal than usual, and begin to shred the materials used for lining the nest box. She may even vomit. As delivery becomes even closer, she usually licks frequently at the abdominal and genital areas. If you have failed to adjust the female to the kindling (kittening) area, your cat may try to nest in your bed, in a closet, or in some other unsuitable spot. Encourage her to remain near the maternity box and stay with her until she becomes comfortable. It is not necessary for the queen to actually be in the box, as mild exercise during the first stages of labor and between kitten deliveries actually helps the process. If she seems particularly distressed about using a designated nest box, however, it is best to let the queen nest where she is most comfortable since emotional stress can inhibit or terminate labor. Queens often move their kittens after delivery, so it is not usually a problem for you to allow them to be delivered in one spot, then move them to a new, more suitable one, once delivery is completed.

During the *first stage of labor* the female kneads and rearranges the bedding and may even pull hair from her body in her attempt to make a nest. Rapid breathing (sometimes panting) and trembling are often seen, and her pulse rate will increase. Frequent changes of position are made; colostrum may drip from her nipples, and blood-tinged discharge may appear at the vaginal opening. Uterine contractions moving the kitten from the uterine horn to the body of the uterus and the cervix are occurring during this first stage, which may last twelve to twenty-four hours. A long first stage is particularly characteristic of a first pregnancy. If the signs last more than a day, if the vaginal discharge is foul smelling or consists of large quantities of pure blood and/or blood clots, or if your cat seems to pass into the second stage then back to the first, or seems unusually uncomfortable, discuss the matter with your veterinarian before assuming everything is all right.

During the *second stage of labor* you will see forceful straining movements caused by the simultaneous contractions of the abdominal muscles and the diaphragm. At the beginning of this stage you *may* see a small amount of straw-colored or greenish fluid passed at the vulva. This is due to the rupture of the *allantois-chorion* (the protective membrane that covers the kitten) as it passes into the vaginal canal. It may take as long as an hour for a kitten to be delivered once the second stage begins. The female may lie on her side or on her sternum (chest), or she will stand and squat as if she were going to have a bowel movement during the most vigorous portions of straining. The *amnion* (membranous sac) enclosing the head of the kitten sometimes appears at the vulva. It may, however, be ruptured before the kitten is delivered. Once the head and paws of the kitten appear, complete delivery should be finished *within* fifteen minutes—if not, call your veterinarian. The nose and feet of the kitten should not appear and disappear each time the female strains. In the classic birth position the kitten is delivered with its sternum on the vaginal floor, nose first and its front paws along the sides of its face. Nearly half of all kittens, however, are delivered rear legs first. This usually causes no problem.

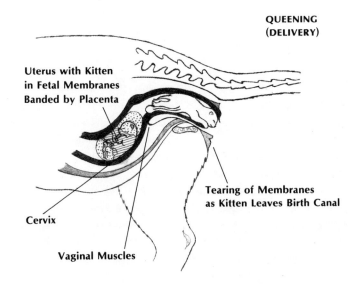

QUEENING
(DELIVERY)

Uterus with Kitten
in Fetal Membranes
Banded by Placenta

Tearing of Membranes
as Kitten Leaves Birth Canal

Cervix

Vaginal Muscles

As soon as a kitten is delivered, the amniotic sac (amnion) should be broken to allow the kitten to breathe. Cats are normally very good mothers and usually do this immediately, but inexperienced or nervous females may not. If this is the case, you must break the amnion or the kitten will suffocate. However, if the umbilical cord is not broken during delivery, it is not necessary to break it immediately. Significant amounts of blood are found in the placenta, and by allowing the umbilical cord to remain unbroken, you allow time for this blood to pass into the kitten. Normally the mother nips the umbilical cord and breaks it as she cleans and licks the kitten following delivery. If she doesn't do this after about fifteen minutes, a clean piece of thread or unwaxed dental floss should be tied around the cord about one-half to one inch from the body wall. Then

TYING THE UMBILICAL CORD

cut or break the cord just beyond (distal to) the tie and dip it briefly in povidone-iodine disinfectant solution. If the mother has a tendency to bite the cords very near the kitten's abdominal wall, you should prevent this and cut the cord yourself, as very short umbilical cords become infected much more often than those of a more usual length.

PREVENT UMBILICAL INFECTION If you have a kitten with a short cord prompt treatment with antibiotics given by your veterinarian will usually prevent umbilical cord infection, a common cause of death in young kittens. Examine the umbilical area for evidence of swelling, discoloration, or drainage that may indicate infection. Untreated infections can easily cause death within three days.

Normally, the placenta (afterbirth) is delivered with or just after the kitten. It is a good idea to count the placentas as they are delivered to be sure all are passed. Retained placentas can cause uterine inflammation and infection (see page 185). It is normal, but unecessary, for the female to eat the placenta following each delivery. It is best to let the queen eat only one or two; the ingestion of too many can cause vomiting and diarrhea.

The time of delivery of the placenta and the period of uterine rest that follows each kitten is the *third stage of labor.* During the rest period the queen often lies still and tends her kittens. Some queens will get up and move about; this can actually help speed delivery. The rest period between kittens varies from about ten to fifteen minutes to several hours. It is not usually more than one to two hours, however. Average-sized litters for cats range from three to five kittens, but as many as fourteen have been delivered and survived! Average delivery times range from about two to six hours. Normal parturitions, however, may take longer than six hours. Some last up to twenty-four or even thirty-six hours, but deliveries lasting longer than this are considered abnormal even though kittens have survived when delivered over a period of three days.

DIFFICULT DELIVERY (DYSTOCIA)

Difficult deliveries are usually caused either by obstruction of delivery of the fetus, or by uterine inertia (see below). *Dystocia* must usually be treated with the help of a veterinarian. If any of the stages of labor seem abnormally long, if large amounts of fresh blood and/ or blood clots are expelled from the vagina for more than ten minutes, or if your cat shows signs of excessive discomfort or extreme quietness, call your veterinarian.

If you can see a kitten at the vulva, but delivery seems slow or the kitten appears and disappears, you may be able to help delivery. Wash your hands and lubricate a finger with a lubricant such as sterile petrolatum or sterile water-soluble jelly. Insert your finger into the vaginal canal and move it around the kitten, trying to determine where the head and the front and rear legs are. You may be able to hook a front leg in an abnormal backward position and bring it forward. If the kitten seems fairly normally placed (see illustration, page 283), grasp him or her with a gauze pad, clean cloth, or your fingers and gently pull with each contraction. It is best to try to grasp the kitten around the shoulders to avoid excessive pressure on the head, and it is best to pull downward because the vagina is angled toward the ground. Do not pull on the amniotic sac surrounding the kitten. If the kitten's head just seems too big to fit through the vulva, you can sometimes gently manipulate the edges of the vulva around the head. A veterinarian will sometimes make an incision at the upper part of the vulvar opening to enlarge it. It is not advisable to perform this procedure at home unless it is impossible to get veterinary help.

If a retained placenta blocks delivery of a kitten, you can often reach it. Grasp it with a gauze pad or clean cloth and gently but firmly pull until it passes out of the vaginal canal. Once an obstruction to delivery is relieved, a female will often have a prolonged rest period before the next kitten is delivered.

Failure of the uterus to contract efficiently (*uterine inertia*) may occur following prolonged straining to deliver a kitten or may be a primary problem, as in the case of an obese or older cat. A form of uterine inertia can be caused by excessive excitement, or by other psychological stresses during delivery. This is why it is important to familiarize your cat with the maternity area well before delivery. It is also why strangers should not be present during delivery unless the cat is extremely calm about them. A labor inhibited by psychogenic stresses can often be helped by having only one or two familiar people remain with the cat during delivery. Rarely, tranquilizers will be necessary. If you suspect uterine inertia, call your veterinarian for advice.

If no obstruction to delivery is found, your veterinarian may have to administer a drug called *oxytocin* to initiate new uterine contractions. Other drugs may be administered as well. If medical therapy does not initiate proper birth or there is some other problem that cannot be relieved with external manipulations, your veterinarian will want to perform a *cesarean section*—surgery in which the kittens are removed through incisions in the abdomen and uterus. It is usually possible to spay your female (see page 269) at the time of such surgery. Unless the difficult birth is solely attributable to the kittens' abnormalities it is probably best to have the spaying done. Mothers who have difficult deliveries tend to repeat them. Most queens are able to nurse and care for their kittens normally following cesarean surgery.

KITTENS WHO WON'T BREATHE

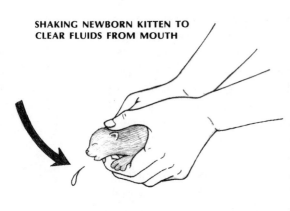

SHAKING NEWBORN KITTEN TO CLEAR FLUIDS FROM MOUTH

If the queen doesn't break the amniotic sac covering the kitten's head within a minute or two, you should. Then hold the kitten in your hands or wrap in a towel. Support the head so it doesn't swing freely, then move the whole kitten vigorously in a wide arc from about chest to knee level. At the end of the arc the kitten's nose should point toward the ground. This helps clear excess fluids from the nose and major airways. Other methods to remove excess fluids are to put your mouth over the kitten's nose and mouth and suck, or to use an infant ear syringe to suck the fluid from the kitten's mouth and throat. After clearing the airways, rub the face, chest, and body of the kitten with a rough towel. If the kitten still does not start to breathe and cry, take in a breath of air, place your mouth over the kitten's nose and mouth, and blow gently until you see the chest expand. Remove your mouth and let the kitten exhale, then repeat. (Using mouth-to-nose and mouth-to-mouth resuscitation and/or airway clearing carries some small risk of infection for humans should the kitten be contaminated with certain bacteria.) Shaking and towel drying even healthy kittens is a good idea if the mother is not interested or is too slow, but this is not absolutely necessary.

CARE OF THE FEMALE FOLLOWING DELIVERY

Although for the first two days the queen will stay almost constantly with her kittens, within twenty-four hours of delivery she should leave the nest for short periods of time, move about, and be normally interested in eating and drinking. For cats who do not eat or drink after delivery, those who have fevers or who seem abnormally quiet or inactive, as well as those who seem to neglect their kittens, there should be no delay in arranging for examination by a veterinarian. Problems following delivery are too complex to be treated well at home without veterinary consultation.

Shortly after delivery a brownish-red vulvar discharge may be seen that may become greenish or greenish black. Such discharges should change to clear mucous or cease within one to three weeks following delivery. A profuse red, bloody discharge following delivery or any vulvar discharge that is odorous or looks like pus or seems to be present in abnormally large amounts or for too many days should alert you to take your cat to a veterinarian for a thorough examination. Such abnormal discharges may indicate excessive internal bleeding, retained placenta or kitten, and/or uterine infection (see page 185).

If all seems well with the mother, little special treatment is necessary. Keep her indoors following delivery. Heat (estrus) often occurs within one to four weeks following delivery, and she may become pregnant while still nursing newborn kittens. Since lactation itself is a great stress and the uterus has not had sufficient time to return to its prepregnancy condition, breeding should not be allowed at this time. Keeping the queen indoors also avoids exposure to diseases that she could catch or carry home to the fragile nursing kittens. Her diet the first few days following delivery can be the same as that just before. As lactation progresses, however, expect her food intake to increase. A rule of thumb to use is to feed the normal maintenance requirement (about 40 calories per pound per day, 85 calories per kilogram) plus 100 to 125 calories per day per pound of kittens (220 to 275 calories per kilogram). And be sure to continue to feed a high-quality, high-protein diet since, as in pregnancy, protein requirements for lactation are higher than normal. By the end of lactation a female may be consuming three to four times as much food as she was prior to breeding; in fact, it is almost impossible to overfeed a nursing queen! But despite all rules of thumb, the best guide to feeding is the appearance of the cat. If she is thin and worn-out looking her diet may need adjustment. Diarrhea in the nursing mother often indicates that a diet inadequate in energy is being fed. Poor-quality high-fiber diets cause the mother to consume large volumes of food in an attempt to meet her nutritional requirements, and diarrhea soon follows. Avoid this problem by offering only good-quality high-protein/high-energy foods to nursing females. Although balanced vitamin-mineral supplements are not required if a proper diet is fed, they are probably most beneficial when used during lactation. Also be sure water is freely available as dehydration will decrease milk production.

The common problems which may affect the female following parturition are infection of the uterus (*acute metritis*), inflammation of the mammary glands (*mastitis*), and milk fever (*puerperal tetany*). These problems are covered on pages 185, 144, and 228.

CARE OF NEWBORNS

It is a rare queen who needs help caring for her kittens following delivery. The most common problem with kittens following delivery is caused by people who are too anxious to handle the kittens, upsetting the mother and causing her to move them from place to place. Since it is not customary for a veterinarian to examine the queen and kittens immediately after delivery (since problems are uncommon and handling may cause psychological upset to the mother), it is wise for a person with whom the queen is familiar to examine the kittens thoroughly within twenty-four hours following delivery to be sure they are free from defects (see page 294). The sex of each kitten can also be checked at this time. After this, restrict handling of the kittens to about fifteen minutes per day until their *eyes are open* and they are moving about freely. Some handling is both physically and psychologically beneficial to kittens, but too much is stressful. A normal litter is quiet, and the kittens sleep most of the time they are not nursing. Most kittens weigh between 3 to 3.7 ounces (90 to 110 g) at birth. Each kitten should gain a minimum of 7 to 10% of his or her birth weight each day following birth. Normally the birth weight will double in about ten days. Kittens who fail to gain weight, or cry and squirm continuously, should alert you to look for signs of neglect or illness, such as weakness, inability to nurse, diarrhea, or lowered body temperature (see page 289). If you find these or other signs of illness or defect, have the litter examined by a veterinarian, since treating young kittens is difficult.

First-time mothers may not have much milk during the initial twenty-four hours following delivery. The first milk is colostrum, which is rich in antibodies (see page 87) to help protect kittens from illness during the first few weeks of life. If at all possible, the kittens should suckle the first milk soon after birth, since they are best able to absorb these special proteins through their intestines for only the first twenty-four hours. Only small amounts are necessary, so don't be alarmed unless the mother's milk supply continues to seem small after the first twenty-four hours. (Test this by looking at the fullness of the mammary glands and squeezing a nipple with a milking action, from near the body to the nipple tip, with your fingers. It should be easy to express a few drops of milk.) Kittens use their sense of smell to locate the nipples, so don't wash the mother's breast area just before or just after delivery.

Cats who ignore or actively reject their litters should be examined by a veterinarian, who can sometimes solve the problem by prescribing tranquilizers. Rejection must be eliminated or the kittens will be unable to nurse, since the mother actively initiates the nursing process during the first two to three weeks of the kittens' lives. In some of these instances, however, nothing helps. In such cases and at times when there is insufficient milk, or if the mother dies, you must take her place. If it has not been possible for the kittens to suckle the colostrum, contact your veterinarian for advice on their immunization.

CARING FOR ORPHANED KITTENS

Then assume care of the kittens or foster them to another nursing mother. (Nursing cats readily accept new kittens.) Try to cross-foster orphan or rejected kittens onto mothers with kittens the same age and size or supervise nursing to be sure all are getting sufficient milk.

Kittens who must be separated from a mother must be kept in an environment free from drafts because they have difficulty controlling their body temperatures. A kitten's temperature may normally be as low as 98.6°F (36°C) at birth, increasing to 100°F (37.5°C) by seven days and it must be maintained for proper nursing to occur. From birth to about five days of age, the room or box temperature should be 85 to 90°F (29.4 to 32.2°C); from about five to twenty days, about 80°F (26.7°C). After twenty days the environmental temperature should be lowered gradually to somewhere between 70° (21.1°C) and 75°F (23.9°C) by the fourth week. Humidity of around 60% helps prevent dehydration.

The best way to provide the proper temperature for orphan kittens if you don't have a incubator is to use a heating pad. Water-circulating pads prevent burns, which may occur when electric pads are used. Hang the heating pad down one side of the box and onto about one fourth of the bottom. Then adjust the temperature control to maintain the proper air temperature. By covering only part of the floor of the box, you allow the kitten to get away from the heat if necessary. For kittens less than seven days of age, place the pad only on the side of the box, since their reflexes are not sufficiently developed to permit them to move if they are becoming overheated by the pad. The heating pad and box bottom should be covered with newspaper, cloth, or diapers that are changed each time they become soiled. Although newborns cannot stand or walk, they move with a swimming motion. The floor covering should provide firm footing to help them move and to avoid splaying of the legs, which can interfere with the normal development of walking.

Many authorities recommend that each kitten be kept in a separate compartment until two or three weeks of age to keep them from sucking each other's ears, tails, feet, and genitals, but if they are allowed to suckle sufficiently at each nursing period, you will probably find that this is not necessary and can thereby avoid this unnatural rearing practice. Research has shown that kittens handled daily are more emotionally stable and resistant to stress. This does not mean, however, that children should handle them without supervision or that they should be handled by strangers (who can carry disease). Handling while feeding is sufficient for kittens less than three weeks old.

NORMAL DEVELOPMENT

Expect the dried umbilical cord to fall off a normal kitten two to three days following birth. Although kittens are blind, vision is present when the eyes open around seven to ten days of age (range of two to fifteen days). The eyes are normally blue-gray when they first open and change to the normal adult color by four to six weeks of age. Newborn kittens can hear even though the ear canals are closed. The ear canals open at about two weeks of age. Kittens can normally support their weight on the front legs between one and two weeks of age and begin walking just after two weeks. They cannot retract their claws until about three weeks after birth and they are not steady

SEXING KITTENS

MALE   FEMALE

on their feet until they are four weeks old. By five to six weeks they are running, jumping, and climbing. Use the illustration on page 290 to help you sex kittens.

Orphan kittens should be fed the formula that most closely approaches the composition of normal queen's milk. Although you can get by with home formulas made from cow's milk, cat's milk is very high in protein (about 60% more on a dry-matter basis than cow's milk, about five times as much as human milk) and comparatively high in fat, and commercial formulas designed for cats (e.g., KMR® and other kitten milk replacers) come much closer to the real thing. These commercial formulas are usually available in pet stores and from some veterinarians, but if they aren't, you can use similar formulas designed for puppies that are usually readily available. Commercial orphan kitten formulas can be used to supplement-feed large litters as well. The best way to determine how much formula each kitten needs is to weigh the kitten and use a table of calorie requirements. The required amount of formula is then divided into three portions fed at eight-hour intervals unless the kitten is very small. Kittens weighing less than 4 ounces will probably do better with feedings spaced at six-hour intervals.

FEEDING ORPHAN KITTENS

CALORIES NEEDED PER POUND BODY WEIGHT	CALORIES NEEDED PER KG BODY WEIGHT	WEEK
190	418	1
125	275	2–5
100	220	5–10

(Example: A 4-ounce [120 g] kitten needs ¼ × 190 = 47.5 calories per day during the first week of life [0.12 kg × 418 = 50 calories]. This is about 1.6 ounces of formula [48 ml], a little over 3 tablespoonfuls, containing 30 calories per ounce.)

If you supply the proper caloric requirements you do not need to feed most kittens more than three times a day. However, if the kitten cannot take in the required volume at three feedings, the number of feedings must be increased. At each feeding the kitten should eat until just comfortably full—not until the abdomen is tight and distended. A steady weight gain (about ¼ to ⅓ pound, 100 to 150 grams per week) and a normal stool are indicators that the kitten is being fed properly.

HOME FORMULAS FOR TEMPORARY FEEDING OF ORPHAN KITTENS

4 oz (120 ml) whole milk
1 egg yolk (15 g)
1 drop multiple infant vitamins
About 30 calories per ounce (30 ml)

16 oz (480 ml) whole cow's milk
1 tsp (5 ml) corn syrup
1 egg yolk (15 g)
pinch table salt
About 30 calories per ounce (30 ml)

All formula is best fed after being warmed to body temperature (about 100°F, 37.8°C). Keep all unused formula refrigerated and all equipment used scrupulously clean to avoid introducing infection. To sterilize feeding equipment, immerse it for fifteen minutes in boiling water. Formula can be administered with an eyedropper, syringe, nursing bottle, or stomach tube. A small syringe or eyedropper is easiest for inexperienced hands. If a nursing bottle is used, the holes in the nipple should be enlarged if the formula does not drip slowly from the nipple when the full bottle is inverted. Be sure the nipple size is suitable for the size of kitten you are trying to nurse. Kittens need to be fed with a special pet nursing bottle or a doll's bottle. Hold the kitten on his or her stomach. Gently separate the kitten's lips with your fingers and slip the nipple in. A healthy, hungry kitten will usually suck vigorously after tasting the milk. Use a towel to give the kitten something to push and knead against as if nursing naturally.

KITTEN NURSING FROM BOTTLE

Weak kittens may have to be held vertically and formula placed slowly in their mouths. *Do not* place a kitten on his or her back for feeding or squirt liquid rapidly into the mouth. These methods can cause aspiration of the fluid into the lungs, which will be followed by pneumonia. If you wish to use a stomach tube for feeding (the fastest method), ask your veterinarian for a demonstration.

After each feeding the kittens should be stimulated to urinate and defecate. Moisten a cotton swab, tissue, or soft cloth with warm water and gently but vigorously massage the anogenital area. Nursing kittens' stools are normally firm (not hard) and yellow. If diarrhea develops, the first thing to do is dilute the formula by about half by the addition of boiled water. If this does not help within twenty-four hours, consult a veterinarian. Cow's milk often causes diarrhea because of its high lactose content.

WEANING

Between the ages of three and four weeks you can start to wean most kittens. Solid foods containing meat should be a part of kittens' diets as soon as possible to prevent iron deficiency. Place a shallow pan of formula on the floor of their box. Change it as needed to keep the food fresh, but leave it out most of the time so the kittens have plenty of opportunity to eat. At first the kittens will step and fall into it and make a general mess, but soon they will be lapping at it. When this stage is reached meat or egg yolk baby food, or commercial cat food can be added to make a gruel. After they are eating the gruel, the amount of formula can be decreased until they are eating solid food and drinking water. Eggs, cottage cheese, yogurt, and meat may be added to their diet as they become adjusted to eating solid food. However, it is best to encourage the consumption of complete, balanced commercial growth foods to avoid developing preferences for nutritionally incomplete food and to avoid causing nutritional deficiencies. Kittens with a natural mother should be allowed to continue nursing during the weaning process until they are eating well-balanced meals of solid food on their own. Although disease-preventing antibodies found in mother's milk cannot be absorbed into the kitten's system, they provide local protection (passive local immunity) in the gastrointestinal tract. Gradual weaning, then, is very desirable to allow time for the kitten's immune system to mature. All changes in feeding should be made gradually to avoid causing digestive upsets.

By five weeks of age the kittens have most of their baby teeth, so that a mother will usually become more and more reluctant to nurse. As the kittens increase their intake of solid food, the mother will gradually restrict nursing time so that weaning can be completed between six and eight weeks of age. Weaning may be achieved this normal, gradual way. But if there is an actual weaning day, offer the queen water but no food, or feed only a small portion of the maintenance diet on that day. Over the following five days gradually increase food back to the normal maintenance level. This procedure helps decrease her milk production.

If milk production does not seem to decrease rapidly enough and the female seems uncomfortable, *do not* remove milk from the glands. This will only prolong the problem. Cold packs applied to the mammary glands may help. If the problem is severe, consult a veterinarian for help as lactation-inhibiting drugs can be administered in cases of extreme discomfort.

UMBILICAL HERNIAS AND OTHER CONGENITAL DEFECTS

Serious birth defects are uncommon in mixed breed kittens, but each member of the litter whether purebred or not should be examined soon after birth and watched as he or she develops to detect any which may be present. Problems to look for soon after birth because they may need veterinary intervention include cleft patate (hole in the hard palate that makes nursing difficult or impossible), imperforate anus (anus sealed closed by skin preventing stool passage), and umbilical hernia.

A *hernia* is a protrusion of a part of the body or of an organ through an abnormal opening in the surrounding tissues. In an umbilical hernia a portion of fat or internal organs protrude through an incompletely closed umbilical ring. Most umbilical hernias are present at birth, but some may be acquired if the mother chews the umbilical cord too short, leaves the placentas attached too long, or through other careless handling of the cord and/or placenta. Congenital umbilical hernias in kittens are usually small, often get smaller as the kitten ages, and usually do not require surgical repair. If your kittens have large umbilical hernias or hernias you can push into the abdomen with your finger, consult your veterinarian about the necessity of repair.

Heart defects are sometimes present at birth and are sometimes the cause of *runting* (smaller-than-average-size kittens). Kittens with such defects who survive until weaning are usually diagnosed abnormal by a veterinarian at their first physical exam.

Problems that are noticed after the first three weeks of age usually consist of abnormalities in the development of walking. Incoordination may result when kittens are infected with the panleukopenia virus while still in the uterus. There are, however, many other causes of locomotor difficulties. If you notice any, a veterinarian should be consulted.

NEONATAL CONJUNCTIVITIS
(*OPHTHALMIA NEONATORUM*)

Signs of infection of the conjunctiva are often seen about the time kittens begin to open their eyes (around seven to ten days). Sticky yellow discharges are present that often seal the eyelids shut until you or the mother cat cleans them, and soon after being cleaned away they return. In some instances the infection is so severe that the lids do not open and severe damage to the eye itself occurs. This type of infectious conjunctivitis of kittens is caused by various bacteria and bacterialike organisms that are thought to be acquired from the mother while the kittens are still in the uterus or soon after birth.

If you notice signs of conjunctivitis in your kittens or if their eyes do not open on schedule, early treatment is important to avoid permanent damage to the eyes. The best procedure is to take the whole litter to your veterinarian who can tell you whether actual eye damage is present or likely to occur. If the infection is simple he or she will provide you with an appropriate antibiotic ointment that you will be instructed to instill into the eyes several times a day after removing the discharges.

Until the kittens can be examined by a veterinarian, home care consists of gently wiping away accumulated discharges with a soft cloth, tissue, or cotton ball moistened with warm water. Follow this by gentle separation of the eyelids and removal of discharges that have become trapped behind them.

For more information on breeding and reproduction in cats, see: Pederson, Neils C., *Feline Husbandry,* American Veterinary Publications, Inc., Goleta, Calif., 1991.

6

YOU, YOUR CAT, AND YOUR VETERINARIAN

HOW TO FIND A "GOOD" VETERINARIAN

Choosing a veterinarian is one of the most important decisions you will have to make concerning your cat's health. Just as in any profession, there are bad veterinarians as well as good ones. There are no specific rules for finding the best one for your cat. However, considering some of the following points may help you in your search.

Find a veterinarian with whom you feel comfortable. No matter how skilled the veterinarian, you cannot make the best use of the services of someone you dislike personally or feel uncomfortable being around.

A good veterinarian explains things thoroughly and in a manner you can understand. However, veterinary medicine is a career that puts great demands on an individual's time, and your veterinarian may sometimes seem rushed or fail to explain things thoroughly to you. This is understandable, but if it happens routinely and you are disturbed about it, let your veterinarian know. There is no need for your veterinarian to give explanations in totally technical terms. Medical terminology is more exact but can be confusing, so most matters should be explained in general terms that you can understand. Veterinarians who continually rely on technical language when discussing your cat's health may be on an "ego trip" or trying to "snow" you, but because they are so familiar with medical terms, sometimes the reason is simply that they forget that you aren't. Let your veterinarian know if you are having trouble understanding and request a simpler explanation.

Good and bad veterinarians exist in all age groups. Don't fall into the trap of believing that an older veterinarian knows more and a younger one less, or vice versa. In general, veterinarians who have been in practice for a while have more experience; but remember, not everyone learns from experience. A recent graduate often has better knowledge of new techniques, but may seem clumsy or insecure. Keep these things in mind and try to evaluate your veterinarian on the quality of care your pet receives. The best veterinarians are always improving their skills through continuing education acquired through courses, videos, and journals. The demand to update medical skills continually will sometimes call your veterinarian away from practice when you wish he or she were in. However, a good veterinarian will always provide a referral or a replacement veterinarian for you at those times.

One way to evaluate a new veterinarian is through your first office call. You should see the veterinarian personally, not be required to leave your cat and "check back later" or have veterinary assistants take care of the whole problem. The people who handle your pet, both the assistants and the veterinarian, should seem capable and use a minimum of restraint on nervous animals unless they have made an attempt to "make friends" without success. A thorough physical examination should be performed and questions regarding your cat's medical history should be asked. Unless your cat sees the veterinarian extremely frequently (more than once a week), a general physical should always be performed at each visit. (Since cats can't tell us their problems, we have to look for them, and new problems can easily arise from one visit to the next.)

A clean office and new equipment are often indicative of good veterinary care. But don't be mislead by a fancy "front room." Most good veterinarians will allow you to see the whole hospital *at a convenient time.* One who won't may have something to hide. Some veterinarians have fancy equipment but don't use it or use it improperly. Veterinarians in small towns or rural areas may not have enough demand to necessitate expensive, specialized equipment in their offices, but even a simple veterinary clinic should be clean and orderly. Again, try to judge your veterinarian on the kind of medicine practiced, not entirely on appearances.

FEES   It is as difficult to judge a veterinarian by his or her fees as it is according to the kind of equipment in the office. What is a reasonable fee varies between geographical areas and types of practices. In general, it is fair to expect to pay more for veterinary services at hospitals, where the latest equipment and specialized services are available, since it costs the veterinarian more to maintain such services. (Remember, most veterinarians, unlike physicians, don't have large central hospitals for patients who need special care and so must maintain their own). *If you are concerned about the fee,* be sure to ask your veterinarian about it if he or she doesn't bring up the matter first. Most veterinarians assume it is their responsibility to practice medicine, the client's responsibility to inquire about the costs. A better rapport is established if you tell your veterinarian at the outset whether there will be monetary limitations. If so, a thorough discussion of what limitations this will place on achieving a diagnosis or a successful treatment can take place before proceeding with a medical plan. (In some states third-party payment, i.e., pet health insurance or pet health maintenance plans may be available. Medical costs are spread among pet owners and can result in lower individual costs for veterinary care. However, many veterinarians believe that the traditional fee for service in veterinary medicine has actually helped keep overall veterinary costs for pet owners lower, since the individual pet owner remains conscious of the actual costs of services, unlike in our human medical system, where patients are covered by medical insurance.) Should there be a fee or treatment dispute you cannot resolve with your veterinarian, contact the ethics committee of your local or state veterinary association and/or the American Veterinary Medical Association Judicial Council in writing. Serious issues of medical competence should also be referred to your state's veterinary medical licensing agency.

REFERRALS

Veterinarians who don't maintain specialized equipment and expertise must refer some cases. A good veterinarian recognizes his or her limitations. Veterinarians who won't make referrals when requested may be trying to hide their own inadequacies.

EMERGENCY CARE

Choose a veterinary clinic that provides emergency service or will be able to refer you to emergency care when necessary. Some communities have central emergency services that work closely with the local veterinarians; others do not. Find out what your veterinarian or the community provides while your cat is healthy so you won't waste precious time when a true emergency arises.

HOW TO BE A "GOOD" CLIENT

Since veterinarians are people and as such aren't infallible or tireless, they appreciate consideration on your part. If you keep a few simple courtesies in mind and try to practice them, these signs of appreciation will make most veterinarians respond with their best efforts.

If your veterinarian makes appointments, try to be on time. This keeps the veterinarian on schedule and helps prevent a long wait for others. Avoid "dropping in" with your cat without an appointment; call ahead if you have a sick pet and cannot wait another day. Never drop in for routine preventive care such as vaccination or deworming unless your veterinarian chooses not to use an appointment system.

When you make appointments, your pet can be scheduled at the best time for a thorough and efficient evaluation of the problem and you can be saved a long wait. And when you do come in, be sure to bring your cat in a secure carrier or on a leash to prevent mishaps and disturbances in the waiting room.

Avoid dropping your cat off for care unless your veterinarian specifically directs you to. Most people would never consider dropping their child off at the pediatrician's, but many seem to expect that veterinarians should provide "one hour, one stop" service. Your cat usually receives better care if you discuss the problem with your veterinarian as the examination is performed. If your animal is very sick and it is impossible for you to wait during an office visit, call ahead and discuss the problem with the veterinarian first. He or she may be able to advise you on home treatment, may be able to make an appropriate drop-off arrangement once the history of the problem is clear, or at least may be able to deal with the problem more calmly than if you show up in a rush hoping to leave your pet.

Do not disturb your veterinarian for nonemergency matters at night, on holidays, or during his or her other time off. If you have any doubts about the emergency nature of an illness, call, but don't call just for general information.

Don't expect your veterinarian to make a diagnosis over the phone or solely on the basis of a physical examination. And don't expect the veterinary clinic to be a drugstore, supplying drugs on demand. Competent veterinarians interested in your cat's health want to examine your pet and may require laboratory tests before prescribing drugs or making a diagnosis, no matter how sure you are of what the problem is. They do this not to "hassle" you, but to protect your cat as well as themselves. *If* you think the doctor may be performing "unnecessary" diagnostic tests, clarify the situation with a thorough discussion of the information expected to be gained by performing them. Though most veterinarians won't diagnose over the phone, don't feel that you can't even call your veterinarian for advice. Just be prepared with some solid facts. If you can tell your veterinarian whether or not your cat has a fever, what the basic signs of illness or injury are, and how long they have been present, he or she will probably be willing to give you some help over the telephone in spite of a busy schedule. If you can't supply such information, though, don't be surprised if you are told that it is impossible to help you over the telephone.

Don't let signs persist for several days without or in spite of home care before consulting a veterinarian. It is extremely frustrating for a veterinarian to see an animal die from an illness that could have been treated successfully if professional care had begun sooner. And once you have consulted a veterinarian *follow directions.* It is quite irritating to a veterinarian to have someone complain that a treatment didn't work, only to find out later that the medication was not used or was used improperly. If you are having trouble, notify your veterinarian, but don't stop treatment without his or her advice.

A long-term relationship with an individual veterinarian is ideally developed over the years of a cat's life starting in kittenhood. The veterinarian becomes the cat's "best friend" in the veterinary clinic and has an excellent opportunity to become familiar with the cat's normal health and behavior as well as with any medical problems. The cat owner and the veterinarian have the opportunity to develop mutual understanding and respect, which are difficult to establish if you first meet over a serious medical problem. Learn to use your veterinarian as a resource for your animal's health. Know that help is there when you need it, but use this book, your patience, your common sense, and your intuition to take most of the responsibility for your cat's health. This book is intended as a tool to help you determine the limits of your responsibility and when you should draw on the veterinarian's resources. By using it in this way you will be practicing preventive medicine and may forestall illness and extra medical costs before they develop. Remember, your relationship to your cat, your moods, and your attitude toward his or her health and well-being are vital factors in the health of your pet and the effectiveness of your veterinarian. If you can temper your concern for your animal with an objectivity acquired through the knowledge you have gained about health care, you will avoid needless emotional upset and promote the growth of the three-way relationship of health among you, your cat, and your veterinarian.

INDEX OF SIGNS

discharge:

  from any body opening,
    234

  from around tail, 13

  at base of toenail, 142

  from ears, 19, 149, 150

  from eyes, 105, 146, 147, 153,
    154, 155, 160, 295

  from incision, 271

  nasal, 31, 104, 134, 150, 153,
    154, 160

  from penis, 177

  from skin, 133, 135

  from vagina, 282, 287

  from vulva, 177, 185

  from wound, 131, 143

discoloration:

  of ear wax, 118

  of gums, 94

  of mammary glands, 144–45, 279

  of milk, 145

  of mucous membranes, 186, 189,
    191, 202, 207, 212

  of pinna in ears, 149

  of skin, 136, 162

  of teeth, 151, 235

  of toenails, 136

discomfort, excessive, 285

distended abdomen, 185, 198

distressed meowing, 228

drinking, increased, 177, 185, 198,
  213, 230, 235, 236

drooling, 89, 112, 151, 153, 154,
  213, 215, 216, 219, 222

dryness:

  of eyes, 128

  of mouth, 128

eating:

  difficulty in, 234

  reluctance, 151

elasticity of skin, decrease in, 128

emaciation, 102

excitability, 215

ferociousness, 88

fever, 88, 90, 94, 104, 126, 127,
  132, 145, 148, 153, 154, 160,
  169, 185, 191, 196, 198, 217,
  228, 271, 287

fighting, 273

flattened ears, 118

flatulence, 98, 172

  with diarrhea, 173

fur matting, 236

gagging, 151

gastrointestinal disturbances: see
  constipation; diarrhea; flatulence;
  vomiting

grooming, excessive, 173

growth:

  poor, 98

  rapid toenail, 236

growths:

  on body, 233

  in mouth, 233

  on skin, 191

hair loss, 112, 119, 134, 143, 225,
  236

  around nipple, 279

  circular areas of, 136

  irregular, 136

haze, on eyes, 232

redness:

    around an incision, 271

    at base of toenail, 142

    of eyes, 105

    of feet, 136

    of gums, 152, 224

    of mouth, 140

    of neck, 112

    on skin, 102

    of skin, 103, 133, 134, 136, 140, 143

reluctance to move, 165

respiratory distress: *see* breathing

responsiveness, lack of, 202, 207

restlessness, 88, 212, 213, 214, 215, 216, 217, 218, 228, 236

retching, 169

rigid body, 133

    see also stiffness

roaming, 273

sandy material protruding from urethra, 180

scabs, 102, 103, 117, 119, 133, 136, 143

    on ear margins, 144

scaly skin, 119, 136

    see also dandruff

scooting anal area, 173

scratching, 102, 103, 133, 134

    ears, 118, 149, 150

secretion: *see* discharge

seizures, 94, 191, 196, 198, 212, 213, 214, 215, 216, 218

    see also convulsions

sensitivity to touch, 94

shedding:

    excessive, 236

    see also hair loss

shivering, 126, 127, 225

shock, 128–29, 200, 202, 205, 211

    followed by urination, 223

shortness of breath, 160

shyness, 88

sitting in crouched or hunched-up position, 171

small pupils, 213, 215, 216

smell, abnormal, 234

    from ears, 19, 149

    from mouth, 235

sneezing, 104, 134, 150, 153, 154, 155, 160

sores that do not heal, 234

spasms: *see* muscle tremors

spinal curvature, abnormal, 165

spontaneous fractures, 165

spraying: *see* urine spraying

squinting, 147, 155

staring expression, 224

stiffness, 106, 228

    persistent, 234

    progressive, 133

stool:

    blood in, 212, 263

    containing large amounts of hair, 168

    see also bowel control; constipation; diarrhea

stupor, 224

sunken eyes, 128

swallowing:

difficulty in, 133, 206, 234

hard, 160

swelling, 162

abnormal, 234

around anus, 174

around an incision, 271

around wound, 143

of chin, 138

in ears, 149

of eyes, 131, 146, 153

facial, 133, 151

of feet, 136, 223

of limb, 163

of lips, 219

of lymph nodes, 94, 196

of mammary glands, 144

of muzzle, 223

of throat, 219

of tongue, 219

under skin, 131

tearing, 134, 147

excessive, 146

teeth marks on skin, small, 221

temperature:

elevated, 224

lowered, 225, 288

subnormal, 189

see also fever

testes, undescended, 275

thickened skin, 119, 134, 139

tremors: *see* muscle tremors

twitching skin, 173

ulcers:

in mouth, 154

on tongue, 154

unconsciousness, 200, 206, 209, 217, 224, 226

with absence of heartbeat, 208

unkempt hair, 126

unresponsiveness, 230

unusual movements:

of lips, 151

of tongue, 151

urination:

abnormal, 177, 49

absence of, 206

bloody, 177, 179, 205, 206

difficult, 172, 177, 178, 206, 234

followed by shock, 223

frequent, 177, 213

inability, 177, 178, 200

increased, 177, 185, 198, 230, 235, 236

loss of control of, 177, 186, 191, 209

urine spraying, 177, 183–85, 268, 273

vocalizing more than usual, 282

voice, change in, 89, 267, 268

vomiting, 90, 94, 101, 103, 106, 112, 134, 167–69, 171, 178, 185, 189, 191, 198, 206, 211, 212, 213, 214, 215, 216, 217, 218, 219, 223, 224, 230, 235, 236, 263, 272, 282, 284

blood, 169

with diarrhea, 169, 170

GENERAL INDEX

ABOUT THE AUTHOR

DR. TERRI MCGINNIS has loved and has had a rapport with animals from the time she was a child living in southern California. Although, or perhaps because, she had few pets while growing up, her ambition was to become a veterinarian. She attained this goal in 1971, when she was awarded her Doctor of Veterinary Medicine degree from the University of California at Davis.

Since that time she has practiced in the San Francisco Bay area and has gradually limited her veterinary practice to care of companion animals. She began writing books for dog and cat owners in 1973. All have been popular, and *The Well Dog Book* and/or *The Well Cat Book* have been published in Great Britain, France, Australia, Germany, Holland, and Japan as well as in the United States. In addition to books, Dr. McGinnis has written articles about pet care for magazines, for an encyclopedia, and as a monthly columnist. She has served on the boards of her local veterinary association and the Oakland Society for Prevention of Cruelty to Animals. She has also made numerous television and radio appearances, hosting her own radio show in San Francisco for three years.